T0291226

NEW GLOBAL DYNAMICS

NEW GLOBAL DYNAMICS

NEW GLOBAL DYNAMICS

Managing Economic Change in a Transforming World

ZIA QURESHI

AND

DAEHEE JEONG

EDITORS

Published by Brookings Institution Press
1775 Massachusetts Avenue, NW
Washington, DC 20036
www.brookings.edu/bipress

Co-published by Rowman & Littlefield
An imprint of The Rowman & Littlefield Publishing Group, Inc.
4501 Forbes Boulevard, Suite 200, Lanham, MD 20706
www.rowman.com
86-90 Paul Street, London EC2A 4NE

Copyright © 2024 by The Brookings Institution
All rights reserved. No part of this book may be reproduced in any form or
by any electronic or mechanical means, including information storage and
retrieval systems, without written permission from the publisher, except
by a reviewer who may quote passages in a review.

The Brookings Institution is a nonprofit organization devoted to research,
education, and publication on important issues of domestic and foreign
policy. Its principal purpose is to bring the highest quality independent
research and analysis to bear on current and emerging policy problems.

Composition by Circle Graphics, Inc., Reisterstown, MD
Typeset in Janson Text

British Library Cataloguing in Publication Information Available
Library of Congress Control Number: 2024940600

ISBN: 978-0-8157-4086-5 (pbk)
ISBN: 978-0-8157-4085-8 (cloth)
ISBN: 978-0-8157-4087-2 (ebook)

The paper used in this publication meets the minimum requirements of
American National Standard for Information Sciences—Permanence of
Paper for Printed Library Materials, ANSI/NISO Z39.48-1992

Contents

Foreword

*N*ew *Global Dynamics* is an apt title for this book. The world is facing a conflux of powerful forces of change. The global economy, and political economy, are experiencing profound shifts. Institutions and policies at both the national and international levels confront new challenges. This book will be valuable not only for policymakers but also for the general reader interested in the implications of transformative change for economies and societies.

Global geopolitics is shifting. The growing economic and geopolitical power of China is challenging the postwar international order led by the United States. The US-China hegemonic rivalry is increasing geopolitical tensions. Nationalist industrial policies and protectionism are on the rise, even in advanced Western economies that have been the champions of a neoliberal vision of free markets and open and rules-based multilateralism. Armed conflicts such as the wars in Ukraine and Gaza are adding to geopolitical tensions.

The digital revolution is transforming markets, work, business models, international trade, and financial networks. Artificial intelligence (AI) and related new technological advances can greatly expand the frontiers of this transformation. The full potential and implications of the latest technologies are still evolving. Today's powerful innovations create enormous new opportunities to advance economic progress, but they also pose complex policy and regulatory challenges. Inevitably, major technological transformation is associated with economic and social disruption. The dislocations, and rising inequality within economies, have been stoking popular discontent and political polarization.

Climate change is adding to this picture of a transforming world. Climate transition will alter economic structures within countries and interconnections among them, profoundly affecting the patterns of production, investment, and trade.

This book analyzes the global implications of these forces of change. It examines how they are affecting the global economy, the future of globalization, and international power structures. It delves into the changing dynamics in industry, trade, and finance and what they mean for national policies and international cooperation to foster the new opportunities and meet the new challenges.

With so much change in the offing, the global outlook will be more uncertain and volatile. The world is not deglobalizing, but there are real risks of globalization fragmenting along lines drawn by major power rivalry, disrupting supply chains and entailing large costs for everyone. Future patterns of globalization will depend crucially on how countries manage the shifting international power dynamics.

In a more contested world, a rules-based international order becomes even more critical. The world would collectively benefit from recommitting to multilateral frameworks governing economic relations between countries—and adding disciplines covering new areas of activity, notably the digital economy and the technologies driving it. A rules-based multilateral economic order developed over decades has not only fostered global economic prosperity but has been an important foundation of geopolitical stability. As economies evolve and economic power structures shift, new competition dynamics in the global economy are inevitable, but it is important that all nations play by internationally accepted rules.

As digital technologies open new avenues for growth and international integration, they also present challenges for policymakers that require new thinking and approaches. New dynamics in industry, labor markets, and trade must be managed to foster inclusive growth, facilitate necessary structural change, and ease social adjustment. New frameworks must be developed to regulate digital markets. Digital innovations in finance must be secured by appropriate oversight. The latest technologies, powered by AI, have immense economic potential but also carry serious risks of misuse. Some are dual-use technologies, with civilian and military applications, that can become a battleground for techno-nationalism in the context of today's major power rivalries. Cooperative frameworks will be needed to balance national and security concerns with broad technology diffusion across nations.

International cooperation has become more challenging in this new and evolving geopolitical environment, but it is essential in matters ranging from trade policies to the global financial architecture to the regulation of new technologies. And it is indispensable for combating climate change, as the climate challenge is inherently universal. Countries will need to rise above nationalist and geopolitical interests in areas such as green technologies and energy transition.

This book is part of a joint research project between the Brookings Institution and the Korea Development Institute (KDI) that examines the implications of today's transformative changes for economies and public policy around the world. The research engages noted scholars from Brookings, KDI, and other institutions. It is the third book in the series supported by this project: the previous two books, *Growth in a Time of Change* and *Shifting Paradigms*, were published in 2020 and 2022, respectively. We hope that this research contributes to a better understanding of some of the big issues and policy challenges of our time.

Changwoo Nam
Senior Vice President and Chief Research Officer
Korea Development Institute

Brahima Coulibaly
Vice President and Director
Global Economy and Development
The Brookings Institution

Acknowledgments

This book is the third in a series produced under a joint research project of the Brookings Institution and the Korea Development Institute (KDI) that examines the implications of the transformative changes occurring in the world today for the global economy and public policy. Zia Qureshi (Brookings) and Daehee Jeong (KDI) coedited the book. The editors thank the leadership of the two institutions for their support for this work.

The book consists of contributions from a team of scholars from Brookings, KDI, and other institutions. The team included, in addition to the editors (who wrote chapter 1, which provides an overview of the book), the following: Laura Tyson, John Zysman, and Brian Judge (chapter 2); Wonhyuk Lim (chapter 3); Diane Coyle (chapter 4); Justin Yifu Lin and Célestin Monga (chapter 5); Bernard Hoekman (chapter 6); Siwook Lee (chapter 7); Eswar Prasad (chapter 8); and Joon-Ho Hahm and Woo Jin Choi (chapter 9). The editors thank their coauthors for their valuable contributions.

These chapters were initially presented as papers at a research conference held at Brookings on July 6, 2023, and subsequently finalized in light of the comments received. Discussants of the papers included Alan Gelb,

Kenneth Kang, Aaron Klein, Susan Lund, Nadia Rocha, Jeffrey Schott, Tom Wheeler, and Andrew Yeo. Their comments and suggestions are gratefully acknowledged. Helpful comments were also received from session chairs, including Youngsun Koh, Jahyun Koo, Amy Liu, and David Wessel. The editors also thank other participants at the conference for sharing their valuable thoughts.

Janina Curtis Bröker provided research and editorial assistance throughout the work. Rohan Carter-Rau, Junjie Ren, Esther Rosen, and Izzy Taylor assisted with the organization of the research conference. For assistance with administrative, budgetary, and coordination matters, thanks are due to Drew Badolato, Mary Conrad, Erin Clements, Yaewon Hyun, Sean Jones, Seonkyeong Kang, Junghyun Lah, Brigette Novak, Samantha Panetta, Kristina Server, and Joowon Yoon.

The publication of this book was managed by the Brookings Institution Press and Rowman & Littlefield Publishers. The editors would like to thank David Lampo, Shavanthi Mendis, Yelba Quinn, Jon Sisk, and the team at Circle Graphics, Inc., of Reisterstown, Maryland, for their advice and support in the preparation and production of the book.

NEW GLOBAL DYNAMICS

NEW GLOBAL DYNAMICS

ONE

Overview

Challenges of Managing Transformative Change in the Global Economy

ZIA QURESHI AND DAEHEE JEONG

To say that we are living in a time of change is to state, or rather understate, the obvious. The world faces a remarkable confluence of transformative changes that are disrupting existing systems and paradigms. These changes have immense implications for both national economies and the global economy, and policymakers face an exceptional array of new challenges.

Global political economy is resetting. A key driver is the growing economic and geopolitical power of China, which is challenging the postwar international order led by the United States. The ensuing US-China hegemonic rivalry has increased geopolitical tensions. The shifting geopolitics has spawned a surge in economic nationalism. Nationalist industrial policies and protectionism have been on the rise. The environment for multilateral cooperation and collaboration has become more difficult.

1

The digital revolution is reshaping economies and societies. It is transforming work, business models and production processes, and international trade and financial networks. Artificial intelligence (AI) and related new advances can take this transformation to a whole new level. The new technologies have great potential to boost economic progress and lift human welfare, but they also pose complex new policy and regulatory challenges as they reshape markets. Associated economic and social disruptions and distributional consequences must be managed. Structural transformations such as technological change, as well as globalization, create winners and losers. Inequality has been rising within economies. The dislocations and widening disparities have been stoking societal discontent and political polarization—and a populist backlash against globalization. Techno-nationalism is on the rise as countries seek dominance and control of the powerful new technologies in the context of today's geopolitical power rivalries. Many of these technologies, especially new generative AI models, also carry serious risks of misuse. The full potential and implications of the latest technologies are still evolving.

Climate change will have profound effects on global patterns of production, trade, and investment. It will alter economic structures within nations and affect interconnections among them. Climate mitigation and adaptation pose major restructuring challenges but also open new avenues for investment and sustainable growth. International cooperation in green technologies and energy transition will be vital, but it faces challenges in today's fraught geopolitics.

The world has also recently experienced major shocks. The COVID-19 pandemic caused pervasive disruptions. Some of its effects will be long-lasting, such as a reconfiguration of global supply chains and increased virtualization of human and economic activity. Indeed, the pandemic may be remembered as a great digital accelerator, marking an inflection point in the advance of digital transformation. Conflicts such as the wars in Ukraine and Gaza also have disrupted supply chains and added to geopolitical tensions.

It is a world of change. Major transformations are rarely smooth, and disruptions are inevitable. Timely and calibrated policy responses and international cooperation on common new challenges, however, can ease such transitions. In this book, we analyze the global implications of the transformative changes we are witnessing. The first section examines how globalization and international power structures may evolve. The next three sections delve deeper into the shifting dynamics in industry, trade, and finance, and this analysis of global trends has implications for national polices and international cooperation. Figure 1.1 provides a schematic representation of the book's structure and main themes.

The Future of Globalization

Globalization has advanced rapidly in recent decades. It has brought enormous benefits to economies by connecting them to international markets, spurring productivity, reducing costs, and boosting economic growth. Both developed and developing economies have gained, notwithstanding that international economic integration inevitably entails important adjustment challenges. How the global economy and globalization evolve in the future will be shaped greatly by the multifaceted change the world faces today, from shifting geopolitics to transformative new technologies to the climate challenge.

Globalization in Transition

Among the several current forces of change affecting global trends, an overarching one is the international power dynamics. In chapter 2, Laura Tyson, John Zysman, and Brian Judge analyze the forces at play and how they may shape the future of globalization. They note that the changing geopolitics is causing a shift from a positive-sum approach to globalization in which interdependence is seen as mutually beneficial to a zero-sum approach in which a country's gain is viewed as another's loss. A key element of this reconfiguration is the rise of China and intensified rivalry with the United States for global dominance. The postwar era of globalization reflected the vision of the world's neoliberal hegemon, the United States. In a bipolar or multipolar world emerging from the rise of China and other new economic powers, however, the framework for globalization could differ significantly from the previous neoliberal vision. In a more contested world, the United States itself has recently been shifting away from that vision, as reflected in an emerging "new Washington consensus" that embraces nationalist industrial policy and trade interventions that depart from open and nondiscriminatory multilateralism. This shift is not confined to the United States but is also evident in many other advanced economies, notably in Europe.

- Shifting geopolitics and international power structures
- Transformative new technologies
- Climate change

- Globalization in transition
- New industrial dynamics
- New trade dynamics
- New financial dynamics

- New challenges for national policies and regulatory frameworks to manage transformative change that is reshaping markets and altering growth and distribution dynamics
- New challenges for international cooperation to refit global governance frameworks to a changing agenda and bolster a rules-based multilateral order against geopolitical headwinds

FIGURE 1.1. New Global Dynamics: Drivers, Change, and Policies

The changing geopolitics and power rivalries will weigh heavily on international trade and investment relations. They will also greatly shape whether today's powerful new technologies act as integrators of the global economy or fragment it along global power blocs. And they will shape whether countries engage in the efforts to combat climate change with more international cooperation or conflict.

The world, however, is not deglobalizing. Globalization is not receding but restructuring, as Tyson et al. argue. Today's global economy is highly interconnected. Globalization has advanced to a stage where countries, large or small, have high, built-in dependence on international trade and investment. Global flows have proven quite resilient to shocks, such as the 2008–2009 global financial crisis and the 2020 COVID-19 pandemic. There has been some slowing of globalization ("slowbalization") but not a reversal. Global trade has continued to hover around 60 percent of world GDP—and global financial integration, as measured by external financial assets and liabilities relative to world GDP, remains around 400 percent of world GDP. What is likely to happen is that globalization will become more fragmented. Economic interconnections among nations will continue to expand but will be reconfigured around competing economic powers and along regional lines. Such geoeconomic fragmentation will disrupt supply chains, raise costs, and likely lead to slower global growth. The emerging landscape will be subject to increased uncertainty and greater risks of instability and conflict.

Digital technologies have been a major driver of globalization in recent decades as they improved connectivity and enabled new types of international trade and financial transactions. AI and other latest advances can drive this process further. Cross-border data flows have been increasing by as much as 50 percent annually, fueling digital trade that is now the fastest growing component of world trade. Globalization is becoming increasingly digital. And it is increasingly services-driven as more services become digitally deliverable across borders. The previous phase of globalization was driven by manufacturing value chains and labor arbitrage as low-cost labor was opened to global companies. The new phase of globalization is led by services intermediated by digital technologies.

But digital globalization also faces challenges. It is closely intertwined with the regulation of the digital economy, in which approaches differ across national jurisdictions. Geopolitical tensions can prompt new barriers to digital trade—digital protectionism—as major digital powers vie for control and supremacy in the new technologies. This includes restrictions on data flows and cross-border digital business and a potential fragmentation of digital networks ("splinternet"). The risks of conflict are especially high in advanced technologies and AI, such as in advanced semiconductors, where the United Stated has deployed government subsidies to favor domestic production combined with restrictions on exports and outbound investment to China. These interventions in advanced dual-use technologies (with both civilian and military applications) involve security considerations but also reflect intensified nationalist competition for global advantage in frontier technologies more broadly.

Climate change epitomizes global interconnectedness as the challenge is universal and requires international collaboration. Cooperation between China and the United States is especially important, as they are the top two greenhouse gas emitters in the world. Unencumbered trade in environmental products would be a strong ally of the efforts to combat climate change by facilitating the diffusion of green technologies and reducing costs. Yet for geopolitical and protectionist reasons, countries are resorting to restrictions, such as domestic content requirements for electric vehicles and renewable energy products and strategic control of technologies and supply chains for minerals critical for energy transition. Years of negotiations at the World Trade Organization (WTO) for an environmental goods agreement have been inconclusive.

In sum, how the global economy and globalization evolve will depend crucially on how countries manage international relations amid shifting geopolitics and a reshuffling of the existing global economic landscape by technological transformation and climate transition. A key factor will be whether the new dynamics play out within a rules-based international order or fray it, with nationalist competition displacing international cooperation. Also important will be how countries address the new policy challenges at the national level and manage domestic economic and political consequences of disruptive change, notably distributional and inequality concerns.

An Asian Century?

Related to the question of the future of globalization is the question of how the fortunes of different regions may evolve in the global economy. The nineteenth century, which saw the first wave of globalization spurred by the Industrial Revolution, is often referred to as the European Century as Britain and other industrializing countries in Europe pulled ahead.

This wave of globalization ended with the major upheavals occurring in the early part of the twentieth century, including the world wars and the Great Depression. The second wave of globalization in the postwar twentieth century saw the growing economic weight and influence of the United States, and thus the twentieth century came to be called the American Century. What is in store for the twenty-first century? Will it be an Asian Century, as some envision? In chapter 3, Wonhyuk Lim addresses this question and analyzes the prospects and challenges for Asia as it navigates shifting dynamics.

Following rapid economic growth in recent decades, Asia now accounts for about half of global GDP, in purchasing power parity (PPP) terms, and more than half of world trade. While China has led the recent surge, rapidly emerging as the second largest economy in the world (or the largest in PPP terms), the dynamics around an Asian Century go beyond China alone. Asia is a vast and diverse region, and its economic dynamism and future potential extend well beyond China.

Asia's economic ascendance has been driven broadly by two factors: internal drive supported by reforms that removed barriers to growth and opened up the economies to connect to world markets; and a favorable external environment in which globalization advanced and international trade and investment grew rapidly. Whether the region's momentum will continue will hinge on how these factors evolve. Lim examines alternative, dramatically different scenarios for Asia based on these factors. In one scenario, wherein the region is able to sustain its growth dynamism and the external environment remains favorable, the current century could indeed turn out to be an Asian Century. Other possible scenarios include a "middle-income trap" if domestic economic management fails to continue to upgrade economies and growth falters; a "perilous prosperity" scenario, wherein the external environment turns unfavorable as geopolitical tensions rise, fueled in particular by intensifying US-China rivalry; and a "crisis and conflict" scenario, wherein a combination of domestic economic weakening and an adverse external environment produces both internal crisis and external conflict.

Asia faces internal and external challenges to sustain its economic success and rising global profile. Internally, the recent slowing of growth in China illustrates the challenges of economic restructuring and rebalancing to recalibrate sources of growth as economies transition. But the region has laid a strong economic foundation to build on and developed capabilities to address the challenges of change. It has the infrastructure, skilled work-force, and technical knowhow needed to take advantage of the transfor-mative technologies of the digital age. This must be done in ways that promote broad improvements in productivity, economic inclusion, and social cohesion—and environmental sustainability. Major economies in Northeast Asia, notably China, Japan, and Korea, face aging and declining popula-tions. However, within the region, countries in South and Southeast Asia, such as India, Indonesia, and Vietnam, have younger and growing popula-tions. Asia can generate mutual benefits by deepening regional value chains between countries with declining populations and those with increasing populations. Economic integration within Asia, already strong, could increase further. The economic and demographic complementarities between North-east Asia and South and Southeast Asia can help generate a third wave of Asia's growth involving the latter, following the first two waves that cen-tered around the former. Asia could become multipolar.

Arguably the biggest challenge to an Asian Century is external, consisting of mounting geopolitical tensions from hegemonic rivalry between major powers and associated risks of a fragmenting globalization. Lim calls upon Asian countries to continue to promote a rules-based order both glob-ally and regionally and build inclusive economic and security frameworks as they navigate changing international power dynamics—and exercise caution on sensitive matters such as the Taiwan issue. The global economy has a vital stake in the preservation of peace and growth momentum in Asia so it can continue to benefit from the region's dynamism. The rise of Asia, from the North to the South, should not be seen in terms of a confronta-tional, zero-sum global game. It benefits not only the 60 percent of humanity that lives there but also promotes global prosperity.

New Industrial Dynamics

Markets and industries are seeing major transformations. Digital tech-nologies are changing how firms compete, altering business models, and reshaping product and labor markets, all of which profoundly affect growth and distribution within economies. They are posing new policy and regula-tory issues. Industries and policymakers also face decarbonization challenges. At the same time, geopolitical tensions and competition for supremacy in the new technologies are driving a resurgence of industrial policy, increasingly wielded as a tool of economic nationalism and global domination. This is particularly evident in recent actions by governments in high-tech industries and in renewable energy industries employing advanced technologies. Chapters 4 and 5 discuss these shifting industrial dynamics.

Digital Transformation of Markets and Policy Challenges

Digital innovations offer new opportunities for economic progress, but also pose significant adjustment challenges. Technology is a key driver of productivity and long-term economic growth. The potential of digital technologies to deliver higher productivity and economic growth is sizable, but, paradoxically, as digital technologies have boomed, productivity growth has tended to slow rather than accelerate. It is too early to determine whether the latest wave of new technologies led by AI will reverse these productivity trends, as the full potential of these technologies is not yet known and they are at an early stage of adoption.

What is clear, though, is that the expected productivity dividend from previous waves of digital technologies has not fully materialized. One reason for this outcome is that the benefits of digital transformation have been predominantly captured by major firms at the technological frontier, which have reaped large gains in productivity and profits (and rents). For the vast majority of other, smaller firms, however, productivity growth has slowed or stagnated, depressing aggregate productivity growth. Market concentration has increased in many industries, with adverse implications for future business entry and innovation. Economies of scale and network effects associated with digital technologies, and advantages derived from proprietary agglomeration of data, have encouraged the rise of dominant firms. These winner-takes-all dynamics are most marked in the high-tech sectors but are increasingly evident in other sectors as digitalization penetrates economies.

At the same time, economic inequality has been on the rise. Not only has inequality between firms increased but so has inequality between workers. Digitalization and automation have shifted labor demand away from workers with low- to middle-level skills to those with higher-level skills, with the former facing diminished job and earnings prospects. As a result, wage inequality has increased. AI and related technologies, the next phase of digital transformation, could accentuate these labor market and distributional impacts, although there is uncertainty associated with how the scope of AI capabilities may evolve.

As technology reshapes markets and alters growth and distribution dynamics, policies must ensure that markets remain competitive and inclusive and support wide access to the new opportunities for firms and workers. The digital economy must be broadened to disseminate new technologies and productive opportunities to smaller firms and wider segments of the labor force. This will help capture the productivity dividend from digital transformation across wider swaths of the economy as well as avert increases in inequality. The policy agenda is broad, ranging from investments in digital infrastructure and reskilling/upskilling workers to strengthening social protection systems to ease adjustment to disruptive change to regulation of changing markets.

In chapter 4, Diane Coyle focuses on the regulatory implications of the digital transformation of markets. One key area is competition policy that needs a revamp for the digital era to ensure that markets continue to provide an open and level playing field, check the growth of monopolistic structures, and promote broader technology diffusion. Antitrust laws need to be aligned with the new market dynamics, with a view to protecting not just consumers but also smaller competitors. New regulatory frameworks are needed for digital platforms, which have emerged as gatekeepers in the digital world, to prevent abuses of their dominant positions. Digital giants that resemble natural or quasi-natural monopolies because of economies of scale and network effects pose the question of whether they should be regulated through frameworks similar to those that govern utilities. Appropriate regulatory standards need to be devised for digital markets on matters such as interoperability and terms of access. The regulation of unfolding AI applications now adds to the new challenges policymakers face. A related set of issues pertains to the regulation of data, the fuel of the digital economy, on questions of privacy, ownership, access, and portability. Intellectual property regimes, established many decades ago, also need to be updated, with the aging patent systems better aligned with the workings of digital innovation and better balancing narrow incumbent interests with the wider promotion and diffusion of innovation.

Regulatory responses typically have lagged well behind the rapid pace of the digital restructuring of markets. The dynamics of the intangible economy of the digital era pose new and complex challenges that require a step-up in institutional policy capabilities—and there is an important political dimension overlaid on policy choices because major structural transformations involve winners and losers. In the past few years, action to address the new regulatory agenda has picked up in Europe, led by the European Union (EU). This has included the enactment of the General Data Protection Regulation in 2018 followed by the Digital Services Act and the Digital Markets Act in 2022 that address some of the agenda relating to data governance and competition policy in digital markets. A recently approved AI Act will come into force in 2024. Some reform momentum has been building also in the United States, but legislative success on new legal frameworks so far has remained elusive, although the enforcement of existing antitrust laws has been strengthened.

Many of the policy challenges, from data governance to competition policy and regulation of tech giants and platforms (whose operations and dominance extend across borders), require international coordination. This is important to avoid regulatory arbitrage, harmonize standards, and avoid conflict. The potential for international conflict is particularly apparent in advanced technology, notably AI-related, industries and their supply chains, driven by strategic, geopolitical considerations. While there have been several statements of general principle on the regulation of AI and related issues from institutions such as the OECD and the G20, international policy development will require detailed work, including addressing questions of governance mechanisms—and greater cooperation in a difficult geopolitical environment.

Resurgence of Industrial Policy

In chapter 5, Justin Yifu Lin and Célestin Monga delve deeper into the recent resurgence of industrial policy. They draw an important distinction between industrial policy and protectionism. Industrial policy actions often are protectionist, as is also true of many of the actions taken by countries recently. However, industrial policy does not have to be protectionist or serve as a tool of economic nationalism. Take the case of subsidies or tax credits for the purchase of electric vehicles. Such government incentives can be justified as industrial policy to promote the electric vehicles industry in view of the environmental externalities involved, but limiting those incentives to vehicles largely manufactured or assembled domestically (or in selected other countries considered "friendly"), as for example is the case with related recent policy actions in the United States, goes beyond industrial policy and into the realm of protectionism. Protectionist actions—not limited to traditional border measures but increasingly an array of behind-the border measures—and discriminatory regionalism are on the rise.

There is great concern today about the risks of global economic fragmentation. But these risks arise not from a resurgence of industrial policy per se but rather from a resurgence of protectionism in a more contested world marked by increased geopolitical tensions.

Lin and Monga also argue that there are a number of misconceptions about industrial policy—such as it being often, and mistakenly, equated with protectionism—that cast it in a rather negative light. A widely held conception views industrial policy in terms of narrow government interventions that aggressively promote certain industries, sometimes even individual firms, regardless of market signals. Such "picking winners" policies are often deployed by governments and often end up as failures and as avenues for rent-seeking. Lin and Monga instead see industrial policy in much broader terms as a process of strategically facilitating structural change in an economy, and doing so not by attempting to go against the grain of an economy's intrinsic comparative advantages in markets but by removing barriers to their realization. In their view, industrial policy is not just direct government interventions to promote certain activities through targeted public investments or incentives provided via subsidies or taxes or tariffs, as it is often conceptualized. Rather, it spans the whole gamut of government actions that affect an economy's structural transformation across sectors and industries, ranging from building infrastructure to upgrading workforce skills to promoting research and innovation. They see the government's role in fostering and disseminating knowledge and learning to unleash an economy's latent strengths as a key element of industrial policy. Industrial policy is thus envisioned as an integral part of economic policy for growth and structural transformation rather than a narrow, fringe element.

The key question, Lin and Monga argue, is not whether economies should engage in industrial policy but how to do it right, that is, how economies at different levels of development can, through collaborative efforts between the public and private sectors, mobilize human, capital, and technological resources and promote knowledge and learning to facilitate the growth of the most productive and competitive sectors and industries—and doing so by not abandoning but working with the forces of competition in markets. The authors critique what they see as a "double standard" in the approach of mainstream economics and its proponents, including the Bretton Woods institutions, that have traditionally discouraged economic strategies employing industrial policy in developing economies but have been more supportive of the recent shift toward such strategies in advanced economies ranging from the United States to Europe.

The resurgence of interest in industrial policy comes at a time when there is also a broader rethinking of the economic role of government. Neoliberal and predominantly market-based approaches are being challenged by new thinking that envisages a more proactive government engagement in matters ranging from growth and employment generation to economic inclusion to management of structural change associated with transformative new technologies and climate transition. Government's role is increasingly being seen as going beyond the traditional rationales of addressing market failures to creating and shaping markets. The "new Washington consensus," mentioned earlier, reflects this shift. Current trends suggest a more active government engagement in economies in the years ahead. With economic nationalism on the rise at the same time, stoked by intensified rivalries for global economic power and technological supremacy, this shift also suggests an increased potential for geoeconomic conflict and fragmentation as governments wield a more activist role to push for global advantage, including through protectionist and discriminatory international trade and investment measures.

New Trade Dynamics

Digital technologies are transforming international trade. Associated with this transformation are new challenges for global trade policy to govern the fast-expanding digital trade. At the same time, global value chains (GVCs) are seeing significant shifts that can shape their future evolution. Chapters 6 and 7 analyze these new dynamics in international trade and their implications.

Digital Trade and Policies

Past gains in establishing rules-based multilateral frameworks for trade and investment are threatened by today's increased protectionist pressures amid elevated geopolitical tensions and a rise in nationalist populism. Not only must the existing multilateral frameworks be shielded from these risks but new rules and cooperative arrangements need to be devised to ensure open access and competition in the next phase of globalization led by digital flows. While digital trade has expanded rapidly and is now the most dynamic component of world trade, the development of necessary international disciplines governing it has been slow and fragmented. In chapter 6, Bernard Hoekman discusses the agenda for international cooperation on digital trade policies. Estimates of digital trade vary depending upon what they include, ranging from digitally intermediated to digitally delivered goods and services. By some estimates, digital trade may already account for between one-fifth and one-quarter of world trade. Services trade has been in the vanguard of digital globalization. Trade in digitally delivered services increased fourfold between 2005 and 2022, rising to about 55 percent of all services trade. Digital technologies are enabling more and more services to be deliverable across borders.

Harnessing the opportunities offered by digital technologies to boost trade and economic growth calls for investment in these technologies and network infrastructure as well as effective regulation to ensure that firms and consumers have digital access at reasonable cost and to safeguard consumers and market competition. Digital trade can be supported by international cooperation to reduce digital trade barriers and promote an open digital trade regime. These barriers range from digital protectionism, such as data localization measures and restrictions on cross-border flows of data and digital goods and services with a protectionist intent, to regulatory heterogeneity and policy uncertainty across jurisdictions as they build their digital governance frameworks. Research suggests that there are significant potential gains for countries that would flow from cooperation to reduce such barriers and associated costs. Restrictive and divergent policies also create risks of trade conflicts and digital fragmentation. International cooperation is needed to agree on common principles and standards and develop good regulatory practices regarding digital trade. There is also a close link between trade policy and competition policy in the digital domain (discussed in chapter 4), such as the regulation of big tech platforms that affect trade and competition across borders.

International cooperation is being pursued through various channels, including preferential trade agreements and plurilateral initiatives that center on the adoption of common regulatory practices and the determination of the equivalence of foreign regulatory regimes covering matters such as consumer protection and data privacy. Past failures of multilateral negotiations at the WTO have led countries to devote greater efforts to negotiate agreements in bilateral, regional, or plurilateral frameworks. Many of the current efforts also focus on specific policy domains—such as data transfer and localization, electronic contracts/invoicing/payment, taxation of electronic transmissions, and cybersecurity and fraud prevention—rather than attempt to reach more comprehensive agreements. Such efforts, especially those that negotiate open plurilateral agreements, have become test beds for broader multilateral cooperation, such as that being pursued through the long-running WTO e-commerce talks.

Differences in societal values regarding issues such as privacy, and noneconomic objectives like national security that impinge on digital policies, will impede broad multilateral agreement on politically sensitive areas of digital regulation, especially in the current geopolitical environment. Digital regulation varies greatly between major digital players, such as Western economies and China, with different political systems and different approaches to regulation and degree of government intervention. But differences in digital regulation pose challenges for cross-border data flows, which drive digital trade, even between players with similar political systems, such as the EU and the United States. Accordingly, digital policy cooperation is likely to comprise a mix of regional, plurilateral, and multilateral arrangements and will be issue-specific rather than comprehensive in scope.

Digital trade is strongly affected by domestic digital regulation. Such regulation motivated by national interests and objectives and influenced by national political orientations has important international effects. Given that national regulatory regimes will continue to differ, and the likely proliferation of initiatives and arrangements between countries, there is a strong case for multilateral scrutiny of the different regulatory regimes and analysis of their effects to inform policy reform, identify good regulatory practices, and underpin the development of internationally accepted standards. The WTO can play an important role in this context.

Shifts in Global Value Chains

While the digital revolution has spawned a rapid rise in digital trade, it has also been instrumental in boosting the growth of GVCs. Advances in global connectivity have increased opportunities for firms to unbundle production processes and organize activities in multiple international locations. The expansion and deepening of GVCs has spurred international trade, boosting productivity, reducing costs, and stimulating economic growth. It has also helped developing economies increase their participation in world trade. The share of GVC-related trade in world trade has increased rapidly, currently accounting for about two-fifths of the total. Looking ahead, however, the growth of GVCs faces structural shifts and risks that cloud its future trajectory. In chapter 7, Siwook Lee examines the GVC dynamics in a changing world and their implications for policy and international cooperation.

There has been some slowing of GVC growth already over the past decade, reflecting a mix of cyclical and structural factors. The recession and the economic slowdown following the global financial crisis dampened trade growth. Structural changes in the Chinese economy, which accounts for the largest share of GVC trade, also played a role, including growing domestic demand and the development of local supply chains for intermediate goods and services inputs into manufacturing. More recently, factors such as the rise of US-China global rivalry, regional conflicts, including the war in Ukraine, and the resurgence of protectionism pose much greater risks that could disrupt GVCs. Increased geopolitical tensions create the risk of fragmentation of supply chains along lines framed by global economic power blocs. The experience with supply chain disruptions caused by the COVID-19 pandemic adds to these risks. Concerns about the security of critical supplies can prompt countries to reconfigure supply lines, opting for diversifying, near-shoring, or friend-shoring such supplies, or even reshoring them back to home.

Given the degree of global connectivity and interdependence that exists today, a widespread rupture or decoupling of GVCs is unlikely. A more likely outcome is selective decoupling in industries of strategic national interest. While the GVC network for traditional industries is likely to remain relatively stable, though not completely unaffected, the pressure to reorganize supply chains will be stronger in high-tech industries related to the quest of major economic powers for supremacy in the new technologies. Such pressures will affect particularly those industries that involve dual-use technologies. This is already evident in the case of advanced semiconductors and AI-related products.

While digital technologies have spurred the growth of GVCs by facilitating the coordination of production across borders, the full range of their potential impacts, particularly that of the latest wave of innovations, is still rather uncertain. On the one hand, they can give a further boost to GVC networks by continuing to lower international communication and coordination costs and creating new business models and new types of international transactions. On the other hand, increased automation may lower the incentive for firms to disperse production geographically in search of lower labor costs. Facilitation of customization by the latest technologies, together with the increasing servicification of manufacturing, may increase the weight of proximity to customers in firms' location decisions. Much would also depend on how policies evolve in relation to trade involving advanced technologies. International trade and investment embodying advanced technologies have recently been subject to increased restrictive actions.

The climate agenda also will shape the future of GVCs. Efforts to reduce carbon footprints are likely to drive GVCs toward greater sustainability. If environmental regulation is wielded in a protectionist or discriminatory way, such as requiring components for electric vehicles or solar panels to be sourced domestically or from a certain group of countries, there is potential for significant disruption of supply chains in related industries. Renewable energy industries are also exposed to the risk of disruption from strategic actions by countries to control the supply of scarce minerals that serve as critical inputs.

Concerns about the disruption and fragmentation of GVCs have prompted countries to undertake cooperative efforts to secure their resilience and viability. As in the case of issues relating to digital trade policies, such efforts are largely taking place in plurilateral formats among like-minded countries outside the WTO. Bringing such plurilateral initiatives within the legal framework of the WTO would not only enhance their perceived international legitimacy but also promote the prospects of other countries joining down the road. This calls for broader acceptance of plurilateral approaches in the WTO, in contrast to its traditional all-or-nothing approach to multilateral negotiations, on issues where broader agreement among members is not feasible at the outset given divergent national interests, especially in the current geopolitical environment. Absent that, there is a risk of further erosion of the role of the WTO as more and more of the policy action and efforts by countries to cooperate occur outside its framework.

New Financial Dynamics

The world of finance also is facing significant change, which creates new opportunities but also poses new challenges. Digital technologies are reshaping financial markets and disrupting existing monetary arrangements with innovative products and mechanisms. At the same time, the institutional and policy framework governing global finance has been slow to respond to changing needs, lagging behind financial globalization and shifts in international financial markets and capital flows. The last two chapters address these dual themes of rapid change in financial markets and a global financial architecture in need of reform to align with the new financial dynamics.

Digital Transformation of Money and Finance

In chapter 8, Eswar Prasad focuses on the implications of digital technologies for the international financial and monetary system. Advances in financial technologies have the potential to substantially improve the efficiency of financial transactions and provide new, lower-cost channels for cross-border financial flows. The innovations of fintech will be a boon to importers and exporters, firms looking to raise capital, investors seeking international diversification opportunities, and migrants sending remittances to home countries. These changes can deepen financial globalization, creating a more global market for capital and enabling it to flow more easily within and across countries to the most productive investment opportunities, in turn spurring the global economy.

With enhanced international mobility of capital, though, many countries will also face increased risks of volatility of capital flows and the complications that creates for managing their exchange rates and economies. The proliferation of channels for cross-border flows will make it increasingly difficult for national authorities to regulate and control those flows to safeguard financial stability. In emerging-market and developing economies, in particular, policymakers will need to pay more attention to increased exposure to capital market volatility and spillovers from monetary policy actions of major central banks. Moreover, the emergence of new conduits for cross-border flows will facilitate not just international investment and commerce but also illicit financial flows, raising new challenges for regulators.

The products of digital financial technologies, such as cryptocurrencies and blockchain-based more decentralized payment systems, are likely to significantly reshape the operation and structure of international financial markets. The reliance on traditional major currencies, and payment systems such as SWIFT, for international transactions may wane. Also, with the rising economic profile of leading emerging-market economies and development of their financial systems, transactions between their currencies will increase as their costs decline and they become easier to execute.

However, the potential disruption of the international reserve system by digital innovations is likely to be more limited, even as they gain traction as mediums of exchange and disrupt the international payment system. Unbacked cryptocurrencies may not be considered reliable reserve assets because of susceptibility to high volatility. Stablecoins may be seen as a less volatile option, but as their value depends on backing by fiat currencies, they may not become independent stores of value—and, like other crypto assets, they lack effective global regulation. While the US dollar could lose some ground as a payment currency, it is likely to maintain its dominance as a reserve currency. This dominance rests not just on the issuing country's economic size and financial market depth but also on a strong institutional foundation that is essential for maintaining investors' trust. A central bank digital currency (CBDC) issued by China—a digital renminbi—will help expand the currency's role in international payments but digitization by itself is unlikely to significantly boost its status as a reserve currency relative to the US dollar, although the renminbi's rise could diminish the role of second-tier reserve currencies, including the euro, the British pound, and the Japanese yen.

Less-developed countries could face greater challenges. Their national currencies could face greater competition from stablecoins or CBDCs issued by major economies. They may also face a tougher external environment if rivalries between major economies and their currencies give rise to currency blocs and a fragmentation of the international monetary system. The risks of geoeconomic fragmentation, noted earlier, could be compounded by the risks of geofinancial fragmentation. How these risks evolve will be linked closely to how today's elevated geopolitical tensions evolve.

Refitting the Global Financial Architecture

The global financial architecture has evolved greatly over time. Typically, significant reform has followed financial crises. As new challenges emerge, the world would benefit from a more proactive approach to reform. In chapter 9, Joon-Ho Hahm and Woo Jin Choi analyze current risks and vulnerabilities and outline key areas where the global financial architecture needs to be strengthened.

Since the global financial crisis, and the reforms that followed, new risks have developed in the global financial system. The composition of capital flows has been shifting, with bond flows rising relative to bank lending and nonbank financial institutions (NBFIs) expanding their role. The increased reliance on debt markets and NBFIs, together with currency mismatches, heighten vulnerabilities for emerging-market and developing economies. Many of them carry increased debt burdens, with a growing number experiencing debt service difficulties. Also, external imbalances have widened again, especially after the pandemic. The pronounced resurgence of US external imbalance creates potential risks for global financial stability from a US rebalancing. Emerging-market and developing economies are facing destabilizing spillover effects from shifts in the global financial cycle and in the monetary policy stance of advanced economies.

The global financial architecture could be strengthened along several dimensions to better address current and emerging challenges and risks. The international lender-of-last-resort capacity should be expanded by augmenting the resources of the International Monetary Fund, enhancing the role of the Special Drawing Rights, and bolstering central bank swap facilities within a more multilateral framework. The global macroeconomic surveillance framework should be broadened, complementing the current focus on individual economies with more attention to global linkages, spillovers, and policy coordination challenges. The financial system regulatory and monitoring framework has been substantially strengthened for banks but needs to be beefed up for NBFIs in view of their expanded role and associated risks. Market-based resilience of the global financial system can be enhanced. For example, the development of local capital markets, harmonization of bond standards, and innovations such as sovereign bond-back securities can help better insulate the financial systems of emerging-market and developing economies from shifts in the global financial cycle. There is a need to establish an improved, multilateral sovereign debt restructuring framework that can respond quickly when needed and that incorporates fair burden-sharing and full participation of both official and private creditors.

Moreover, adequate regulation and oversight need to be developed for the new forms of money and funds transfer mechanisms created by digital technologies. The potential of digital financial technologies must be harnessed in ways that foster their benefits while containing their risks.

Another new challenge for the global financial architecture is to facilitate the mobilization of large amounts of funds to support countries' efforts to combat climate change—including by augmenting public funding, bolstering the role of the World Bank and other multilateral development banks, and incentivizing private investment—and to build the resilience of the financial system to climate-related risks. Progress in addressing all of these challenges will depend crucially on the ability of the international community to shield global economic and financial cooperation from geopolitical headwinds.

Conclusion

The global economy faces multifaceted, transformative change. Disruptions to existing systems and paradigms are inevitable and must be managed. The global outlook will be more uncertain and volatile. Global integration has been enormously beneficial for economic progress in developed and developing countries alike, but it faces risks from shifting geopolitics. The world, however, is not deglobalizing. Built-in economic interdependence gives globalization resilience. Major powers competing for global dominance have been huge beneficiaries of global economic integration and have a continuing stake in not undermining it. But there are real risks of globalization fragmenting along lines drawn by major-power rivalry, entailing large costs for all involved and the global economy—and potential for conflict. Future patterns of globalization will depend crucially on how countries manage the shifting international power dynamics.

In a more contested world, the need for a rules-based international order is even greater. Rather than letting the multilateral framework of rules governing economic relations between countries be frayed by rising nationalist competition and protectionism, the world would collectively benefit from recommitting to it—and strengthening it to add governance frameworks for new areas of interconnection between nations, notably the digital economy and the technologies driving it. Past gains in establishing a rules-based multilateral economic order have not only fostered global economic prosperity but have been an important underpinning of geopolitical stability. New competition dynamics in the global economy are inevitable as economies evolve and economic power structures shift. But a lesson of history is that all must play by internationally accepted rules.

Digital technologies are opening new avenues for growth and international integration, including leapfrogging opportunities for development and structural transformation for developing economies. But they also pose new challenges for national policies and international cooperation. New dynamics in industry, labor markets, and trade must be managed to foster inclusive growth and facilitate adjustment to change. Digital innovations in finance must be secured by appropriate oversight. New frameworks need to be developed for regulating digital markets, where international cooperation will be important to encourage agreement on common principles and standards while recognizing that policy approaches will differ across countries. Some of the powerful new technologies, notably AI applications, have immense potential to expand the frontiers of human advancement, but they also carry serious risks of misuse and are dual-use technologies. There is a risk that they can become a battleground for technological supremacy weaponized for advantage in major-power rivalries. Cooperative frameworks will be needed wherein countries balance national and security concerns with broad technology diffusion across nations.

Geopolitics will make needed international cooperation more challenging in matters ranging from trade policies to the global financial architecture to regulation of new technologies. In combating climate change, international cooperation is inherently essential given the universal nature of the climate challenge. The international community will need to rise above nationalist and geopolitical interests in areas such as green technologies and energy transition to address the climate imperatives. The future of the global economy, and indeed of humanity, will depend on how nations engage on matters of the global commons—from a rules-based international order to climate.

PART I

The Future of Globalization

TWO

The New Logic of Globalization

Uncertainty, Volatility, and the Digital Economy

LAURA TYSON, JOHN ZYSMAN, AND BRIAN JUDGE

The global economy in the decades ahead will be volatile and uncertain.[1] The first driver of the volatility and uncertainty is the reconfiguration of the global political economy reflecting what we term the new zero-sum logic of globalization and its implications for cross-border flows of goods and services. An important element of this reconfiguration is the growing economic and geopolitical power of China. The post–World War II period of globalization reflected the neoliberal vision of the United States, but American economic and political power is declining, at least in relative terms. The rise of China and other new economic powers means the emergence of a multipolar or perhaps a bipolar framework for globalization that differs from the neoliberal vision in significant ways. A second driver is ongoing technological changes in both the digitalization of goods and services and the automation of work via artificial intelligence (AI). Over the past thirty years, as the digital economy has matured, it has become inter-twined with and has supported globalization. AI will continue to transform work and society, but it remains to be seen whether it acts as an integrator of the global economy or, equally likely, fragments it along national or regional lines with the restructuring of global politics. A third driver is climate change and its effects on global patterns of production, employment, and investment.

In this chapter, we examine how the patterns and the rules for global trade and investment are changing as a result of these three drivers of change. Based on our reading of the evidence and current trends, we posit four conclusions for the advanced industrial democracies.

First, the economic world remains highly interconnected. It is not deglobalizing; it is restructuring. All nations have significant dependence on international trade and investment, and thus self-sufficiency is not an option for any nation, regardless of size. Cross-border flows proved remark-ably resilient during the COVID-19 pandemic. Even before the pandemic, there had been a slowdown in global integration after more than two decades during which global trade grew twice as fast as global GDP. The period of "slowbalization" after the 2008 global recession was marked by a plateauing of the global flow of goods, but that plateau did not mean a reversal: global trade flows have continued to hover around 60 percent of global GDP. No single region or country is anywhere close to economic self-sufficiency.[2]

Economic interconnections, however, are being reconfigured along more fragmented and regional lines as a zero-sum approach to globalization displaces the previous positive-sum approach in the United States and many other advanced industrial countries. The United States, long the champion of neoliberal globalization, has embraced onshoring, near-shoring, and friend-shoring to bolster national security, mitigate vulnerabilities that can lead to supply chain disruptions, and promote national production and employment. The zero-sum logic is likely to result in higher costs and slower global growth. According to the International Monetary Fund (IMF), the fragmentation of the global economy could reduce global GDP by a sober-ing 7 percent.[3] According to the World Trade Organization (WTO), the separation of the global economy into two blocs could lead to a 5 percent reduction in global GDP.[4]

Second, globalization is increasingly "services-driven," enabled by digital technologies. Global trade and financial flows are being driven by services and, within services, by flows of data, knowledge-intensive services, intangibles, and talent. Cross-border data flows are growing by 50 percent annually as they enable remote-working and the production of digital services around the world, surpassing the flows of physical trade. Half of all trade in global services depends on digital technologies, and exports of digital services account for more than half of total exports of services. Digital technologies allow actors, from small businesses to multinational companies, to participate in cross-border transactions. Having a website can give small firms an immediate global presence, and e-commerce platforms provide support with financial payments and logistics.

The neoliberal era of globalization was driven by manufacturing deconstruction and labor arbitrage as low-cost labor became available to global companies and was facilitated by the integration of Russia and China into the global economy. Now, that era of globalization is giving way to the globalization of services production and trade based on new sources of labor-market arbitrage in digitally enabled services. Patterns of interconnections are also being changed by AI and its effects on the production and delivery of both goods and services.

Third, globalization is being reshaped by the resurgence of industrial policies in the United States and around the world, particularly as nations search for "strategic autonomy" and competitive advantage in AI and other technologies deemed crucial to national security, the energy transition, the fight against climate change, and high-wage employment opportunities. These four goals drive the resurgence of industrial policy with multiple objectives, which at times can pull in opposing directions. Industrial policies, unless developed cooperatively, are, by definition, zero-sum in the sense that they promote domestic—as opposed to and at the expense of global—production and employment in favored sectors. But industrial policies can also have positive-sum effects across nations, for example, by promoting scientific and technological advances through investments in research and development. The "subsidy war" between the United States and Europe in green technologies may speed and scale investment and production with a positive-sum effect on global collective efforts to address the shared "common goods" challenges of climate change. No nation has a monopoly on the technological advances necessary to address climate change, however, and there is a danger that dueling industrial policies and differing standards will impede rather than accelerate the development and adoption of the most effective mitigation technologies.

Fourth, US-China economic and national security relations will be a defining force for the future course of globalization. China's entry in the WTO and its resulting growing share of global trade and GDP were key outcomes of neoliberal globalization as China emerged as the center of complex global supply chains throughout manufacturing. The "designed in the US, produced in China" description of the Apple iPhone, which transformed lives around the world, applied to a growing array of sophisticated manufactured goods, including many dual-use goods with both civilian and security applications. Despite higher tariffs, pandemic supply-chain disruptions, and heightened geopolitical tensions, US trade with China set a new record in 2022. Primarily for national security reasons but also for concerns about the eroding US lead in key technologies relative to China, the United States today is committed to "de-risking and diversifying" its economic relations with China, while pursuing its own ambitious "industrial and innovation strategy."[5]

This new emerging Washington consensus view is evident in US policies in the semiconductor industry, which include both direct incentives to build semiconductor facilities in the United States and the unilateral imposition of US controls with extraterritorial reach on exports of advanced semiconductors to China, together with restrictions on outbound US investments to China in this and related advanced technologies. The goal of these controls is to keep China several years behind the technological frontier in this militarily critical dual-use digital technology while the United States strengthens its lead. Although the United States denies a zero-sum approach in its economic relations with China, the zero-sum logic is a foundation of US policies to restrict its exports and outbound investments in technologies deemed to have significant national security implications.

Where We Are and How We Got Here

The old logic of globalization was perhaps best encapsulated by John Williamson's "Washington Consensus" in the early 1990s.[6] This consensus, championed by the United States, emphasized private property rights, the elimination of cross-border trade and investment barriers, competitive exchange rates, market liberalization, and other pro-market reforms. In contrast, the new logic of globalization is driven by the reassertion of national interests. Nations around the world, including the United States, are now acting assertively to shape and position their economies to generate advantage in the reconfigured global economy. Decisions that were formerly considered to be the primary, if not exclusive, domain of profit-driven corporate managers are increasingly the subject of intense political scrutiny, policy intervention, and conflict as states engage in a competitive struggle to generate jobs and income for their populations, combat climate change, and secure strategic autonomy in critical digital technologies like semiconductors and AI.

The net effect is a shift from a positive-sum to a zero-sum logic in national decision-making and a departure from the previous emphasis on the benefits of free trade and global cooperation. Several examples illustrate this shift: the increasing regulation of the private sector on the basis of national security concerns; the explicit focus of policies on creating good jobs at home by attracting production, investment, and employment from other nations; the embrace of industrial policies, including government subsidies and protections to promote domestic capacity in favored sectors; and the undercutting of possibilities for global cooperation on issues like climate change by national rivalry for dominance in key sectors and technologies. This new logic of globalization emphasizes advancing national interests rather than promoting global cooperation and mutual benefit. The jobs lost in the previous era or, more precisely, the effort to offset those losses and generate future employment are a significant driver of industrial policy today.

The new nationalist logic of globalization is heightening volatility and uncertainty in the global economy. The certainties that could once be relied upon in an earlier phase of globalization are being upended by this new logic. Countries are now attempting to secure their positions in a rapidly changing and highly competitive global economy. The fast pace of technological change has also brought significant challenges in areas like privacy, cybersecurity, and the impact of automation on employment. Although the evolving zero-sum logic will not bring globalization to an end, it will significantly impact its shape and structure, with deleterious effects on efficiency and global growth.

We emphasize, however, that the economic transformations of the last several decades cannot simply be undone. The global system is not disintegrating but transforming.[7] Accordingly, deglobalization is the wrong term for describing what is unfolding. Rather, what is emerging is increasing fragmentation and regionalization, not diminished international connections.

The new logic of globalization is especially evident in the digital economy, in which the tensions between globalization and nationalism are quite visible. Digital technology and the digital economy are ubiquitous: chips are embedded, it has become conventional to note, in everything from toasters and cars to mobile phones and computers. Our economic and social lives are mediated by interconnected webs of data, and digital fabrics underpin everything from product repairs to restaurant deliveries. Products are increasingly differentiated by the information and communications technology (ICT) services they offer in their use and maintenance.[8] Digitalization has also led to the emergence of the large tech platforms that challenge traditional industries and create new value chains.

Today, the rules for data, AI, and digital platforms are taking significantly different forms throughout the world, making it likely that even without geopolitical rivalries intensifying, the internet will splinter and become a "splinternet."[9] Digital tools are also reshaping warfare via cyberattacks on critical infrastructure, misinformation campaigns in elections, new forms of battlefield surveillance, and the deployment of autonomous drones. Moreover, national strategies to adapt to and create advantage in the transition to a hopefully green but certainly digital future will create tensions amongst erstwhile allies.[10] The digital economy—from software to semiconductors—will be a key battleground on which governments seek to balance the benefits of openness against national interests.

The trajectories of the digital economy and the neoliberal global system are intertwined and mutually supporting and overlapping in time. The commercial internet dates either from 1993, when Tim Berners-Lee released the code that would become the World Wide Web, or 1995, when the National Science Foundation (NSF) retired the NSF Network internet backbone, enabling the rise of private internet service providers.[11] The maturation involved a shift from a focus on the power of particular devices, the speed of processors, and memory in personal computers, to the ways internet bandwidth permitted interconnected computer systems to be built at massive scale. Microprocessors were suddenly everywhere and in everything. The spread of cloud computing, mobile networks, and the rise of the platform economy changed business practices, market structures, and social arrangements.

The phone system itself became part of the digital universe, with 5G networks delivering an increasing share of existing digital services and enabling entirely new ones. Computing power arguably contributed to the 2008 financial crisis by enabling derivatives, securitized assets, and high-speed trading.[12] More formally stated, the maturation of the digital economy involved the interlinked and compounding increase in network capacity, storage capacity, and semiconductor power. Cloud-based systems replaced standalone systems to capture economies of scale. Global cloud storage capacity increased twenty-five-fold, while global data center internet traffic increased eleven-fold between 2010 and 2020.[13] Digital transformation was not limited to the advanced economies. Mobile phone networks and simple payment systems such as M-PESA in Africa and the Unified Payments Interface (UPI) in India, for example, fundamentally transformed market dynamics in those countries.[14] Estonia became a recognized leader in the digital provision of government services to its population.

At about the same time the commercial internet was launched, the fall of the Berlin Wall in 1989 and the collapse of the Soviet Union in 1991 signaled a new structure of the global economy. The heyday of neoliberal globalization was marked by the entry of China into the WTO at the end of 2001. A political consensus in favor of neoliberal globalization in the advanced economies enabled this transformation: policymakers seemed to agree that increasing economic integration would provide benefits for all. The "global economy" became a vision and a goal for some. In practice, however, globalization has not been uniformly beneficial. It has had quite different consequences for different groups, with real winners, including substantial parts of the emerging economies, and real losers, notably many in the former industrial belts of the advanced economies. These events were not the end of history, but rather a new geopolitical chapter.

The diverse experiences of neoliberal globalization generated what Roberts and Lamp identify as the "six faces" of globalization.[15] They argue that political attitudes toward globalization crucially depend on one's perspective. The dominant view of globalization, which they term the "establishment narrative," focuses on the benefits of globalization for everyone. The evidence supporting this view includes lower prices, strong growth around the world, the millions lifted from poverty and the emergence of strong middle classes in the developing world, and the emergence of a global consensus around boosting trade and cross-border investment. This view, however, has become "besieged from all sides."[16] The other "faces" of globalization focus on the relative winners and losers from globalization and the distributive flows.[17] Right-wing populists emphasize how blue-collar workers in developed countries have been disproportionately harmed relative to workers elsewhere, while left-wing populists see the gains of globalization as having been disproportionately captured by a small economic elite.

The two stories—technology and geopolitical economy—are intimately interconnected. Cross-national supply networks emerged as firms headquartered in the advanced economies sought lower costs for parts of their operations, both in production (for example, manufacturing/assembly) and services (for example, call centers). ICT permitted the deconstruction and reconfiguration of the production and distribution of both goods and services. New trade and finance regulations, framed in general theory but benefiting specific groups more than others, were sought to facilitate these new arrangements, and the possibilities of global gains became the ideological framing for the particular demands of these groups. Nevertheless, the winners were not just in the advanced economies: millions in countries now integrated with global production systems and supply networks were pulled out of poverty and, indeed, into middle incomes. But as production moved out of the advanced economies, it meant job losses, wage stagnation, and devastated communities in the industrial heartlands of the United States and other advanced industrial nations.

To set the stage for the future, let us consider some of the economic consequences of the maturing and increasingly ubiquitous digital infrastructure and the digitalization of the global economy. We cannot, of course, do justice to the full skein of developments, only spotlight some of the most important ones reconfiguring economies and societies.

The Domestic Side of the Story

ROUTINE-BIASED TECHNOLOGICAL CHANGE. Digitization enabled routine-biased technological change in production that has been a major driver of the decline in the share of routine middle-income, middle-skill jobs as a share of overall employment; the stagnation of wages for middle-skill workers; and increasing income inequality in the advanced economies. These effects were most dramatic in the manufacturing sector, where the declines in employment were far larger than the declines in production, attesting to the substantial labor productivity gains from routine and skill-biased technological change. Digitally driven gains in information, communications, and logistics facilitated the outsourcing of jobs—the deconstruction and relocation of manufacturing employment from the advanced industrial economies to China and other low-cost labor locations. Despite popular

perceptions, the reality is that technological changes have been more important than trade based on labor arbitrage and China's policies in the loss of
manufacturing employment in the advanced industrial economies.[18]

RISE OF THE PLATFORM ECONOMY. The rise of the platform economy is arguably the most visible transformation driving cross-border data flows and
digital services. Ten years ago, the arrival and significance of platforms
enabled by digitalization and driven by powerful network effects and first-
mover advantages were already recognized. By the early 2020s, the maturation and pervasiveness of platforms were evident across the economy.[19]
Platforms have reshaped retail commerce (Amazon), libraries (Google search),
travel (Expedia, but more powerfully, Google Maps), entertainment (Spotify
to Netflix and all the other streaming services), and more:

> A digital platform economy is emerging. Companies such as Amazon,
> Etsy, Facebook, Google, Salesforce, and Uber are creating online
> structures that enable a wide range of human activities. This opens
> the way for radical changes in how we work, socialize, create value in
> the economy, and compete for the resulting profits. Their effects are
> distinct and identifiable, though certainly not the only part of the
> rapidly reorganizing global economy.[20]

Platforms are no longer a surprise, but rather are a maturing if not mature
technology penetrating a vast array of sectors and affecting the way work
itself is organized.[21]

CLOUD COMPUTING AS THE FOUNDATION. Digital platforms rest on a revolution in computing, loosely referred to as cloud computing:

> [There is a] Cloud Computing revolution in computing architec-
> ture, transforming not only the "where" (location) of computing,
> but also the "how" (the manner in which software is produced and
> the tools available for the automation of business processes).[22]

Fundamentally, the rise of cloud computing marks the enormous abundance of computing resources and the move past scarcity. The basics of

contemporary cloud computing, now often referred to as hyperscaling, were long understood in theory but emerged in practice from the computing needs of companies like Google and Facebook.[23] They required large-scale operations and could achieve them only with the new abundance of resources. Cloud offerings from the likes of Amazon and Google permit firms to spin up offerings quickly and at very low cost. There is no need for a startup or a unit in an established company to build out an entire— and extremely expensive—IT infrastructure. Rather, they simply "rent" the computing power on an ongoing basis or long enough to assess the offering.

SERVICES WITH EVERYTHING.   The emergence of cloud computing has transformed services. Capital costs for computing and data storage infrastructure have plummeted and have been transformed into an operating cost, enabling an array of service functions that can be cheaply produced and easily rented.[24] The avalanche of firms providing these services is a direct consequence of the dramatic decline in computing costs. Startups no longer need to purchase expensive equipment to provide a specific business function:[25]

> With the Algorithmic Revolution, tasks underlying services can be transformed into formalizable, codifiable, computable processes with clearly defined rules for their execution. The inexorable rise in computational power means that an ever greater range of activities are amenable to expression as computable algorithms, and a growing array of activities are reorganized and automated.[26]

A wide range of services—accounting and book-keeping, x-ray diagnostics, order-taking in a restaurant, to name a few—are now facilitated and delivered with AI and digital tools. Value creation and work are being reconfigured.[27] At the same time, physical products become portals to service offerings. The "television" is now really just a tablet hanging on the wall, functionally more limited than the computer, which also offers a portal to an ocean of services. Many physical products, from tires to jet engines, are sold in service packages made possible by sensors and digital analytics.

The combination of routine-biased technological change, platforms, cloud computing, and ICT-enabled services profoundly affects work, its location, the economic structures within nations, and the global inter-connections among them. This transformative combination is also recon-figuring politics and societies within nations and the geopolitical relations among them.[28]

The International Counterpart

Neoliberal globalization connected domestic economies with the global economy. The result was widespread, albeit unevenly shared, economic growth and prosperity. It produced a period of converging growth rates around the world that brought millions of people out of poverty and into the global middle class in the emerging-market economies while reducing the size of the middle class in the advanced industrial economies. The expansion of trade in manufactured goods was perhaps the most visible aspect of this era, but its defining characteristics were the emergence of cross-border supply chains and production networks that enabled the decon-struction, decomposition, deverticalization, and outsourcing by large firms to low-cost sites and to growing markets around the world. A dramatic instance of that decomposition was when IBM, eager to duplicate Apple's personal computer, outsourced processors to Intel and operating systems to Microsoft. The label "Wintelism"—Windows from Microsoft and pro-cessors from Intel—captured the notion that crucial innovation could come from outside.[29]

A more general expression of that argument is "open innovation," the concept that firms should be open to and incorporate innovation outside their own company boundaries.[30] What emerged was not an atomic system of competing nodes but rather regions and ecosystems specializing in dif-ferent phases of the overall production system. Examples range from ser-vice centers and help desks to semiconductor foundries.[31] Echoing this earlier arrangement, Apple focuses on design and software while outsourcing semiconductor fabrication to the Taiwan Semiconductor Manufacturing Company (TSMC) and assembly to Foxconn. Hence the phrase on every Apple product: "Designed by Apple in California. Made in China."

Moreover, globalization enabled the Pearl River Delta region to become the global leader in electronics assembly and Taiwan to become the global leader in advanced semiconductor fabrication, with Samsung a close second or third. The entire global value chain in semiconductors is enabled by advanced lithography machines made by the Dutch firm Advanced Semiconductor Materials Lithography (ASML). The decomposition and globalization of production have created geographic nodes of supply chains rooted in expertise and know-how rather than simple labor-cost advantages. The overall effect has been an exponential decrease in the cost of storage, computing power, and bandwidth, enabling large platforms to capture massive economies of scale without historical precedent. Thus, over the last decade, global flows have been driven by services and intellectual property rather than physical resources and manufactured goods. Growth in global data flows has been particularly sharp, nearly doubling since 2020.[32]

The benefits of the global economy, however, have not been distributed equally. The famous "elephant chart" captures the fact that while globalization enabled high income growth among middle-income countries and the very wealthy, the 80th to the 95th percentile of the global income distribution experienced flat or negative income growth during the same period.[33] Income inequality within many countries increased while income inequality between countries declined. More recent work complicates the exact shape of the curve, but the general conclusion that the benefits of globalization were not widely shared remains.[34] It is essential to note, however, that skill- and routine-biased technological change enabled by the digitalization of production, rather than globalization, was the major source of the loss of middle-skill, middle-income jobs and the resulting decline in the share of the middle class in the advanced industrial economies. In popular thinking, neoliberal globalization bears a disproportionate share of the blame for the rise in income and wealth inequality in these economies. Moreover, despite the fact that these economies had similar experiences with globalization and technology, they exhibit differences in wage and income inequality, indicating the importance of policies to mitigate the distributional effects.[35]

What Lies Ahead for the Globalization of the Digital Economy

The neoliberal political economy dominated by the United States is shifting toward a yet-to-be-defined global architecture and governance regime. The rapid advancement of digital technologies, the changing geopolitical landscape, and climate change are certain, but the specific outcomes shaped by these forces are uncertain. It is difficult to make accurate predictions about the direction and speed of developments in the digital economy and their implications for the global economy given the significant uncertainties that are embedded in these certainties. Despite this, identifying emerging issues can help to shed light on the potential paths and directions that the increasingly digital global economy may take.

We identify three key issues:

- The United States and other nations are embracing more activist industrial policies to gain competitive advantage in strategic technologies like semiconductors and green technologies. This approach risks sparking subsidy wars and tensions with other countries, including allies. Will competing national industrial policies in a struggle for digital technology leadership and the "de-risking and diversifying" of US economic relations with China force difficult adaptation?
- The internet could splinter as countries impose diverging regulations on data, platforms, and digital infrastructure. However, the extent of the fragmentation is unclear. Will geopolitical conflict accelerate the splintering of the internet?
- AI, especially new generative models, will likely transform economies and societies. But the precise impacts on jobs, productivity, and international trade are debated. How will AI's impact on productivity and work influence global patterns of production, employment, and investment? How will nations differ in their regulation of AI?

The United States was once the champion of neoliberal globalization, with its multinational corporations playing a major role in global trade and investment. Now, the landscape has shifted: global flows are increasingly shaped by nations with policies to bolster their own companies and economies. Both security and commercial interests play key roles in this shift. The belief that integrating China and Russia into the US-led global order would stabilize global geopolitics has been shattered by Russia's invasion of Ukraine and by rising tensions between the United States and China. Whether there will be a destructive decoupling, to use Michael Spence's phrase, or a diversification and derisking of economic relations with China, is now a significant concern for both the United States and Europe.[36]

Despite these tensions, most nations, especially in Asia, are not interested in decoupling from China. South-South trade is growing and now accounts for more than a quarter of global trade. Asia has doubled its share of world trade, with more than half remaining within Asia itself. Countries in the Association of Southeast Asian Nations (ASEAN) have negotiated several trade agreements and supported China in creating the Regional Comprehensive Economic Partnership (RCEP), which includes fifteen countries representing about one-third of global GDP and is currently the largest free trade agreement in the world.

Regional and bilateral trade agreements may continue to eclipse multilateral rules. Supply chains may also become shorter and more regional to boost resilience. Supply chains in services and trade and investment flows in intangibles are likely to expand, resulting in new global hubs and requiring new rules. Recognizing the importance of digital trade in services, a group of ninety members of the WTO, including members of the European Union (EU), the United States, and China, is negotiating to develop new multilateral rules for digital trade. Despite the increased challenges, multilateral cooperation on trade rules is still possible, as evidenced by recent WTO agreements to curb subsidies to fisheries, remove barriers to food aid, and enhance access to the intellectual property behind COVID vaccines.[37]

Global trade and finance aggregates as such do not appear to be in retreat, though the pace of the overall expansion has certainly slowed.[38] However, the pattern of who trades what with whom will be shaped by the character and intensity of geopolitical conflicts. There are several important factors affecting the outlook:

- The war in Ukraine and the ensuing sanctions have certainly been disruptive, especially shifting patterns of grain and oil trade.
- The confrontation with China and related sanctions suggest the possibility of a destructive decoupling. Setting aside the chip wars, the battle to control the pace and direction of a host of strategic technologies, including AI and climate technologies, will likely have significant effects on production networks and supply chains. Only ponder the adjustments that Foxconn will need to make about what it produces and where.
- The rise of new powers, notably India, will likely also change the patterns of trade, particularly trade and investment in services.

- Climate mitigation strategies as well as migration flows driven by climate, not just war, will have consequences.
- Challenges to big tech domination running from defensive regulation in Europe, tougher antitrust policies in the United States, rupture in China, and open-source development of digital public utilities in India will shape data flows and commerce more generally.

There are diverse possibilities that range from destructive decoupling to a reconfiguration of economic linkages around geopolitical blocs rather than geographic regions. The most dramatic outcome would be a confrontation aligning China, Russia, and their allies with the rest of the world. The emerging architecture might involve a different regional concentration as, for example, reflected in Japan's push for closer engagement with India. There will be tensions as competing national objectives foster different regional and global arrangements. National security confrontation with China will strain the ability to arrange global agreements to address climate change. The final global architecture will shape who is a "friend" and affect patterns of trade and finance.

The Rise of Industrial Policy and Its Implications for the Global Economy

The United States remains the largest economy in the world by GDP, the largest importer (accounting for about 13 percent of global imports in 2022), and the second largest exporter after China (accounting for close to 10 percent of global exports in 2022). Given its shares of global trade and its leadership in shaping the WTO and the prevailing multilateral rules of trade, the resurgence of industrial policy in the United States is a major driver of the new logic of globalization. Although the overall size of industrial policy in the United States is relatively small—for example, subsidies to favored industries are currently only around 0.5 percent of GDP—a new era in US economic policy is emerging. There are multiple, interrelated goals of US industrial policy: strengthening national security; maintaining leadership in key technologies, including those related to climate change; slowing China's advancement in these technologies; and boosting domestic investment, production, and employment. In both trade policy and industrial policy, the Biden administration emphasizes the need for an inclusive "bottom-up, middle-out" approach, with a special focus on labor and disadvantaged communities. This approach is reflected in policies in both the

CHIPS Act and the Inflation Reduction Act (IRA) enacted in 2022 and in the actions and priorities of the United States Trade Representative.[39]

Neoliberal globalization rested on the assumption that investment decisions should be made by managers and shareholders, not by governments. This market logic reflects the belief that markets always allocate capital productively and efficiently, regardless of what other nations do to create competitive advantage, the existence of market imperfections and market power, the effects of markets on income inequality, and externalities like climate change that markets overlook. Driven by this logic, national economic interests in the United States and other advanced industrial economies receded into the background as global rules and incentives along with routine and skill-biased technological change and digitalization tilted production, employment, and investment away from the industrial heartlands of the North Atlantic world toward the South and the East.

It is important to reiterate that neoliberal globalization generated significant returns for the US economy and for most of the world. This period was not a race to the bottom but a race to the top—most nations became richer, and income inequality between nations declined. Neoliberal globalization was driven by a positive-sum logic with positive-sum results.[40] But globalization, particularly the rapid emergence of China as a manufacturing powerhouse, offshoring through complex supply chains, and the development of labor-saving technologies also imposed significant costs on the firms, workers, and communities that lost economic activity to lower-cost locations around the world. The globalization of manufacturing production to low-cost locations based on labor-arbitrage contributed to rising income inequality and the stagnation of middle-class wages in the United States and other advanced industrial economies. These in turn fed rising political discontent, reflected in the UK's decision to break from the EU and the election of President Trump in the United States in 2016.

Recent speeches by the US Treasury Secretary Janet Yellen and National Security Adviser Jake Sullivan signal the shift in US thinking about globalization and in favor of industrial policy—what US officials are calling "industrial and innovation strategies."[41] It is important to acknowledge that industrial policy is not new to the United States. The US competitive position in major industries, including aircraft and space vehicles, the internet, social media, fracking, pharmaceuticals, and medical equipment has been supported–some might say created—by numerous policies, including research and development (R&D), taxation, and government procurement. Now, however, the United States has become more explicit about the need for industrial policy for three reasons: to strengthen the supply-side foundations and productive capacity of the US economy, especially in technologies and products like semiconductors critical to national security; to strengthen the US technological lead and secure global supply chains for such products, including through friend-shoring and near-shoring investments; and to encourage investment in green industries and jobs and create US competitive advantage in new products and technologies to combat climate change.

In her recent remarks, Secretary Yellen linked the new industrial policy focus to what she called "modern supply-side economics"—investing in infrastructure and physical capital, in R&D and knowledge capital, and in human capital to counter the harm that US underinvestment and what she termed China's unfair economic practices have imposed on US workers and firms around the world. At the same time, she emphasized national security concerns with China as a major factor in the development of a robust industrial policy in semiconductors, including subsidies, tax credits, and controls over exports and cross-border inflows and outflows of investment.[42] In his comments, Sullivan emphasized the need for industrial policy on national security grounds to protect "foundational technologies" with a "small yard and a high fence" and to usher in a new wave of the digital revolution to ensure that next generation technologies work for, not against, democracy and security.[43] Sullivan's comments presage additional US industrial policy measures on digital technologies beyond semiconductors. Although Sullivan was explicit that the intent was not to impose a "technology blockade" on China, the United States has also been clear that the national security objective is to maintain a technological edge over China in semiconductors and in other high-value and dual-use technologies.

Will the US industrial policy in semiconductors be successful? There are many formidable obstacles to onshoring a meaningful percentage of advanced semiconductor manufacturing. Running a semiconductor fabrication plant requires more than just the factory itself. It also requires an entire ecosystem of advanced inputs and high-skill engineering talent. TSMC is headquartered in the Hsinchu Science Park in Taiwan that is also home to four hundred technology companies, their suppliers, and two leading technical universities. The park was established in 1980 by the Taiwanese government on the model of Silicon Valley. Building such an ecosystem from scratch in the outskirts of Phoenix is a tall order.[44]

TSMC founder Morris Chang referred to the CHIPS Act as an "expensive exercise in futility." On an earnings call, TSMC's chief financial officer estimated that the cost of building a US plant might be upwards of four times as expensive as building a similar plant in Taiwan.[45]

In the absence of cooperation with allies in Europe and Asia, US industrial policy in semiconductors is triggering similar policies in other countries. Cooperation among allies is giving way to competition and commercial friction to gain competitive advantage in semiconductors and other strategic technologies, including green technologies. Germany has already announced plans to build semiconductor fabrication facilities and is inviting foreign companies to invest in such facilities. Samsung has announced that it will invest $228 billion to create a new semiconductor cluster in Korea, with significant support from the Korean government. Samsung is already the largest producer of semiconductors in the world and is in a race to close the gap with TSMC in advanced semiconductors within five years.

Given the shared strategic importance of the semiconductor industry and its location in many allied countries, the United States should have worked to coordinate industrial policies with its allies. Instead, it has fostered competition and potential commercial conflicts with them. An effective industrial policy for a global strategic industry requires coordination, not zero-sum policies to attract employment and production from one nation to another. Cooperation with allies on both semiconductors and green technologies is essential to prevent tit-for-tat measures that could potentially slow both digitalization and the energy transition.[46]

It is also possible that competition among countries to gain competitive advantage in semiconductors will result in overproduction, with poor market returns. It is certain that this competition will not create many jobs. The semiconductors industry is capital and research intensive; it relies on expensive educated engineering talent, not low-cost talent. It is very likely that moving a significant share of the semiconductor supply chain back to the United States will significantly increase the production costs and prices of semiconductors that are a key input to all digital products and services. This in turn could impede the pace of digitalization in the global economy. Some bottom-up and middle-out provisions of the CHIPS Act, such as labor requirements and benefits, including childcare benefits, and requirements that investments include small minority-owned businesses and disadvantaged communities, are likely to further increase chip production costs. The US Semiconductor Industry Association estimates the

CHIPS Act, if successful, will create only about 42,000 permanent jobs in the semiconductor industry.[47]

The US embrace of industrial policy is also apparent in the IRA that includes numerous policies to create competitive advantage for US-based production, employment, and private investment in green goods and services to combat climate change. Many provisions of the IRA are zero-sum in the sense that they reward economic activity in the United States, whether by domestic or foreign firms, relative to activity in the rest of the world. In response to strong allied opposition, the United States has already eased some of the most glaring IRA zero-sum policies, such as its buy American provisions. But commercial frictions are likely to continue as the EU and the United States compete to create their own competitive companies and clusters in green products and services. Such frictions are already apparent in the battery industry and in the critical materials needed to produce them.

The IRA also contains positive-sum measures, however, like generous R&D subsidies, to encourage the development of new green technologies and products and to speed and scale their deployment. Indeed, the IRA has triggered a "subsidy war" between the United States and Europe that could have beneficial effects on hastening the energy transition to achieve net-zero goals. Policymakers in the United States have been clear that a key objective for them is to maintain a technological edge over China in high-value technology sectors. Billion-dollar subsidies to profitable multinational firms may be a small price to pay for continued technological dominance. Even before the CHIPS Act, the top five corporate spenders on R&D were all American (Amazon, Alphabet, Meta, Apple, and Microsoft). Whether or not the chip war or the IRA subsidy war escalates further remains to be seen.[48] It is clear, however, that the return of industrial policy marks a significant inflection point for the global economy: the United States is now openly embracing the strategic importance of technological leadership in place of its erstwhile free-market principles.[49] Moreover, the emphasis on high-value technology sectors risks neglecting other areas of the economy that also require investment while precipitating an arms race in other digital technologies deemed significant for national security, particularly AI.

Splinternet

The internet emerged as a crucial dimension of the global economy during the highpoint of neoliberal globalization in the 1990s. The United States pursued a laissez-faire regulatory approach facilitating global access to information and services. By the late 1990s, the internet had become ubiquitous in developed countries and was rapidly expanding in the developing world.

In the mid-2010s, the impact of internet platforms became evident, which led to increased attention from regulators. The United States, as the primary beneficiary of the previously unregulated online environment, has been hesitant to introduce substantial regulatory measures, instead focusing on stricter antitrust enforcement to curb the market power of the global platform giants, headquartered in the country. Outside the United States, however, national responses vary greatly depending on political objectives and available policy tools. All are framed by the strength of the US platform companies.

The EU's response has been evolving. Initially aligned with neoliberal ideology, the EU did little to impede the adoption of larger, better-funded US platforms. The EU's push for a digital single market in the 1990s and 2000s led to policies that facilitated cross-border data flows and harmonized national laws that ultimately favored US platform firms over domestic rivals. However, this shifted as the influence of the US platform firms, fears of cybercrime, and US surveillance programs became more apparent. The EU and national European governments established regulations to limit the power of platform giants, beginning with the General Data Protection Regulation (GDPR) on data privacy, attempts to limit platform self-preferencing, and the introduction of the Digital Markets Act and the Digital Services Act. The lack of native platforms and technical expertise in managing truly large datasets leaves Europe with limited homegrown capacity to emerge as a substantial player in the platform economy or the AI field.

In contrast, China acted early to develop a domestic high-technology industry and internet economy separate from the rest of the world. In a speech on China's ascension to the WTO in 2000, President Clinton remarked: "Now there's no question China has been trying to crack down on the Internet. Good luck! That's sort of like trying to nail jello to the wall."[50] Within the borders of the "Great Firewall," the Chinese government supported the growth of its own domestic platform giants like Alibaba, Tencent, and Baidu, and it is currently rolling out a program to migrate government IT infrastructure from Microsoft Windows to homegrown KylinOS. Even though Chinese platform firms have so far failed to penetrate global markets, the massive domestic market provides the scale necessary for growth and innovation. And recently, some Chinese app companies like TikTok, Shein, and Temu have become some of the most popular apps globally.

Differences in national priorities and policies might potentially lead to a fragmentation of the global internet—splinternet. Splintering can be broadly defined as the establishment of varying regulations or technical protocols for the operation of online platforms across jurisdictions. These regulations could pertain to the flow of data, news, and services through the internet within and across political boundaries, motivated by economic, political, or national security reasons. Additionally, nations could also differ in the rules mandating the pre-installation of an application or operating system.[51] The Chinese case reveals that there never was a truly "global" internet. The outcome of these struggles and divergent national goals and policies could impact not only the US platform giants that dominate the global internet but also the interoperability of the underlying systems. The question now is how far down the technological "stack" splintering will go.

AI: Is This Time, At Last, Different?

Regardless of how the splinternet story plays out, the crucial question at hand is how the current wave of innovation in AI will affect national economies and societies and the global connections among them. Our digital infrastructure has been built in successive stages, with each wave of innovation laying the foundation for the next. Radical increases in processing capabilities, data storage, and networking and communications have enabled the realization of radical ideas once constrained by technological limitations. Throughout each phase, both economies and societies have undergone adaptations, sparking serious debates about the benefits and drawbacks, and the winners and losers. Will the AI technological revolution mark a significant departure from the past? According to many observers, the answer is yes because AI is a general-purpose technology (GPT), much like electricity and the steam engine, with potentially wide-ranging effects. Historically, GPTs have been responsible for driving economic growth and structural change, and they are defined by three characteristics: they are pervasive, they improve over time, and they spawn complementary innovations.[52]

As a GPT, AI has broad applications that will transform economies, societies and even geopolitics. Moreover, AI technologies can be rolled out rapidly through the internet, the ubiquitous digital infrastructure already in place. Both Microsoft and Google are already incorporating AI tools in their search engines and office suites, and humans are already interfacing with large language models (LLMs) using natural language rather than special codes or commands. And the social consequences of AI are already apparent in digital platforms from Amazon to Twitter (now X) to TikTok that can target information to and surveil particular groups or even individuals.

A recent phase of AI, beginning around 2010, was based on machine learning using deep learning.[53] In a 2022 article, we characterized this first phase as "routine-biased technological change on steroids," noting that it adds intelligence to automation tools that substitute for humans in physical tasks and also for humans in routine and increasingly nonroutine cognitive tasks.[54] For this phase, we predicted that AI will displace humans from existing tasks while increasing demand for humans in new tasks in both manufacturing and services. Overall, our conjecture was that AI will continue, even intensify, automation's adverse effects on labor, including the polarization of employment, stagnant wage growth for middle- and low-skill workers, growing inequality, and a lack of good jobs. Though there likely will be enough jobs to keep pace with the slow growth of labor supply in the advanced economies, we were skeptical that AI and ongoing automation will support the creation of enough good jobs. We doubted that the anticipated productivity and growth benefits of AI will be widely shared, predicting instead that they will fuel more inequality.

A new phase of "generative" AI is emerging with the development of LLMs based on "transformers." OpenAI released the first commercially viable LLM (GPT-3) in the middle of 2020. The subsequent releases of ChatGPT in late 2022 and GPT-4 less than six months later showcased the remarkable ability of these models to perform a wide range of useful tasks. Today, many companies are offering and advancing their own LLMs. Microsoft and Google, for instance, have both integrated their LLMs into their respective business productivity suites. Since the cost of assembling and processing the data for these new tools is extremely high (the cost of training GPT-4 is rumored to have exceeded $100 million), it is likely that giant tech firms will dominate the development game and enhance their market power. But while LLMs may be expensive to develop, they are cheap to operate and can be built on top of the existing ICT infrastructure, reducing expenditure on complementary capital equipment. Consequently,

LLMs may deploy much more rapidly compared to previous transformational technologies.

The applications of these tools are expected to have far-reaching effects, although the exact nature and extent of these consequences for the economy, society, and politics are uncertain and difficult to predict. In its most basic form, ChatGPT predicts the next word within a sequence, spanning a dozen to several thousand words. However, despite lacking a true understanding of queries or directives, it has showcased the capacity to generate responses that are remarkably relevant and applicable. Such proficiency has led the majority of users to believe that it will ultimately enhance their productivity. Importantly, the mechanisms at work are not fully understood, nor are the limits, nor the sources of often bizarre errors. Loosely put, what we do know is that LLMs can create highly credible "deepfakes" not just of text but of image and sound. With the reach of the internet, the consequences of these fake, or alternate, realities can be enormous.[55] Let us set aside for this discussion the likely extraordinary impacts on social and political life and focus on the economy.

What will be the consequences of this phase of AI for work and productivity? According to a recent paper, 80 percent of the workforce could have at least 10 percent of their tasks affected by LLMs, while about 19 percent could have at least 50 percent of their tasks affected, where the exposure threshold is a 50 percent reduction in time to complete a task while maintaining quality.[56] This study found that while there are many low-wage occupations with high exposure and many high-wage occupations with low exposure, higher-wage occupations overall are associated with increased exposure. This conclusion is consistent with the findings of another recent study by Goldman Sachs that found that generative AI could substitute for humans in one-fourth of current work tasks and globally expose the equivalent of 300 million full-time jobs to AI automation.[57] The exposure varies significantly by industry and by job, with high exposures in administrative and office support, legal services, business and financial operations, management, and sales, and low exposures in physically intensive professions such as construction and maintenance and in services like personal care and food/hospitality services. Many of these low-exposure occupations are in the nontraded goods and services sector.

With ever increasing digital capabilities, AI-based automation has moved from the factory into agriculture and services and from routine physical and cognitive jobs to many high-level complex cognitive jobs.

Instead of middle-skill jobs bearing the brunt of disruption, many of the highest-paying jobs, with significant educational credentials, are likely to be affected. An array of professions, including legal and accounting services, will be vulnerable, along with many middle management tasks. There is uncertainty about which tasks will be augmented, which tasks will be displaced, which new tasks will be generated, and the implications for skill requirements and wages. But the overall disruption in labor markets is likely to be significant, although it may take considerable time.

Whether the technology is used to automate or substitute for human labor or to complement and enable human labor is not primarily a technical matter but one of costs and incentives. In the United States and other market economies, profit-motivated businesses rather than governments will make these decisions. Governments, however, can affect these decisions through different policy choices to achieve different outcomes, just as they did to mitigate the labor market consequences of routine-biased technological change.[58]

In any case, we must push beyond that dichotomy and pose the questions we have often heard: given the new AI capabilities, how can a business reimagine its mission and offerings as well as the organization and delivery of its existing products? More than a decade ago, for example, firms began imagining themselves selling services rather than just physical products, such as fleet provision of tires or aircraft engines as ongoing maintenance and services. If the cost of particular tasks is reduced by AI, the bar for choices of projects to be implemented is lowered. Consider, for example, the challenge in a major corporation of maintaining sales and service materials in multiple languages. Will AI improve translation? Reduce the number of translators? Or increase the array of materials and languages in which a company can operate? To avoid translation errors, and increase the translation capacity for client firms, Lilt inserts a native-speaking translator into the process.[59] It can undertake a range of translation tasks that is not otherwise possible, and at lower costs. Does the ChatGPT tool become a less expensive law clerk allowing lawyers to handle more materials? Because generative AI makes mistakes, it is now assumed by some firms that keeping humans in the loop is a necessity. As the technical obstacles to automating some tasks go down, and the number of projects that are then above the adoption bar go up, the employment and productivity consequences will shift and will be harder to predict.

Early studies suggest, however, that the potential productivity gains are real and substantial as are the effects on employment, skills, and wages.[60]

To date, the overall adoption of AI in both the United States and Europe has been limited, but the rollout of LLMs has been more rapid, producing some of the fastest growing apps ever. Larger and more digitalized firms are more likely to adopt AI technologies than smaller ones, with a handful of US and Chinese digital platforms far ahead. Adoption has also varied across activities and sectors, with greater adoption in activities like office and administrative support and business and financial operations and in sectors like finance and retail.

A significant increase in productivity growth and the creation of new occupations are likely to accompany and offset some of the disruptions in labor markets as AI changes existing tasks and occupations, automating some and augmenting others. Historically, the emergence of new occupations following technological innovations accounts for the vast majority of long-term employment growth. But history also confirms that the disruption effects on labor markets can be rapid, while the pace of both the productivity gains and the creation of new occupations can be considerably slower. In the United States, technological change displaced workers and created new occupations at roughly the same rate for the first half of the post–World War II period, but displacement has occurred at a faster pace than new occupation creation since 1980, when neoliberal globalization took hold.

History also confirms that there are both winners and losers from technological innovations and that the winners and losers are different— different in education, sectors, location, access to capital, income and wealth, gender, and ethnicity. While such innovations produce aggregate benefits, they impose significant costs that are not compensated and tend to increase income and wealth inequality. A new book by Daron Acemoglu and Simon Johnson presents a sobering assessment of how past technological change has affected the majority of workers and the middle class in the United States and other advanced industrial economies and warns that generative AI will have similar negative effects unless they are offset by policy.[61] Rather than simply accept the future that AI technologies will generate, policymakers should act boldly to create a better and more equitable and sustainable future—in education, health care, climate policy, and work—made possible by these innovations.

The effects of AI on the economic interconnections among nations—the next phase of globalization—are uncertain and difficult to predict. Trade will likely become increasingly based on services, and digital flows will continue to expand rapidly. But if AI displaces or augments human labor in the provision of services and digital products in the developed economies, it could reduce their demand for inexpensive cognitive labor and dampen trade between them and the developing economies. Take the example of call centers, where generative AI can speed up, scale, and improve customer experience and reduce the demand for inexpensive workers running call center services in developing economies. If AI further increases the productivity of manufacturing in the developed economies, it could reduce their demand for imports of manufactured products from lower-cost developing economies and support the reshoring of such activities. Take the example of how workers in a US global manufacturing company can ask generative AI technical questions about operating procedures.

The energy sector in the United States provides an illustrative example of how technological innovation can affect productivity, product innovation, and trade. In recent years, the country has emerged as the world's largest oil producer and is now a net oil exporter, driven in part by fracking technologies supported by the US government. In a similar fashion, AI could increase competitiveness, productivity, incomes, employment, and trade in sectors of importance to many developing economies such as agriculture, forestry and other natural resources, and certain services. What appears to be clear, however, is that China's export-led rapid growth as a global manufacturing center based on offshoring by the developed economies, its low-cost labor, digitally enabled supply chains, and neoliberal globalization rules cannot be replicated by other emerging nations. Instead, many developing economies will have to grapple with "premature deindustrialization" and pursue other growth strategies focusing on services, infrastructure, natural resources, education, and health care—much of which will be nontraded activities.[62]

Finally, it is essential to acknowledge that although discussions of globalization focus on things that can be traded across borders, most workers throughout the world, regardless of the development level of the countries where they work, are employed in nontraded activities—for example, local construction, local infrastructure, the provision of products and services for local markets, education, health care, and government services. AI technologies may affect both routine and nonroutine physical and cognitive tasks in nontraded activities, with important effects on local labor markets—wages, training, job security, career ladders, surveillance, and bias. But these effects will not show up in international trade and globalization measures. A question for a separate discussion is how digitalization and, in particular, AI will affect workers in nontraded activities throughout the world.

Conclusion

US power is in relative decline and the global order is fragmenting. The emergence of transformative technologies raises important questions about the potential reshuffling of the existing global system. As technological advances redefine the economic landscape, they may well also disrupt existing power structures and give rise to new geopolitical tensions.

The world is moving from a positive-sum approach to globalization, in which interdependence is perceived as mutually beneficial, to a zero-sum approach, in which one nation's gain is viewed as another's loss. Nationalist competition is displacing collaboration and cooperation, straining relations even among allies. In the absence of a liberal hegemon to maintain global order and stability, the emerging landscape will be defined by increased volatility, unpredictability, and uncertainty. This instability will be more costly as nations grapple with the consequences of increased uncertainty and the resulting conflicts.

As the leading global power, the United States has enjoyed immense economic prosperity. For domestic politics, however, the growth argument— a rising tide lifts all boats—has been overwhelmed by distributional and inequality concerns. The era of neoliberal globalization was beneficial for the nation, but today, many US policymakers take a different view. While Yellen argues that the US economy is strong, Sullivan presents a contrasting narrative of decline over several decades, attributing it in part to globalization and in part to the rise of China.[63] Sullivan advocates a "domestically led foreign policy," focusing on rebuilding the United States from the middle out and bottom up to regain its competitive edge.[64] Surprisingly, in their recent speeches, neither Yellen nor Sullivan acknowledged the role of technology as a major source of job displacement and growing income and wealth inequality.

In the realm of international trade, economic interconnections among nations are projected to expand, albeit in a more fragmented and regional manner that could disrupt supply chains and drive up costs. Digital trade is set to increase as a proportion of total trade, reflecting continuing digital transformation of trade and new labor dynamics in the services sector. And the weight of Asia—both south and east—in the global economy and South-South trade will continue to grow.

Climate change presents a shared global challenge requiring enforceable international agreements. This issue is directly related to global interconnectedness: the challenge is universal and the solution requires collaboration among all nations. Cooperation between China and the United States is essential—they are the number one and number two carbon emitters in the world, respectively. A free trade agreement for green technology could be a powerful platform for strengthening global cooperation via trade and investment. A case in point is the trade agreement in the information technology sector introduced in 1996 under the auspices of the WTO and expanded since then: it reduced tariffs on almost all world trade in IT products, which spurred innovation, trade, investment, and the creation of global supply chains that reduced the costs and increased the use of these products.

Just as digital technologies drove globalization during the last several decades, new digital technologies, especially AI, will have profound economic, social, and political effects within individual nations and on the interconnections among them. Even industry leaders argue that there is a clear need for robust regulations and industry standards in AI to navigate through these effects and foster its benefits while containing its risks. In a sobering recent open letter, a group of leading technology experts from around the world warned that AI should be considered a societal risk of the same priority as pandemics and nuclear war.[65]

A variety of regulatory initiatives responding to the potential impacts of AI are currently underway around the world. However, as of the time of this writing, there have been relatively few proposals for the statutory regulation of AI.[66] Building on the GDPR, the EU is currently finalizing an AI Act that envisages a tiered risk-based approach to regulating AI. China has announced a comprehensive framework to regulate generative AI. China's framework is not likely applicable for use in Western industrial democracies, however, as it has a system with strong state control over business and society. In the United States, President Biden has issued an executive order to coordinate the federal government's efforts around the development and deployment of AI, and Senate Majority Leader Chuck

Schumer has convened several "AI Insight Forums" to educate lawmakers about the possibilities and perils of AI. In November 2023, the United Kingdom hosted an AI Safety Summit that produced a joint declaration to foster an inclusive global dialogue on AI safety. The G7 has outlined its "Hiroshima Process" for disseminating voluntary guidelines to ensure the safe, secure, and trustworthy deployment of AI. Overall, these different approaches to AI regulation will affect its deployment and may lead to different regional trade and investment outcomes from this key transformative technology.[67]

Different societies will adopt different AI norms on privacy, dissent, and personal rights, reflecting their unique cultural contexts and values. But all societies face common AI risks: for example, the risk that AI will disrupt labor markets, eliminate good jobs, and increase income inequality; the risk that AI can be weaponized to build chemical and nuclear weapons; the risk that AI will drive an increase in the volume and spread of misinformation that undermines trust in governance and governments; the risk that AI could further increase the market power of a handful of global companies; and the risk of cybercrime and cyberwarfare enabled by AI. In a recent essay, Ian Bremmer and Mustafa Suleyman argue that AI marks the beginning of a world-changing technological revolution, which will initiate a seismic shift in the structure and balance of global power and threaten the status of nation-states as the world's primary geopolitical actors.[68] In their words, AI is a global commons issue that requires a global AI governance structure to contain the common risks. As the two leading nations in AI development, the United States and China share the responsibility to spearhead the creation of the governance rules and institutions required for a stable and secure interconnected global economy in the age of AI.

NOTES

1. Tyson and Zysman (2022a).
2. McKinsey Global Institute (2022a).
3. International Monetary Fund (2023).
4. World Trade Organization (2022) and Góes and Bekkers (2022).
5. Sullivan (2023).
6. Williamson (1990).
7. Lund and Tyson (2018).
8. Zysman et al. (2013).
9. Garcia Calvo, Kenney, and Zysman (2023).

10. Tyson and Zysman (2023) and Meckling (2021).

11. Harris and Gerich (1996).

12. Breznitz and Zysman (2013).

13. Masanet et al. (2020).

14. https://www.vodafone.com/about-vodafone/what-we-do/consumer-products-and-services/m-pesa.

15. Roberts and Lamp (2021).

16. Roberts and Lamp (2021), p. 7.

17. For a summary, see Roberts and Lamp (2021), pp. 166–68.

18. Tyson and Zysman (2022b).

19. Kenney, Bearson, and Zysman (2021).

20. Kenney and Zysman (2016), p. 61.

21. Garcia Calvo, Kenney, and Zysman (2022).

22. Kushida, Murray, and Zysman (2015), p. 5.

23. To define terms: Cloud computing delivers computing services—data storage, computation and networking—to users at the time, to the location, and in the quantity they want, with costs based only on the amount of resource used (Kushida, Murray, and Zysman 2013).

24. Our World in Data (n.d.).

25. A few years ago, an entrepreneur whom we know sold her company to Microsoft. She remarked that she needed to raise $70 million for the necessary infrastructure, whereas today she could have started the whole project on her credit card by purchasing the required computing power from Amazon's cloud.

26. Zysman et al. (2013).

27. Frey and Osborne (2016).

28. Fourcade (2021).

29. Borrus and Zysman (1998).

30. Chesbrough (2006).

31. Breznitz (2021) argues that the global economy sees nodes of specialization in four phases and that regions specialize in one particular phase in the innovation process: novelty (stage 1); design, prototype development, and production engineering (stage 2); second-generation product and component innovation (stage 3); and production and assembly (stage 4).

32. McKinsey Global Institute (2022b).

33. Lakner and Milanovic (2013).

34. Kharas and Seidel (2018).

35. Autor et al. (2022).

36. Spence (2023) and Acemoglu and Johnson (2023).

37. Georgieva and Okonjo-Iweala (2023).

38. Nye (2023) writes: "Globalization is simply the growth of interdependence at intercontinental, rather than national or regional, distances."

39. Office of the United States Trade Representative (2023).

40. Irwin (2022).
41. Yellen (2023) and Sullivan (2023).
42. Yellen (2023).
43. Sullivan (2023).
44. Locating the new TSMC plant in Arizona and the new Intel plant in Ohio suggests the centrality of domestic political considerations.
45. Liu and Mozur (2023).
46. Kammer (2023).
47. Semiconductor Industry Association (2021).
48. Miller (2022).
49. Posen (2023).
50. Clinton (2000).
51. For example, visitors to the 2022 World Cup in Qatar were required to download the Hayya app.
52. Bresnahan and Trajtenberg (1995).
53. Nitzberg (2023).
54. Tyson and Zysman (2022b).
55. Kenney (2023).
56. Eloundou et al. (2023).
57. Goldman Sachs (2023).
58. Autor, Mindell, and Reynolds (2020).
59. http://www.lilt.com.
60. Baily, Brynjolfsson, and Korinek (2023).
61. Acemoglu and Johnson (2023).
62. Rodrik (2016).
63. Yellen (2023) and Sullivan (2023).
64. For a very different assessment of the role of US power in the world, see *The Economist* (2023).
65. https://www.safe.ai/statement-on-ai-risk.
66. Russell, Nitzberg, and Judge (n.d.).
67. Luo et al. (2023).
68. Bremmer and Suleyman (2023).

REFERENCES

Acemoglu, Daron, and Simon Johnson. 2023. *Power and Progress: Our 1000-Year Struggle Over Technology & Prosperity.* New York: Public Affairs.

Autor, David, Kaushik Basu, Zia Qureshi, and Dani Rodrik. 2022. "An Inclusive Future? Technology, New Dynamics, and Policy Challenges." Brookings Institution, Washington, DC.

Autor, David, David Mindell, and Elisabeth Reynolds. 2020. "The Work of the Future: Building Better Jobs in an Age of Intelligent Machines." MIT,

Cambridge, MA. https://workofthefuture.mit.edu/wp-content/uploads/2021/01/2020-Final-Report4.pdf.

Baily, Martin, Eric Brynjolfsson, and Anton Korinek. 2023. "Machines of the Mind: The Case for an AI-Powered Productivity Boom." Brookings Institution, Washington, DC.

Bremmer, Ian, and Mustafa Suleyman. 2023. "The AI Power Paradox." *Foreign Affairs*, September-October. https://www.foreignaffairs.com/world/artificial-intelligence-power-paradox.

Bresnahan, Timothy, and M. Trajtenberg. 1995. "General Purpose Technologies 'Engines of Growth?'" *Journal of Econometrics* 65 (1): 83–108.

Breznitz, Dan. 2021. *Innovation in Real Places: Strategies for Prosperity in an Unforgiving World*. Oxford: Oxford University Press.

Breznitz, Dan, and John Zysman. 2013. *The Third Globalization: Can Wealthy Nations Stay Rich in the Twenty-First Century?* Oxford: Oxford University Press.

Borrus, Michael, and John Zysman. 1998. "Globalization with Borders: The Rise of 'Wintelism' as the Future of Industrial Competition." In *Enlarging Europe: The Industrial Foundations of a New Political Reality*. Berkeley: University of California Press.

Chesbrough, Henry. 2006. *Open Innovation: The New Imperative for Creating and Profiting from Technology*. Cambridge, MA: Harvard Business Review Press.

Clinton, Bill. 2000. "Speech on China Trade Bill." Paul H. Nitze School of Advanced International Studies of the Johns Hopkins University, Washington, DC, March 8.

Economist. 2023. "America's Economic Outperformance is a Marvel to Behold." April 13. https://www.economist.com/briefing/2023/04/13/from-strength-to-strength.

Eloundou, Tanya, Sam Manning, Pamela Mishkin, and Daniel Rock. 2023. "GPTs are GPTs: An Early Look at the Labor Market Impact Potential of Large Language Models." arXiv preprint arXiv:2303.10130.

Frey, Carl, and Michael Osborne. 2016. "The Future of Employment: How Susceptible Are Jobs to Computerisation?" *Technological Forecasting and Social Change* 114: 254–80.

Fourcade, Marion. 2021. "Ordinal Citizenship." *The British Journal of Sociology* 72 (2): 154–73.

Garcia Calvo, Angela, Martin Kenney, and John Zysman. 2023. "Will National Sovereignty Splinter the Internet?" BRIE Working Paper 2023-3. Berkeley Roundtable on the International Economy, Berkeley. https://brie.berkeley.edu/sites/default/files/publications/will_national_sovereignty_splinter_the_internet_brie-wp-2023-3.pdf.

———. 2022. "Understanding Work in the Online Platform Economy: A Critical Review." BRIE Working Paper. Berkeley Roundtable on the

International Economy, Berkeley, May 10. https://brie.berkeley.edu/publications/understanding-work-online-platform-economy-critical-review.

Georgieva, Kristalina, and Ngozi Okonjo-Iweala. 2023. "World Trade Can Still Drive Prosperity." International Monetary Fund, Washington, DC, June. https://www.imf.org/en/Publications/fandd/issues/2023/06/world-trade-can-still-drive-prosperity-georgieva-okonjo-iweala.

Góes, Carlos, and Eddy Bekkers. 2022. "The Impact of Geopolitical Conflicts on Trade, Growth, and Innovation." WTO Staff Working Paper ERSD-2-22-09. World Trade Organization, Geneva.

Goldman Sachs. 2023. "Generative AI Could Raise Global GDP by 7%." Goldman Sachs & Company, New York.

Harris, Susan, and Elise Gerich. 1996. "Retiring the NSFNET Backbone Service: Chronicling the End of an Era." ConneXions 10 (4).

International Monetary Fund. 2023. "Geoeconomic Fragmentation and the Future of Multilateralism." Staff Discussion Note 2023/001. International Monetary Fund, Washington, DC.

Irwin, Douglas. 2022. "Globalization Enabled Nearly All Countries to Grow Richer." Peterson Institute for International Economics, June 16. https://www.piie.com/blogs/realtime-economic-issues-watch/globalization-enabled-nearly-all-countries-grow-richer-recent.

Kammer, Alfred. 2023. "Europe, And the World, Should Use Green Subsidies Cooperatively." IMF Blog, May 11. https://www.imf.org/en/Blogs/Articles/2023/05/11/europe-and-the-world-should-use-green-subsidies-cooperatively.

Kenney, Martin. 2023. "New Digital Political Economy of Deepfakes." Berkeley Social Sciences Matrix, Berkeley, May 10.

Kenney, Martin, and John Zysman. 2016. "The Rise of the Platform Economy." Issues in Science and Technology 32 (3): 61–69.

Kenney, Martin, Dafna Bearson, and John Zysman. 2021. "The Platform Economy Matures: Measuring Pervasiveness and Exploring Power." Socio-Economic Review 19 (4): 1451–83.

Kharas, Homi, and Brina Seidel. 2018. "What's Happening to the World Income Distribution? The Elephant Chart Revisited." Brookings Global Economy & Development Working Paper 114. Brookings Institution, Washington, DC.

Kushida, Kenji, Jonathan Murray, and John Zysman. 2013. Clouducopia: Into the Era of Abundance, CLSA Blue Book.

Kushida, Kenji, Jonathan Murray, and John Zysman. 2015. "Cloud Computing: From Scarcity to Abundance." Journal of Industry, Competition and Trade 15: 5–19.

Lakner, Christoph, and Branko Milanovic. 2013. "Global Income Distribution: From the Fall of the Berlin Wall to the Great Recession." Policy Research Working Paper 6719. World Bank, Washington, DC.

Liu, John, and Paul Mozur. 2023. "Inside Taiwanese Chip Giant, a U.S. Expansion Stokes Tensions." *New York Times*, February 22.

Luo, Yan, Xuezi Dan, Vicky Liu, and Nicholas Shepherd. 2023. "China Proposes Draft Measures to Regulate Generative AI." *Covington Inside Global Tech*, April 14.

Lund, Susan, and Laura Tyson. 2018. "Globalization Is Not in Retreat: Digital Technology and the Future of Trade." *Foreign Affairs* 97 (3): 130–40.

Masanet, Eric, Arman Shehabi, Nuao Lei, Sarah Smith, and Jonathan Koomey. 2020. "Recalibrating Global Data Center Energy-Use Estimates." *Science* 367, no. 6481: 984–86.

McKinsey Global Institute. 2022a. "On the Cusp of a New Era?" McKinsey & Company, New York.

———. 2022b. "Global Flows: The Ties that Bind in an Interconnected World." McKinsey & Company, New York.

Meckling, Jonas. 2021. "Making Industrial Policy Work for Decarbonization." *Global Environmental Politics* 21 (4): 134–47.

Miller, Chris. 2022. *Chip War: The Fight for the World's Most Critical Technology.* New York: Simon & Schuster.

Nitzberg, Mark. 2023. "Deceit at Scale." UC Berkeley Social Science Matrix, Berkeley, May 10.

Nye, Joseph. 2023. "Is Globalization Over?" *Project Syndicate*, March 31.

Office of the United States Trade Representative. 2023. "Fact Sheet: In Year 2, Ambassador Katherine Tai and USTR Continued to Execute President Biden's Vision for Worker-Centered Trade Policy."

Our World in Data. n.d. "Historical Cost of Computer Memory and Storage." https://ourworldindata.org/grapher/historical-cost-of-computer-memory-and-storage.

Posen, Adam. 2023. "America's Zero-Sum Economics Doesn't Add Up." *Foreign Policy*, March 24.

Rodrik, Dani. 2016. "Premature Industrialization." *Journal of Economic Growth* 21 (1): 1–33.

Roberts, Anthea, and Nicolas Lamp. 2021. *Six Faces of Globalization.* Cambridge, MA: Harvard University Press.

Russell, Stuart, Mark Nitzberg, and Brian Judge. n.d. "When Code Isn't Law: Rethinking Regulation for Artificial Intelligence." University of California, Berkeley, unpublished manuscript.

Semiconductor Industry Association. 2021. "Chipping In." https://www.semiconductors.org/wp-content/uploads/2021/05/SIA-Impact_May2021-FINAL-May-19-2021_2.pdf.

Spence, Michael. 2023. "Destructive Decoupling." *Project Syndicate*, March 30.

Sullivan, Jake. 2023. "Remarks by National Security Advisor Jake Sullivan on Renewing American Leadership." Brookings Institution, Washington, DC, April 27.

Tyson, Laura, and John Zysman. 2022a. "Preparing for A Volatile Global Economy." *Omidyar Future of the Global Economy Project.*

———. 2022b. "Automation, AI & Work." *Daedalus* 151 (2): 256–71.

———. 2023. "Cooperation or Conflict? Will Industrial Policy Produce Solutions or Generate Unmanageable Conflicts." In *A New Industrial Policy for Europe.* Brussels: Bruegel Blueprint.

Williamson, John. 1990. *Latin American Adjustment: How Much Has Happened.* Washington, DC: Peterson Institute for International Economics.

World Trade Organization. 2022. *The Crisis in Ukraine: Implications of the War for Global Trade and Development.* World Trade Organization, Geneva.

Yellen, Janet. 2023. "Remarks by Secretary of the Treasury Janet L. Yellen on the U.S.-China Economic Relationship." Johns Hopkins School of Advanced International Studies, Washington, DC, April 20.

Zysman, John, Stuart Feldman, Kenji Kushida, Jonathan Murray, and Niels Christian Nielsen. 2013. "Services with Everything: The ICT-Enabled Digital Transformation of Services." In *The Third Globalization: Can Wealthy Nations Stay Rich in the Twenty-First Century?*, edited by Dan Breznitz and John Zysman. Oxford: Oxford University Press.

THREE

Globalization and the Asian Century

WONHYUK LIM

"In 1968, the answer to whether the twenty-first century would be the 'Asian Century' almost certainly would have been clearly negative. . . . Today most people would consider the answer to be obviously yes."[1] Beginning in about 2010, with China surpassing Japan as the second largest economy in the world, several studies promoted the idea of the "Asian Century," including a 2011 Asian Development Bank (ADB) report titled *Asia 2050: Realizing the Asian Century*. In 2012, the Australian government released a white paper titled *Australia in the Asian Century*, seemingly taking the arrival of the Asian Century as a given. Conspicuously absent from these studies were concerns about geopolitical tensions and risks, even though the United States had already declared "a pivot to Asia," turning to meet the challenge of China's rise after the ill-conceived wars and nation-building efforts in Iraq and Afghanistan.[2] Also missing from these studies was a deeper understanding of the changing trends in globalization in the wake of the 2008 global financial crisis, including increasing discontent among workers in advanced industrial economies and shifts in global patterns of production. Instead, they assumed that geopolitical and economic conditions prevailing after the end of the Cold War would remain fairly stable, and they essentially extrapolated ongoing structural trends to project the Asian Century.

Over the subsequent decade, however, the pendulum has swung in the opposite direction. Geopolitical considerations now dominate international economic discussions, with the risk of geoeconomic fragmentation highlighted by international organizations.[3] Widespread discontent among workers is a well-recognized driver of domestic politics in advanced economies, making the United States, among others, reluctant to take on the challenge of further trade liberalization.[4] It is no longer assumed that the division of labor that prevailed between advanced and emerging economies after the end of the Cold War will continue in some version of the flying-geese pattern of development, where advanced and emerging economies fly together harmoniously without any drastic change in their ranks.[5] Instead, advanced economies today recognize that emerging economies can catch up and forge ahead. The Asian Century has become a contentious term, loaded with "are you with us or against us" connotations, as many Western observers mistakenly equate the Asian Century with the Chinese Century. Although Asia is a vast region characterized by diversity and historical multipolarity, they tend to assume China's dominance.[6]

Yet, some of the structural trends that justified the talk of the coming Asian Century in the first place have continued over the past decade. According to the World Bank's World Development Indicators, Asia's share of global GDP at purchasing power parity (PPP) exchange rates has exceeded 50 percent since 2020. The intraregional share of Asia's trade and investment flows has increased as well, as multinational corporations from China, Japan, and Korea, among others, have expanded their regional production networks. The intraregional trade share of the Asia-Pacific region averaged 74 percent in the 2010s, substantially higher than that for the twenty-seven members of the European Union (EU) and for the United States, Mexico, and Canada (USMCA) over the same period, at 62 percent and 44 percent, respectively.[7] ADB's Asia-Pacific Regional Cooperation and Integration Index, covering not only trade and investment but also cooperation in such areas as environment, finance, infrastructure, and technology, increased steadily from 2006 to 2020.[8] Although the early studies on the Asian Century tended to overlook geopolitical risks and emerging problems for globalization, their economic projections were not off the mark. A key question looking ahead is whether countries can manage geopolitical tensions and challenges to globalization so that they collectively can benefit from the growth momentum that most likely will be centered around Asia for at least the next few decades—what Khanna (2017) has called "the third wave of Asia's growth" centered around South and Southeast Asia, following the first two waves that involved mainly Northeast Asia.

This chapter is organized as follows. The first section provides an overview of globalization. It looks at technical and institutional barriers to globalization, briefly reviews theoretical perspectives, and analyzes two waves of globalization since the second quarter of the nineteenth century. The second section places the Asian Century in a historical perspective over the same period, examining the evolution of population and GDP shares by region and what the two waves of globalization meant to Asia in terms of its policy space and trade and industrial development. The third section focuses on current challenges and prospects, exploring Asia's alternative futures based on different scenarios for both external cooperation and internal reform required for economic upgrading, social cohesion, and environmental sustainability. Using this framework, it examines Asia's current external and internal challenges and offers policy recommendations. The last section provides brief concluding remarks.

Globalization: An Overview

Globalization may be defined as the process through which interaction among individuals and societies increases to such a degree that it is meaningful to think of a single, worldwide system rather than just a disparate collection of national or regional systems. Economically, globalization denotes an increase in the international movement of goods, services, and people to such a degree that it is meaningful to think of a single global market. The extent of price convergence around the world can be a good indicator of globalization.[9] Alternatively, international trade and financial flows relative to global GDP can be used as indicators of globalization even though these metrics are less reliable than price convergence measures because they depend on the configuration of domestic and global value chains. For example, if a country that used to process imported intermediate inputs for exports now produces these intermediate inputs on its own, its trade-to-GDP ratio would decline, without negatively affecting price convergence.

The threshold at which the international movement of goods and services is significant enough to merit the term "globalization" is subject to debate, but convergence in prices should be such that there are no huge price disparities across different continents.[10] This implies that ancient trade routes such as the Silk Road, typically dealing in low-volume, high-price products across two or three continents (namely, Asia, Europe, and Africa), were not sufficient to support economic globalization. It required the integration of all continents through circumnavigation and the dramatic expansion in the variety of tradable products. From this perspective, economic globalization was not substantial until the second quarter of the nineteenth century, marked by a significant reduction in transportation costs as well as a rapid imperialist expansion after the First Industrial Revolution.

In theory, economic globalization can continue until it reaches the point where there is a completely free flow of goods and services, capital and labor, and information and ideas around the world. However, in practice, globalization is impeded by a variety of technical and institutional barriers. Technical barriers have to do with transportation and communication costs. Economic theories on trade, geography, and growth tend to focus on these issues. Institutional barriers have to do with political economy costs, as increased trade and financial flows create winners and losers, both domestically and internationally. Various regulations and tariffs, as well as political-military blocs and conflicts, constitute institutional barriers to globalization. Political economy and geopolitical theories deal with these issues.

Technical and Institutional Barriers to Globalization

Technological breakthroughs and reductions in transportation and communication costs over the past few centuries have dramatically reduced technical barriers to globalization. Historically, international trade routes such as the Silk Road depended on animal-based land transportation or small-scale river and sea transportation. After the fifteenth century, they were supplemented by new maritime routes that used large ships. In the nineteenth century, land vehicles using fossil fuels as their source of energy began to overtake animal-based transportation. Advances in shipping, containerization, and logistics reduced transportation costs. Similarly, advances in communication such as printing, post, telegraph, telephone, and the internet drastically reduced the cost of conveying information and ideas. Overall, technical barriers to globalization have exhibited a secularly declining trend over time (figure 3.1).

FIGURE 3.1. Trends in Technical Barriers to Globalization

A. ICT Use, 1960–2017

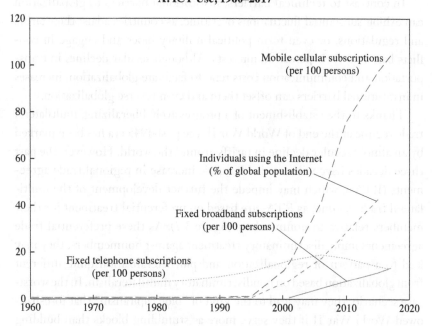

B. Transport and Communication Costs, 1920–2015

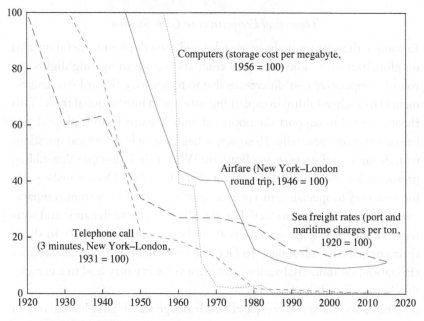

Source: World Bank (2020).

Note: ICT = Information and communication technology.

In contrast to technical barriers, institutional barriers to globalization can exhibit substantial fluctuations over time, as countries adjust their tariffs and regulations, or even form political-military blocs and engage in conflicts based on their perceived interests. Although secular declines in transportation and communication costs tend to facilitate globalization, increases in institutional barriers can offset them and even reverse globalization.

Thanks to the establishment of a progressively liberalizing, multilateral trade regime at the end of World War II, the post-1945 era has been marked by an almost secular decline in tariffs around the world. However, the past three decades have witnessed a dramatic increase in regional trade agreements (RTAs), which may impede the further development of the multilateral trade regime, as RTAs are based on preferential treatment for their members relative to nonmembers (figure 3.2). As these preferential trade agreements imply discriminatory treatment against nonmembers, they may lead to a pattern of regionalization and plurilateralization quite different from globalization based on nondiscriminatory multilateralism. In the worst-case scenario, they may lead to the kind of "bloc capitalism" that foreshadowed World War II if they serve more as stumbling blocks than building blocks for economic integration.

Theoretical Perspectives on Globalization

Economic theories on trade, geography, and growth provide useful insights on globalization.[11] The theory of comparative advantage highlights the role of comparative cost differences due to technology (Ricardo) or endowment (Heckscher-Ohlin) in explaining patterns of international trade. This theory is used to support the notion of mutual gains from trade and globalization more generally. However, it begs a couple of critical questions with dynamic and strategic implications: What if the long-run value-adding prospects for one product are greater than the other? Does it make sense for a country to specialize in a product just because of its current comparative advantage in that product? For globalization, these dynamic and strategic implications raise questions about how countries may try to shape their comparative advantage. In fact, the combination of commodity specialization, de-industrialization, and price volatility may lead to a correlation between trade and poverty.[12]

Unlike the theory of comparative advantage that highlights the role of cross-country differences in motivating international trade, the theory of new economic geography notes that much of international trade takes place

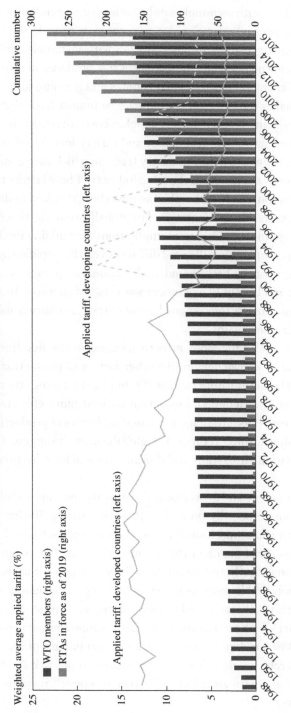

FIGURE 3.2. Trends in Institutional Barriers to Globalization

Source: World Bank (2020).

Note: WTO = World Trade Organization.

between countries with seemingly similar technology or endowment.[13] This theory focuses on agglomeration due to economies of scale and backward and forward linkages. Even among countries with seemingly similar technologies or endowments, a historical accident that produces an early lead can facilitate agglomeration in a particular country and generate such an advantage that it makes sense for other countries to import from that country instead of producing on their own at a higher cost. Alternatively, a combination of increasing-returns technology and variety-loving preferences can lead countries to engage in intraindustry trade, in which each country produces a different variety within the same industry. These factors that facilitate agglomeration should be weighed against those that lead to dispersion, such as rising costs due to congestion. For globalization, the theory of new economic geography has important implications for building international value chains, as seemingly small initial differences can be amplified by increasing returns. Against this background, multinational corporations must consider the cost and benefit of agglomeration versus dispersion. In the same vein, they must consider the cost and benefit of fractionalization and coordination of their value chains.

The theory of endogenous growth focuses on the nondiminishing returns nature of knowledge, unlike other factors of production that are characterized by diminishing returns.[14] It implies that a country can build on its stock of knowledge and maintain its lead more effectively than would be the case if its advantage was based on factors of production characterized by diminishing returns. For globalization, it suggests that strategic accumulation, utilization, and dissemination of knowledge can play a key role.[15]

Political economy and geopolitical theories also provide useful insights on globalization, especially on its institutional barriers. Realist perspectives start with the proposition that the clash of interests is real and that power is an essential factor in the resolution of actual or potential conflicts, both domestically and internationally, where power may be defined in terms of mobilizable resources, such as military and economic capabilities.[16] Major realist theories tend to view international peace and prosperity as a precarious phenomenon, with states competing for power either out of sheer lust for dominance[17] or as a rational pursuit of security in a perceived anarchic world.[18] It requires a great deal of work and favorable conditions to maintain an effective balance of power[19] or achieve hegemonic stability.[20]

In contrast, liberal perspectives contend that rational actors should be able to see the advantages of interdependence and find ways to resolve conflicts without resorting to force, even in the absence of a complete harmony of interests.[21] The economic interdependence theory argues that high levels of trade and investment among states make them unlikely to fight each other, for war would destroy mutual gains. It views globalization as less precarious. However, much depends on an expected payoff structure that favors cooperation rather than unilateral deviation. Democratic peace theory claims that democracies tend not to go to war against other democracies because they can be more certain of each other's intentions, which they believe are generally benign.[22] But democracies are distrustful of nondemocracies. According to this perspective, internal state characteristics matter for international peace, and democratization facilitates economic globalization because it reduces distrust. It is worth noting that the democratic peace theory takes a somewhat different view on the relationship between internal state characteristics and war from that put forward by Immanuel Kant (1795), who supported a free federation of republican states with universal human rights, or by Giuseppe Mazzini, who saw an international society of democratic nation-states as key to world peace, with citizens imbued with a sense of civic duty beyond utilitarian self-interest.[23] Liberal institutionalism holds that international institutions can facilitate cooperation among states through repeated interactions, information transparency, and credible commitments.[24]

Constructivist perspectives hold that membership in a society based on the construction of a common identity, with shared interests and values, is key to sustained cooperation. Only a society sharing a common identity can guarantee peace and order, either at the national or international level.[25] Polanyi's "double movement" pits laissez-faire forces attempting to expand the free market against social forces attempting to establish social protection and market regulation.

The pain and tragedy of the two world wars and the Great Depression led to a rethinking of international peace and prosperity and produced "embedded liberalism," or liberalism embedded in multilateralism and social democracy.[26] Unlike the economic nationalism of the 1930s, the post-1945 international economic framework was based on nondiscriminatory multilateralism and progressive liberalization. Unlike the laissez-faire liberalism before World War I, the post-1945 framework was predicated on social democracy, supported by market regulation and social safety nets. According to this perspective, domestic and international political economy conditions must be aligned for globalization to be sustained.

Two Waves of Globalization

The history of globalization shows that the increasing integration of the world is not preordained but rather must be carefully nurtured by addressing external and internal risks. While the technical costs of globalization, relating to transportation and communication, have declined secularly, institutional costs, driven by international relations and domestic politics, have fluctuated over time. To understand the evolving patterns of globalization, it is important to identify changes in international and domestic political economy that impact institutional costs associated with globalization. As a first approximation, inequality both between and within countries provides useful information on international and domestic political economy.[27] However, the relationship between inequality and the probability of conflict at either the international or domestic level is not linear. In fact, the probability of international conflict may go up when inequality between countries has either decreased to such an extent that an emerging challenger thinks it can take on an incumbent power or increased to such an extent that an incumbent power thinks it can easily conquer other countries. Similarly, the probability of domestic conflict may increase when within-country inequality changes in ways to produce "rising expectations."[28]

Trends in trade and financial flows relative to GDP show two waves of globalization since the second quarter of the nineteenth century. Despite their limitations due to their dependence on the configuration of global value chains, trade and financial flows relative to GDP are often used as indicators of globalization because of their superior data availability compared to measures of international price convergence (figure 3.3). The first wave of globalization consisted of three phases. The rising phase (1830–1870) was driven by the combination of the First Industrial Revolution and imperialism under the ideology of imperialistic liberalism, which preached liberalism at home but supported racial hierarchy abroad.[29] The First Industrial Revolution led to inventions such as the steam engine and railways and greatly reduced transportation costs. It also provided Britain and other industrializing countries in Europe with significant technological and military advantages, which they utilized in their imperialist aggression against non-European states to open up their markets, if not conquer them outright. Within Europe, the Concert of Vienna helped

FIGURE 3.3. Trade and Financial Globalization

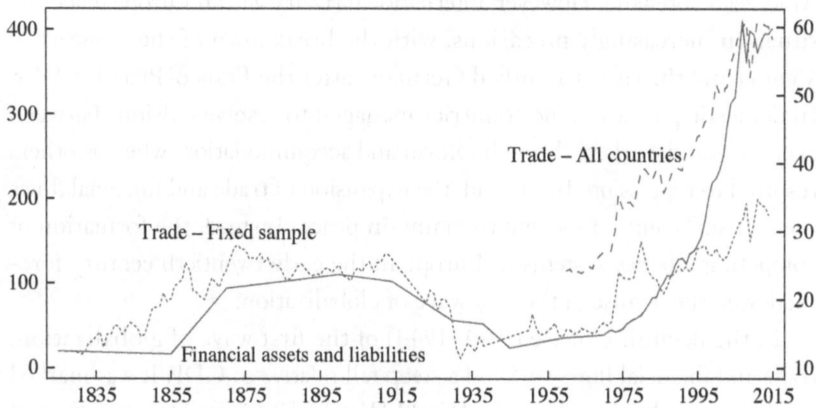

Source: Bank for International Settlements (2017).

Note: Trade openness is measured as percent of exports plus imports to GDP (right y-axis). Financial openness is measured as percent of external financial assets plus liabilities to GDP (left y-axis). External financial assets and liabilities prior to 1970 were calculated as external financial assets multiplied by two. Fixed sample includes eighteen major economies.

to facilitate peace and prosperity after the Napoleonic Wars.[30] The ideology of imperialistic liberalism justified European powers' aggression abroad as a so-called civilizing mission, even though this was questionable in practice as demonstrated by the example of the Opium Wars, among others. The confluence of these factors led to a dramatic increase in trade and financial flows, not just in absolute levels but relative to GDP as well.

In the expansion phase (1871–1913), trade and financial flows increased in volume, but their ratios to GDP were relatively stable because, among other factors, the kind of fractionalization and coordination of value chains observed since the late twentieth century was not viable back then. Facilitated by the gold standard, international trade in this period mostly involved simple commodities and manufactured products that did not cross national borders multiple times in their production process. During this phase, the Second Industrial Revolution, centered around electricity and chemistry, further widened the gap between Western and non-Western states. Transportation costs continued to fall, and communication costs declined thanks to the invention of the telegraph and telephone. Imperialist aggression reached the heart of Africa and Asia, not just coastal areas, following the Indian precedent—and the precedents in North and South America beforehand. However, international rivalry within Europe made the situation increasingly precarious, with the breakdown of the Concert of Vienna and the rise of a unified Germany after the Franco-Prussian War. In domestic politics, some countries managed to resolve tensions between capitalists and workers through reform and accommodation, whereas others resorted to repression. In the end, the expansion of trade and financial flows was not sufficient on its own to maintain peace. Instead, the formation of competing alliance systems in Europe in the early twentieth century fore-shadowed the demise of the first wave of globalization.

In the declining phase (1914–1944) of the first wave of globalization, trade and financial flows suffered a steep fall relative to GDP. It was marked by three worldwide upheavals: World War I, the Great Depression, and World War II. World War I and its contentious postwar settlement led to a decline in trade and financial globalization, and this trend accelerated in the wake of the Great Depression, as countries increasingly adopted pro-tectionist measures and competitive devaluations.[31] High unemployment led to social turmoil in many countries, setting the stage for the rise of totalitarianism, most notably in Germany, Italy, and Japan. By the middle of the 1930s, the world was divided into competing blocs, which culminated in World War II. Competition between liberalism and totalitarianism pro-vided an ideological context for the great conflict.

The second wave of globalization also consists of three phases. The rising phase (1945–1978) was characterized by a strong recovery in international trade and financial flows under the ideology of "embedded liberalism," as emphasized by Ruggie (1982). The Bretton Woods institutions—the International Monetary Fund, the World Bank, and the General Agree-ment on Tariffs and Trade—established after World War II together with the United Nations (UN) promoted nondiscriminatory multilateralism and progressive liberalization. The ascendancy of social democracy in advanced economies led to a compression of inequality in those economies and broad-based growth.[32] The Third Industrial Revolution, centered around information technology, helped to set the stage for a sustained eco-nomic expansion. However, this resurgence of globalization was really "half-globalization," as it took place mainly in the capitalist bloc, led by the United States, against the communist bloc, led by the Soviet Union, in the context of the Cold War. Economic interaction between the two blocs was quite limited. Mutually assured destruction (MAD) preserved peace between the two nuclear-armed superpowers, although several proxy wars flared up in this period, often in the context of decolonization. The Vietnam War was the best-known example of such a war in this phase. Although ideological competition between the United States and the Soviet Union was intense, the logic of MAD helped to prevent World War III.

The expansion phase (1979–2008) of the second wave of globalization saw the increasing influence of neoliberalism, as social democracy (or the welfare state) was weakened in many Western countries in the wake of the oil shocks and stagflation in the 1970s. As restrictions on international capital flows were eased, financial globalization accelerated. At the same time, beset with economic stagnation, socialist countries went through market-oriented transitions, starting with China in 1978, Vietnam in 1986, Central and Eastern European countries in the late 1980s, and the Soviet Union itself in the early 1990s. The end of the Cold War came without a major conflict and led to a dramatic increase in economic integration. In addition, the establishment of the World Trade Organization (WTO) in 1995 and China's accession to the WTO in 2001 were critical to the sharp acceleration of globalization, ushering in a period of "hyperglobalization" from the 1990s to the global financial crisis of 2008.[33] In fact, the expansion phase of the second wave of globalization was even more impressive than the expansion phase of the first wave, as multinational corporations took advantage of drastically reduced technical and institutional barriers to globalization and set up extensive regional and global value chains. The rise of emerging economies such as China and India highlighted the latter part of this phase.

Finally, the current phase (2009–present) corresponds to a potential crisis or even reversal in globalization—a slowdown in globalization combined with growing inequality and intensifying geopolitical competition. The combination of skill-biased technological change, expanding trade, and declining social protection has undermined workers' positions in many advanced economies since the 1980s. The Fourth Industrial Revolution, centered around smart robots, and the response to climate change seem to provide opportunities for leap-frogging, at least to those countries that made successful catch-up efforts in industrialization. During this phase, under its dual circulation strategy, China has pushed for the vertical integration of production and has become central to global value chains, accounting for the largest share of exports of intermediate goods globally. Although international price convergence has continued, trade relative to global GDP has tended to stagnate. In recent years, three main shocks have hit global value chains: the US-China trade war (2018), the COVID-19 pandemic (2020), and the Russian invasion of Ukraine (2022). Countries are now reconfiguring global value chains with strategic stockpiles and domestic production, diversification and multisourcing, and geopolitical realignment and friend-shoring, toward a China-plus strategy.

Unlike the declining phase of the first wave of globalization, however, the current phase has not been stricken with a world war or a Great Depression and has avoided the dangerous dynamic of belligerently competing blocs, at least so far. Recognition of MAD continues to prevent a major war among nuclear-armed powers. Having benefited from the second wave of globalization, especially since the end of the Cold War, most emerging and developing economies would like to avoid another Cold War and maintain their strategic autonomy. In contrast, advanced economies have had to cope with difficult domestic politics of globalization in recent years, marked by tensions between nationalist populism and neoliberalism, for example, in countries such as Britain and the United States.

Table 3.1 summarizes the different phases of the two waves of globalization, including the leading ideology, major elements, and "finishing shocks," that triggered major changes in the trajectory of globalization. In the first wave, the dynamic of competing blocs and the outbreak of World Wars led to the decline of globalization. In the second wave, it is the logic of MAD that has helped to prevent another world war, and the challenges to globalization have been more economic in nature, related to domestic discontent and international rivalry for economic power.

The Asian Century in Historical Perspective

The history of globalization can be viewed in a different light by looking at the shifting fortunes of different regions. This exercise helps to see Asia's evolving position in the two waves of globalization, as the world shifted from the European Century in the nineteenth century to the American Century in the twentieth and toward an Asian Century in the twenty-first.

In 1820, Asia accounted for the lion's share of global population and GDP (Table 3.2). Northeast Asia's shares in global population and GDP were 41.4 percent and 38.4 percent, respectively. South and Southeast Asia's population and GDP shares were 24.7 percent and 19.6 percent,

Table 3.1. Two Waves of Globalization

Phase	Ideology	Major elements	Finishing shocks
Rise I (1830–1870)	Imperialistic liberalism	First Industrial Revolution, Concert of Vienna, imperialist aggression	Franco-Prussian War
Expansion I (1871–1913)	Liberalism vs. socialism	Second Industrial Revolution, breakdown of the Concert of Vienna, competing alliance systems	World War I
Decline I (1914–1944)	Liberalism vs. totalitarianism	World War I and contentious postwar settlement, Great Depression, competing blocs	World War II
Rise II (1945–1978)	Embedded liberalism	Third Industrial Revolution, social democracy, multilateralism, Cold War, MAD, decolonization	Oil shocks and stagflation
Expansion II (1979–2008)	Neoliberalism	Weakening welfare state, socialist transition and end of Cold War, financialization, rise of emerging economies	Global financial crisis
Decline II? (2009–Present)	Rise of nationalist populism	Fourth Industrial Revolution and climate response, worsening inequality and populist reaction, US-China strategic competition	Major risks to future trajectory: domestic discontent, geoeconomic/ geopolitical tensions

Source: Author's formulation.

Table 3.2. Population Share vs. Income Share by Region

Region	1820 Pop.	1820 GDP	1870 Pop.	1870 GDP	1900 Pop.	1900 GDP	1950 Pop.	1950 GDP	1990 Pop.	1990 GDP	2018 Pop.	2018 GDP
NE Asia	*41.4	*38.4	32.3	21.3	29.7	14.6	26.7	8.9	25.8	19.2	21.7	23.3
South & SE Asia	24.7	*19.6	25.8	14.7	23.8	10.7	26.0	8.3	29.8	9.3	*32.5	16.3
MENA	3.4	2.9	3.9	3.1	3.6	2.1	4.1	2.9	5.9	4.6	*7.1	*8.7
Western Europe	12.8	25.2	14.7	*32.4	*15.1	32.2	12.0	26.1	7.2	22.1	5.6	14.7
Eastern Europe	8.8	6.1	11.2	11.7	*12.6	*15.4	10.6	12.9	7.8	9.8	5.4	7.4
Western Offshoots	1.1	2.3	3.6	11.3	5.6	19.6	*7.0	*31.0	5.7	24.7	5.3	18.7
Latin America	1.9	1.6	3.0	2.6	4.0	3.1	6.3	7.0	8.2	*8.1	*8.3	7.7
Sub-Saharan Africa	5.8	*4.0	5.5	2.9	5.0	2.1	7.2	2.9	9.7	2.1	*14.0	3.3
Total Level	1.0b	$1.2t	1.3b	$1.9t	1.5b	$3.4t	2.5b	$8.4t	5.2b	$43.0t	7.5b	$113.6t

Source: Author's calculations based on Maddison Project Database (2020).

Note: Values in the table are shares of world population and GDP except in the last row, which shows total global levels in absolute terms (b = billion; t = trillion). GDP is adjusted for PPP at 2011 prices. An asterisk denotes the peak population or GDP share for the region during the 1820–2018 period. Underlined population and GDP shares correspond to the year of the region's peak GDP-to-population ratio. For example, Northeast Asia recorded its peak population and GDP shares in 1820 and its peak GDP-to-population ratio in 2018. Western Europe recorded its peak population share in 1900, its peak GDP share in 1870, and its peak GDP-to-population ratio in 1990.

respectively. In other words, even without including Central Asia and West Asia (or the Middle East), the Asian region accounted for more than 50 percent of global population and GDP in 1820. Its GDP share was only modestly lower than its population share, implying that its per capita GDP was basically on a par with the world average. In fact, except for Western Europe and Western offshoots such as the United States, Canada, and Australia, other regions around the world had similar levels of per capita GDP in 1820. By comparison, although Western Europe's population share was only 12.8 percent in 1820, its GDP share was 25.2 percent, implying that its per capita GDP was about twice the world average. Western offshoots had levels of per capita GDP similar to that of Western Europe, but their collective population share in 1820 was only 1.1 percent. Overall, thanks to technological and military advantages supported by its lead in industrialization as well as commercial gains from its colonies, Western Europe was positioned to make the nineteenth century the European Century.

By 1870, Western Europe's population and GDP shares had increased to 14.7 percent and 32.4 percent, respectively. Western offshoots' population and GDP shares had also increased, to 3.6 percent and 11.3 percent, respectively. In contrast, the Asian region's shares had declined, with its GDP share declining more sharply than its population share. In particular, Northeast Asia's GDP share plummeted from 38.4 percent in 1820 to 21.3 percent in 1870, while its population share declined from 41.4 percent to 32.3 percent. The Asian region's per capita GDP fell relative to the world average over the 1820–1870 period, as it lagged behind in industrialization and also became subject to imperialist aggression. The English East India Company, among others, played a key role in bringing globalization to Asia, a process that involved military defeats and major concessions on the part of Asian countries. Starting with trading posts established in the seventeenth century, the company dramatically expanded its influence in India and Malaya over the next two centuries and precipitated the first Opium War to open up the Chinese market. The Dutch and the French similarly subjugated Indonesia and Indochina in the nineteenth century. The only notable exception in Asia in this period was Japan. Although Japan was forced to open up and sign unequal treaties in the 1850s, it managed to avoid internationalized civil war and launched the Meiji Restoration in 1868. Maintaining national unity and learning from best practices from around the world, Japan pursued a strategy of *Datsu-A* (a shift of focus away from Asia) to become an imperialist power of its own.

By 1900, the European Century seemed secure, with Western Europe enjoying a comfortable lead in economic and military power over other continents, where it had acquired numerous imperialistic possessions. However, the European Century came to an end in the first half of the twentieth century as European countries were engaged in two horrific world wars, and the United States and, to a lesser extent, the Soviet Union surged ahead.

By 1950, Western offshoots' GDP share had become larger than Western Europe's, with the United States accounting for most of the increase. The American Century had replaced the European Century. In contrast, 1950 marked the lowest point for Asia's share of global GDP, with Northeast Asia's GDP share at only 8.9 percent and South and Southeast Asia's at 8.3 percent. Many Asian countries had been subject to imperialist aggression, with little policy space to pursue industrialization on their own, and then suffered wartime damages and political turbulence. Japan, the only Asian country to industrialize before World War I, suffered a decisive defeat in World War II after trying to create the Greater East Asia Co-Prosperity Sphere through military invasion.

By 1990, however, Asia's fortunes had turned around. First, giving up military adventurism after World War II, Japan channeled its national energy into economic reconstruction and innovation and successfully rode the second wave of globalization to become the world's second-largest economy by the early 1970s. Second, newly industrializing economies, including Hong Kong, Korea, Singapore, and Taiwan, made a rapid transition from agriculture and trading to more sophisticated industry and services, taking advantage of expanding global trade to overcome the limits of small domestic markets. Third, Southeast Asian countries such as Indonesia, Malaysia, and Thailand also recorded high rates of economic growth, even though their structural transformation was not as complete as that of successful Northeast Asian countries.[34] Fourth, China launched its reform and opening-up drive in the late 1970s and greatly improved its productivity in both agriculture and manufacturing, on its way to becoming "the world's factory." Based on these trends, the World Bank published a report titled *The East Asian Miracle* in 1993. At that time, the only Asian countries to be regarded as disappointing performers were those in South Asia and those undergoing postcommunist transition. Northeast Asia's GDP share had increased dramatically, from 8.9 percent in 1950 to 19.2 percent in 1990, while the share of South and Southeast Asia had increased only modestly, from 8.3 percent to 9.3 percent.

The latest data, for 2018, show that Asia's surge continued and broadened in the post-1990 period. Northeast Asia's global GDP share rose to 23.3 percent, higher than its population share of 21.7 percent, indicating that its per capita income exceeded the world average. Given the region's strong investment in human capital, technology, and industry, this trend is likely to continue, at least for the next few decades. South and Southeast Asia's GDP share also increased significantly, from 9.3 percent in 1990 to 16.3 percent in 2018. Showing a pattern similar to that recorded by Northeast Asia, South and Southeast Asia's global GDP share is likely to catch up with its population share in the next few decades. The expansion of regional production networks from Northeast Asia to South and Southeast Asia is likely to facilitate this trend.

Studies estimating shifts in the world's economic center of gravity corroborate the trends revealed by the above review of historical world GDP and population shares. These studies estimate the average location of the world's economic activity, measured by GDP, across geographies on Earth.[35] Their results show the world's economic center of gravity shifting to Western Europe in the nineteenth century (the European Century), followed by a shift across the Atlantic toward the United States in the twentieth century (the American Century), and then a shift toward Asia starting in the late twentieth century and continuing into the twenty-first (setting the stage for an Asian Century).

Asia's surge is also reflected in the region's share of the world's 5,000 largest firms. In 1995–1997, Asia had 1,695 firms in the top 5,000 list, or about one-third of the total. Japan accounted for 1,215 firms, Korea and Southeast Asia had about 140 firms each, and Mainland China and India had only 57 and 25, respectively. In 2015–2017, Asia had 2,027 firms in the top 5,000 list, or about 41 percent of the total. Mainland China accounted for 738 firms, Japan had 644, India had 142, and Korea and Southeast Asia had about 160 each. Asia's large firms had not only increased in number to account for a larger share of globally prominent firms but had also become more widely distributed within the region.[36]

Current Challenges and Prospects

The question is whether the Asian region as a whole can sustain its growth momentum. Particularly relevant to this question is how the region will address geopolitical risks, which put an end to the European Century in the first half of the twentieth century and created so many problems for the Asian region later in that century, including the Cold War and a series of conflicts such as the Korean War, the Indo-Pakistan conflict, the Sino-Soviet conflict, the Vietnam War, and the Yom Kippur War.

Asia's Alternative Futures

Figure 3.4 outlines Asia's four alternative futures, depending on how external cooperation and internal reform evolve. ADB (2011) basically assumed that Asian countries and extraregional powers would successfully manage changing international power dynamics and achieve greater cooperation, and it analyzed only two main scenarios depending on the path of internal reform for economic upgrading, social cohesion, and environmental sustainability. These two scenarios lead to two potential, dramatically different outcomes for the year 2050. The "Asian Century" and "Middle-Income Trap" scenarios project that Asia's share of global GDP at market exchange rates in 2050 will be 51 percent and 32 percent, respectively, compared to 27 percent in 2010. The same two scenarios project Asia's GDP per capita at PPP exchange rates in 2050 at $38,600 and $20,300, amounting to 105 percent and 78 percent of the world's average, respectively. For comparison, in 2010, Asia's GDP per capita at PPP exchange rates was $6,600 (62 percent of the world's average). In this ADB study, Asia was defined to include East Asia, South Asia, Southeast Asia, Pacific Islands, and Central Asia but not West Asia (the Middle East)—unlike the UN definition, which includes West Asia.

If external cooperation cannot be assumed, however, the divergence in scenario outcomes could be even more dramatic. For this case, figure 3.4 presents two additional scenarios: "Perilous Prosperity" and "Crisis and Conflict." In the "Perilous Prosperity" scenario, Asian countries carry out internal reforms to upgrade their economies, maintain social cohesion, and ensure environmental sustainability. However, as they and extraregional powers have trouble managing their relations, prospects for Asia's prosperity are undermined by rising geopolitical tensions. In "the Crisis and Conflict" scenario, Asian countries fail to carry out internal reforms and also face difficult international relations, leading to both internal crises and external conflict risks. For these scenarios, it is difficult to put numbers on Asia's GDP share and per capita GDP as in ADB (2011). Nevertheless, the scenarios help bring out a wider range of possible risks and outcomes.

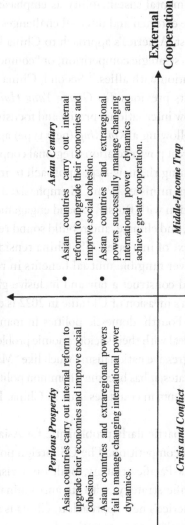

FIGURE 3.4. Asia's Alternative Futures

Internal Reform

Perilous Prosperity

- Asian countries carry out internal reform to upgrade their economies and improve social cohesion.

- Asian countries and extraregional powers fail to manage changing international power dynamics.

Crisis and Conflict

- Asian countries fail to upgrade their economies and improve social cohesion.

- Asian countries and extraregional powers fail to manage changing international power dynamics.

External Cooperation

Asian Century

- Asian countries carry out internal reform to upgrade their economies and improve social cohesion.

- Asian countries and extraregional powers successfully manage changing international power dynamics and achieve greater cooperation.

Middle-Income Trap

- Asian countries fail to upgrade their economies and improve social cohesion.

- Asian countries and extraregional powers successfully manage changing international power dynamics and achieve greater cooperation.

Source: Author's formulation.

Managing External and Internal Risks

Asia's current challenges include geopolitical risks and changing trends in globalization, in addition to internal reforms for economic upgrading, social cohesion, and environmental sustainability as emphasized in ADB (2011). In the context of these external and internal challenges, four developments are noteworthy. First, America's approach to China has changed from strategic engagement to strategic competition, or "competition without catastrophe," in coordination with allies.[37] Second, China has become more assertive. In place of its previous *Tao Guang Yang Hui* strategy of mostly keeping a relatively low international profile and focusing on building itself, China has been following a *Xin Xing* (new type) approach of a more active engagement in great power relations, regional cooperation, and global governance.[38] Explaining the new-type approach to international relations, the Chinese foreign minister Wang Yi emphasized the need to strengthen strategic cooperation with Russia, expand engagement with the EU on multilateralism, trade, and climate, and rebuild sound relations with the United States in a context of increased US-China tensions. He also highlighted the need to deliver tangible mutual benefits in regional and international cooperation and construct a fair and inclusive global governance system.[39] Third, Russia's invasion of Ukraine in 2022 is exacerbating the risk of a new Cold War. Fourth, domestic politics in many countries, either unable or unwilling to deal with their socioeconomic problems directly, is turning to nostalgic and aggressive nationalism. Much like "Make America Great Again" in the United States, it has become a common political practice to appeal to nationalist sentiments in countries such as China, India, Japan, and Russia, as well as Europe.

Against this background, particularly problematic for Asian countries is the intensifying US-China competition. The US foreign policy appears to have shifted from an Asia-Pacific strategy, built on a vision of open regionalism, to an Indo-Pacific strategy, with its anti-China stance and security focus. Although America's new approach to China is supposed to pursue competition, confrontation, or cooperation depending on the issue area, the formation and expansion of groupings such as the Quadrilateral Security Dialogue, or the Quad (including Australia, India, Japan, and the United States), and AUKUS (including Australia, the United Kingdom, and the United States) are giving the impression that America is intent on building a maritime arc to contain China. The overall anti-China stance implicit in US policy is having negative spillovers even in those areas where cooperation would be mutually beneficial. Moreover, the US focus on security issues in the region, while understandable, risks exacerbating the security dilemma. Certainly, given China's increasing assertiveness in the region against the backdrop of long-running territorial disputes, many Asian countries would like to work with the United States to enhance their security. However, without a common security framework for the region, one side's effort to enhance its security can trigger a reaction from the other side, producing an escalation dynamic heightening tensions and risks. The history of Europe over the past two centuries offers valuable lessons in this regard: the Concert of Vienna and its breakdown, competing alliance systems on the road to two World Wars, and the Helsinki process and the unfinished work on common security.

In addition, America's Indo-Pacific strategy seems to lack tangible resource commitments abroad. It is as if the United States were trying to maintain its primacy "on the cheap." Although the United States launched the Indo-Pacific Economic Framework (IPEF) in 2022 to complement its security wing, it stopped short of providing market access benefits to the participating countries due to its concern about domestic backlash against trade liberalization.[40] The IPEF does include technical cooperation and economic assistance, but what the United States has offered so far is very limited. In effect, without being offered tangible trade and economic assistance benefits, participating countries are being asked to go along with the United States to upgrade their labor and environmental standards, write new rules for the digital economy, ensure supply chain resilience, and uphold international anti-corruption and tax conventions. By contrast, at the onset of the Cold War, the United States sent a clear signal of its commitment by launching the Marshall Plan, which provided approximately 2.5 percent of Western Europe's combined GDP at the time.[41] This time, however, despite bipartisan concerns among its politicians about the need to respond to China's rise, the United States has so far made no comparable resource commitment to its Indo-Pacific strategy. For example, there is no "Green Marshall Plan" designed to facilitate energy transition and climate-change mitigation, which would demonstrate US commitment and bring tangible benefits not only to the IPEF members but to the American economy as well. Instead, the United States is using trade and industrial policy to promote investment at home, as demonstrated by the tariffs and subsidies included in the Inflation Reduction Act and the CHIPS and

Science Act. The combination of America's anti-China stance, security focus, weak resource commitments abroad, and recent protectionist actions has made Asian countries uneasy. They would like to construct a more reassuring mechanism for peace and prosperity in the region.

Having suffered so much through past proxy wars, Asian countries should not take a new Cold War as preordained. In this regard, it is worth remembering that Willy Brandt of West Germany launched *Ostpolitik* only a year after the Soviet Union's invasion of Czechoslovakia in 1968, during the heyday of the Cold War. Brandt believed that if another war were to break out in Europe, West and East Germany would become the central battle ground and suffer devastating destruction once again. Instead of shunning the Soviet Union and its allies and letting geopolitical risks build up, he felt that it would be better to promote change through rapprochement. Similarly, Asian countries should continue to promote international cooperation and contribute to an inclusive, rules-based order both regionally and globally. Asian countries should enhance their security in such a way that it contributes to the security of all countries without exacerbating the security dilemma in the Asia-Pacific region and beyond.

Consequently, Asian countries should improve not only bilateral relations but make efforts to build an inclusive economic and security architecture. In the economic area, Asian countries should actively participate in cooperative groupings, with a view that the Regional Comprehensive Economic Partnership (RCEP) and the Comprehensive and Progressive Trans-Pacific Partnership (CPTPP) could eventually become useful building blocks for a broader framework of cooperation, such as some variant of the proposed Free Trade Area of the Asia-Pacific (FTAAP) that would include both the United States and China (figure 3.5).[42] In the security area, Asian countries could look at both the accomplishments and limitations of the Organization for Security and Co-operation in Europe (OSCE), going beyond exclusive groupings like the Quad and exercising caution with regard to sensitive issues like the Taiwan Question.[43]

Internally, Asian countries have to address a number of challenges if they are to continue their economic success. In this context, much of the focus is on China, the largest regional economy, although Asia includes much more than China and other regional countries have opportunities and challenges of their own. Some observers have pointed to China's recent slowdown in economic growth and argued that the Chinese Communist Party's politically driven policies are largely responsible for it. For example,

FIGURE 3.5. **Regional Trade Architecture in the Asia-Pacific**

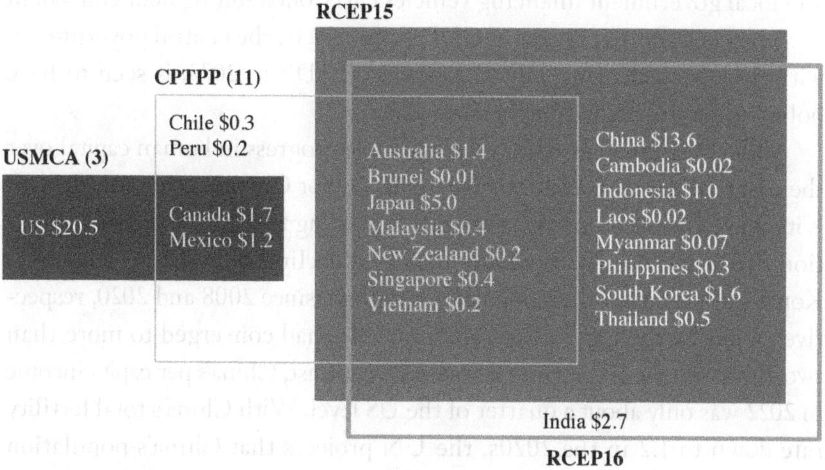

RCEP15

CPTPP (11)

USMCA (3)

Chile $0.3			
Peru $0.2	Australia $1.4	China $13.6
	Brunei $0.01	Cambodia $0.02
	Japan $5.0	Indonesia $1.0
Canada $1.7	Malaysia $0.4	Laos $0.02
Mexico $1.2	New Zealand $0.2	Myanmar $0.07
	Singapore $0.4	Philippines $0.3
	Vietnam $0.2	South Korea $1.6
		Thailand $0.5

US $20.5

India $2.7

RCEP16

Source: Petri and Plummer (2020).

Note: Each country's 2018 GDP in trillions of dollars is calculated at market exchange rates. India was part of the initial negotiations for the RCEP but decided to opt out. It was invited to join later at any time.

claiming that China's economic miracle is over, Posen (2023) states that even though authoritarian regimes tend to start out on a "no politics, no problem" compact, they increasingly disregard commercial concerns and pursue interventionist policies whenever it suits their political goals. He argues that the Chinese Communist Party has finally succumbed to this temptation after more than four decades of economic reform and opening-up efforts and, as a result, entrepreneurs have become reluctant to invest and consumers have cut back on spending.

Some long-time China watchers separate the short-term impact of China's recent policies from long-term structural factors and trends.[44] They note that while policy interventions to promote "common prosperity" and combat inequality may have negatively influenced entrepreneurs' confidence, the government more recently has taken steps to reassure the private sector. They point to China's overly strict and prolonged COVID-19 response and new regulation of the real estate sector as important factors contributing to the growth slowdown. Even though the latter measure was necessary to cool down the Chinese real estate sector before it overheated like Japan's real estate did in the late 1980s, it had a dampening effect on the economy. At the same time, even though China's local governments and local government financing vehicles carry outstanding debt equivalent to 55 percent and 30 percent of GDP, respectively, the central government, with debt equivalent to only 25 percent of GDP in 2023, is seen to have policy space to safeguard debt sustainability.[45]

Although China has achieved remarkable progress in human capital over the past four decades, a key current challenge for Chinese economic growth is its aging and declining population.[46] According to the UN World Population Prospects, China's population started declining in 2022.[47] Japan and Korea have also seen their populations decline (since 2008 and 2020, respectively), but by then, their per capita incomes had converged to more than two-thirds of that of the United States. By contrast, China's per capita income in 2022 was only about a quarter of the US level. With China's total fertility rate down to 1.2 in the 2020s, the UN projects that China's population could shrink from 1.4 billion in 2020 to 1.3 billion in 2050, and the population share of those over 65 years of age could jump from 13 percent to 30 percent over the same period. However, about 25 percent of the Chinese labor force is still employed in agriculture, compared with the average of 3 percent in the OECD countries.[48] Rural-urban migration could allow China to overcome the negative effect on growth of population aging over the 2020–2035 period, after which the population aging effect could surpass the migration effect.[49] Further reforms in the household registration system could facilitate labor mobility.

It is important to note that South and Southeast Asia, including countries such as India, Indonesia, and Vietnam, are projected to have increasing populations up to 2050, unlike Japan, Korea, and China, and they also have more room to catch up in human capital and industrial development. Asia can generate mutual benefits by deepening regional value chains between countries with declining populations and those with increasing populations.

Many observers argue that China's investment-driven growth may have run its course. China's investment-to-GDP ratio, at more than 40 percent, is double that of the United States, but China's returns on assets have declined: private sector returns declined from 9.3 percent in 2017 to 3.9 percent in 2022, while state-owned enterprise returns declined from 4.3 percent to 2.8 percent over the same period.[50] China's households save as much as 35 percent of their disposable income to support the large and increasingly low-return national investment. In 2019, China's household consumption amounted to only 39 percent of GDP, compared with 48 percent in Korea, 53 percent in Japan, 58 percent in Germany, and 65 percent in the United States.[51] China could strengthen its social safety net and increase tax progressivity to reduce households' incentives to save and provide more disposable income to those with a higher marginal propensity to consume. Some other Asian countries may also need to rebalance their investment and consumption, although they seem to have much less of an imbalance relative to China's in this regard.

China's total factor productivity (TFP) growth contributed about three percentage points to its GDP growth in the 1980–2000 period, or about one-third of total growth. Over the past decade, this contribution has declined to one percentage point, or less than one-sixth of total growth.[52] Although China has made major strides in terms of patents granted and articles published in scientific and technical journals, advanced into high-tech fields, and leap-frogged over other countries in such sectors as electric vehicles, it needs to continue to improve resource allocation so that its research and development efforts promote broader TFP improvement. As a large, populous country with a good foundation of digital infrastructure and skills, China has major advantages in the emerging data economy, but it needs to stay the course on reform and opening-up the economy. Other large, populous countries in the region such as India and Indonesia have similar latent advantages, but they need to improve their human capital, digital infrastructure, and the innovation ecosystem to a much greater degree than does China.[53]

Conclusion

Asia faces both internal and external challenges to sustain its economic success and rising global profile. However, these challenges seem to be more manageable than those that beset the region in the third quarter of the twentieth century, when several countries in the region suffered from internal turmoil and international wars. The regional countries have stabilized their domestic politics. They have built up their economic capabilities while also addressing social issues and facing up to the emerging environmental challenges. Their strengths and economic potential position them well to take advantage of the transformative technologies of the digital age. The main challenge to the Asian Century is geopolitical, notably the rising US-China tensions and the risks of geoeconomic fragmentation. But even this challenge can be managed if regional countries exercise their strategic autonomy to work toward a common security and economic framework with extraregional powers, all while the logic of MAD continues to prevent war among nuclear-armed states. Steady progress in regional cooperation since the end of the Cold War provides a solid base from which broader cooperation can be pursued.

There are demographic and economic complementarities between Northeast Asia and South and Southeast Asia that can help generate a third wave of Asian growth, which could serve as a locomotive for global growth. Ongoing trends suggest that Asia is likely to become multipolar, much like its historical experience, rather than being dominated by a single country.

The global economy has a vital stake in the preservation of peace and growth momentum in Asia so it can continue to benefit from the region's dynamism. Northeast Asia, in combination with South and Southeast Asia and working with extraregional powers, can build an Asian Century that boosts the region's prospects but also promotes global prosperity and cooperation.

NOTES

1. Findlay (2019, p. 98), in an article commemorating the fiftieth anniversary of the publication of *Asian Drama* by Gunnar Myrdal (1968).
2. The "pivot to Asia" is a term often used to describe the rebalancing of US foreign policy under the Obama administration (2009–2017).
3. Aiyar et al. (2023).
4. Sullivan (2023).
5. Schroeppel and Nakajima (2002).
6. Khanna (2017).
7. Huang (2021).
8. ADB (2023).
9. O'Rourke, Taylor, and Williamson (1996).
10. O'Rourke and Williamson (2002, 2004).
11. Baldwin (2016).
12. Williamson (2011).
13. Krugman (1981).
14. Romer (1986).
15. Grossman and Helpman (1991).
16. Carr (1939).
17. Morgenthau (1948).

18. Waltz (1979).
19. Mearsheimer (1981).
20. Kindleberger (1973).
21. Angell (1912).
22. Russert (1994).
23. Mazower (2012).
24. Keohane (1984).
25. Polanyi (1944).
26. Ruggie (1982).
27. Milanovic (2016).
28. Brinton (1965) and Dalio (2021).
29. Mazower (2012).
30. Kissinger (2014).
31. Eichengreen and Irwin (1995).
32. Krugman (2007).
33. Subramanian and Kessler (2013) and Rodrik (2019).
34. Studwell (2013).
35. Quah (2011); McKinsey Global Institute (2012); Huang (2021).
36. McKinsey Global Institute (2019).
37. Campbell and Sullivan (2019).
38. Pang (2020).
39. Wang (2020).
40. The IPEF currently has fourteen members: Australia, Brunei Darussalam, Fiji, India, Indonesia, Japan, Korea, Malaysia, New Zealand, Philippines, Singapore, Thailand, the United States, and Vietnam.
41. De Long and Eichengreen (1991).
42. The FTAAP is a proposed free trade area that has been under discussion for some time in the Asia Pacific Economic Cooperation (APEC) forum. APEC has twenty-one member countries, including China, Russia, and the United States.
43. The OSCE has fifty-seven participating states from Europe, Central Asia, and North America, including Russia and the United States.
44. Garcia-Herrero (2023) and Hofman (2023).
45. Garcia-Herrero (2023).
46. Dalio (2021).
47. UN (2022).
48. Hofman (2023).
49. Garcia-Herrero (2023).
50. Garcia-Herrero (2023).
51. Hofman (2023).
52. Hofman (2023).
53. WIPO (2023).

REFERENCES

Aiyar, Shekhar, Jiaqian Chen, Christian Ebeke et al. 2023. "Geoeconomic Fragmentation and the Future of Multilateralism." Staff Discussion Note SDN/2023/001. International Monetary Fund, Washington, DC.

Angell, Norman. 1912. *The Grand Illusion* Toronto: McClelland and Goodchild Publishers.

Asian Development Bank (ADB). 2011. *Asia 2050: Realizing the Asian Century.* Manila.

————. 2023. *Asian Economic Integration Report 2023.* Manila.

Australian Government. 2012. *Australia in the Asian Century: White Paper.* Canberra.

Baldwin, Richard. 2016. *The Great Convergence: Information Technology and the New Globalization.* Cambridge, MA: The Belknap Press of Harvard University Press.

Bank for International Settlements (BIS). 2017. Annual Economic Report. Basel.

Brinton, Crane. 1965. *The Anatomy of Revolution.* Revised and Expanded Edition. New York: Vintage Books.

Campbell, Kurt, and Jake Sullivan. 2019. "Competition without Catastrophe: How America Can Both Challenge and Coexist with China." *Foreign Affairs* 98 (5): 96–111.

Carr, E. H. 1939. *The Twenty Years' Crisis 1919–1939.* New York: Harper & Row.

Dalio, Ray. 2021. *Principles for Dealing with the Changing World Order.* New York: Avid Reader Press.

De Long, J. Bradford, and Barry Eichengreen. 1991. "The Marshall Plan: History's Most Successful Structural Adjustment Program." NBER Working Paper 3899. National Bureau of Economic Research, Cambridge, MA.

Eichengreen, Barry, and Douglas Irwin. 1995. "Trade Blocs, Currency Blocs and the Reorientation of World Trade in the 1930s." *Journal of International Economics,* 38 (1–2): 1–24.

Findlay, Ronald. 2019. "Asia and the World Economy in Historical Perspective." In *Asian Transformations: An Inquiry into the Development of Nations,* edited by Deepak Nayyar, pp. 80–105. Oxford: Oxford University Press.

Garcia-Herrero, Alicia. 2023. "Can Chinese Growth Defy Gravity?" Policy Brief 14/2023. Bruegel, Belgium.

Grossman, Gene, and Elhanan Helpman. 1991. *Innovation and Growth in the Global Economy.* Cambridge, MA: MIT Press.

Hofman, Bert. 2023. "Diminishing Expectations: China's Economy in the Runup to the Third Plenum." August 9. https://berthofman.substack.com/p/diminishing-expectations.

Huang, Francoise. 2021. "The World Is Moving East, Fast." Allianz Research, Munich, January 18.

Kant, Immanuel. 1795. *Perpetual Peace: A Philosophical Sketch.* Königsberg: Nicolovius.

Keohane, Robert. 1984. *After Hegemony: Cooperation and Discord in the World Political Economy*. Princeton, NJ: Princeton University Press.

Khanna, Parag. 2017. *The Future Is Asian: Global Order in the Twenty-First Century*. London: Wiedenfeld & Nicolson.

Kindleberger, Charles. 1973. *World in Depression 1929–1939*. Berkeley: University of California Press.

Kissinger, Henry. 2014. *World Order*. New York: Penguin Press.

Krugman, Paul. 1981. "Intraindustry Specialization and the Gains from Trade." *Journal of Political Economy* 89 (5): 959–73.

———. 2007. *Conscience of a Liberal*. New York: W. W. Norton.

Maddison Project Database. 2020. https://www.rug.nl/ggdc/historical development/maddison/releases/maddison-project-database-2020.

Mazower, Mark. 2012. *Governing the World: The History of an Idea, 1815 to the Present*. New York: Penguin Books.

McKinsey Global Institute. 2012. *Urban World: Cities and the Rise of the Consuming Class*. New York: McKinsey & Company. https://www.mckinsey.com/featured-insights/urbanization/urban-world-cities-and-the-rise-of-the-consuming-class.

———. 2019. *Asia's Future Is Now*. New York: McKinsey & Company.

Mearsheimer, John. 2001. *The Tragedy of Great Power Politics*. New York: W. W. Norton.

Milanovic, Branko. 2016. *Global Inequality: A New Approach for the Age of Globalization*. Cambridge, MA: The Belknap Press of the Harvard University Press.

Morgenthau, Hans. 1948. *Politics among Nations*. New York: A. A. Knopf.

Myrdal, Gunnar. 1968. *Asian Drama: An Inquiry into the Poverty of Nations*. New York: Pantheon Press.

O'Rourke, Kevin, and Jeffrey Williamson. 2002. "When Did Globalization Begin?" *European Review of Economic History* 6 (1): 23–50.

———. 2004. "Once More: When Did Globalization Begin?" *European Review of Economic History* 8 (1): 109–17.

O'Rourke, Kevin, Alan Taylor, and Jeffrey Williamson. 1996. "Price Convergence in the Late Nineteenth Century." *International Economic Review* 37 (3): 499–530.

Pang, Zhongying. 2020. "From Tao Guang Yang Hui to Xin Xing: China's Complex Foreign Policy Transformations and Southeast Asia." Series: Trends in Southeast Asia. ISEAS-Yusof Ishak Institute, Singapore.

Petri, Peter, and Michael Plummer. 2020. "East Asia Decouples from the United States." Working Paper 20-9. Peterson Institute for International Economics, Washington, DC.

Polanyi, Karl. 1944. *The Great Transformation*. Boston: Beacon Press.

Posen, Adam. 2023. "The End of China's Economic Miracle." *Foreign Affairs* 102 (5): 118–30.

Quah, Danny. 2011. "The Global Economy's Shifting Centre of Gravity." *Global Policy* 2 (1): 3–9.

Rodrik, Dani. 2019. "Globalization's Wrong Turn." *Foreign Affairs* 98 (4): 26–33.

Romer, Paul. 1986. "Increasing Returns and Long-Run Growth." *Journal of Political Economy* 94 (5): 1002–37.

Ruggie, John. 1982. "International Regimes, Transactions, and Change: Embedded Liberalism in the Postwar Economic Order." *International Organization* 36 (2): 379–415.

Russert, Bruce. 1994. *Grasping the Democratic Peace: Principles for a Post-Cold War World*. Princeton, NJ: Princeton University Press.

Schroeppel, Christian, and Mariko Nakajima. 2002. "The Changing Interpretation of the Flying Geese Model of Economic Development." *Japanstudien* 14: 203–36.

Studwell, Joe. 2013. *How Asia Works. Success and Failure in the World's Most Dynamic Region*. New York: Grove Press.

Subramanian, Arvind, and Martin Kessler. 2013. "The Hyperglobalization of Trade and Its Future." Working Paper 13-6. Peterson Institute for International Economics, Washington, DC.

Sullivan, Jake. 2023. "Remarks by National Security Advisor Jake Sullivan on Renewing American Economic Leadership at the Brookings Institution," April 27.

United Nations (UN). 2022. *World Population Prospects 2022*. New York.

Waltz, Kenneth. 1979. *Theory of International Politics*. New York: McGraw-Hill.

Wang, Yi. 2020. "Serving the Country and Contributing to the World: China's Diplomacy in a Time of Unprecedented Global Changes and a Once-in-a-Century Pandemic." Speech at the Symposium on the International Situation and China's Foreign Relations, Beijing, December 11.

Williamson, Jeffrey. 2011. *Trade and Poverty: When the Third World Fell Behind*. Cambridge, MA: MIT Press.

World Bank. 1993. *The East Asian Miracle: Economic Growth and Public Policy*. Oxford: Oxford University Press.

———. 2020. *World Development Report 2020: Trading for Development in the Age of Global Value Chains*. Washington, DC.

World Intellectual Property Organization (WIPO). 2023. *Global Innovation Index 2023: Innovation in the Face of Uncertainty*. Geneva.

PART II

New Industrial Dynamics

FOUR

Digital Transformation, Digital Markets, and Economic Strategy

DIANE COYLE

The global economy is undergoing two fundamental technological trans- formations: the first is the transition from fossil fuels to renewables, and the second is digitalization. Both involve "general purpose technolo- gies" spanning energy and information, the two fundamental economic resources. Such technological transformations are never smooth transi- tions. Prompted also by the succession of large economic shocks, starting with the 2008 global financial crisis, there is a significant shift underway in the climate of ideas about economic policy and policy rhetoric. Indus- trial policy is being widely discussed after some four decades when it was "the policy that shall not be named," although it was nevertheless widely practiced in various forms in most countries.[1]

There are some general lessons from past experiences with strategic economic or industrial policies. Implementation of industrial policies has mostly been undertaken by rich countries, mainly selectively targeted to sectors in which they have a revealed comparative advantage in inter- national trade.[2] Governments use a wide range of different policy tools, from encouraging research and development (R&D) and innovation to export credit finance or trade subsidies.[3] There are continuing debates about the effectiveness of individual policy interventions, and about the channels through which innovation contributes to higher income and living standards, yet it is evident that differing rates of adoption and use of technology account for a substantial part of the differences in economic performance between countries and between businesses within countries.[4] This chapter focuses on the policy implications of digitalization. Digital computation, especially artificial intelligence (AI), involves the rewiring of economic relations, offering new opportunities for progress and at the same time posing significant adjustment challenges. It is impossible to imagine how countries (at any stage of their development) can navigate the digital transformation without purposive government economic strategies, encompassing industrial policy but also broader policies concerning worker skill development, competition in markets, and access to new technologies.

The importance of technology in shaping national economic trajectories increases at times when the technological frontier is advancing. Although the origins of modern information and communications technologies (ICTs) date back at least to the second world war, and recent waves of innovation arguably to the creation of web protocols and broadband infrastructure in the 1990s, digital innovation is still extremely rapid. The latest example to receive public and policy attention is the launch of generative or large language AI models that are rapidly being adopted by some users. These models' capabilities are continually advancing and their costs declining. They in turn will form the basis for a multitude of new commercial services and apps when paired with plug-ins or Application Programming Interfaces (APIs).

In this environment, some of the lessons of the past remain as relevant as ever for policymakers. One lesson is that innovation policies are important, but for most countries the bleeding edge of the research frontier is not the critical domain of innovation. Rather, the diffusion and use of new technologies, and the adoption of process innovations, are more important, as is a policy framework that ensures the benefits are widely shared. This means that innovation policies will be context-specific and will need to be coordinated with complementary policies for skills and for infrastructure. For example, very few countries will be at the AI frontier, but all will need adequate broadband (wired and wireless) infrastructure. All need to consider the skills their workforces will need.

Another key lesson is that competition determines whether the strategic policy framework succeeds or fails. If incumbents can capture the policy process and keep out either new entrants (in domestic markets) or foreign competition, there will be less innovation and less economic gain from innovation. The past neuralgia about industrial policy stems from "picking winners" or encouraging "national champions" that turned out instead to be highly effective rent-seekers. Active competition policy can mitigate such risks but faces new challenges in digital markets.

These lessons—support innovation and enforce competition—are at the same time more relevant and harder to implement in the emerging, increasingly digital economy. They are more relevant because of the extent of structural change that is under way and because the dynamics of digital markets—as described below—mean such shifts occur quickly. They are harder to implement because the technologies are highly sophisticated and require significant change in skills and organizational structures to adopt, as well as agile policymaking.

The extent and degree of structural change may also offer some new opportunities. For example, for countries experiencing or fearing premature deindustrialisation,[5] there may be niches or scope for leapfrogging linked to provision of digital services.[6] The evidence that countries' growth trajectories depend on expanding their extensive margin of trade using the capabilities they have available implies that any technology that opens up the space of the "adjacent possible"[7] is to be welcomed.[8] The rapid spread and impact of mobile technologies in developed and emerging economies alike from the mid-2000s may offer an encouraging early example. The policy framework will affect the extent to which new opportunities can be realized.

On the other hand, the challenges are significant. The challenges of scale (and a high ratio of fixed to variable costs) and digital dynamics (slow, then extremely rapid) create a different kind of market and regulatory landscape than most institutional systems can respond to sufficiently flexibly. These characteristics mean there are new requirements for state capacity to manage the economy,[9] some of them already apparent in the new debates about industrial policy. The more advanced or the more disruptive the technology, the greater the demands it will place on tacit knowledge and complementary assets; these assets include management quality, organizational capital and state capacity, and costly physical assets (such as data centers or fiber-optic cables).

In an illuminating thought experiment, Mancur Olson (1996) imagined an unskilled worker who migrated from Haiti to New York to work as a janitor. By merely crossing the national border, the worker's productivity increased many times over, thanks to the other assets the janitor used—perhaps better cleaning equipment—but mainly due to more productive modes of organization and more highly educated coworkers. While the physical capital matters, intangibles matter more, including tacit knowledge as well as codifiable intangibles.[10] Tacit knowledge is by definition hard to convey and requires on-the-job experience to acquire. The importance of tacit knowledge makes technology transfer harder; in general, it requires the movement of people.[11]

The landscape of opportunities and challenges posed by digital transformation will in short require a purposive, strategic approach to economic policy, embracing a more active but better-designed and more broadly conceived industrial policy than in the recent past. Most governments fall short. It has been described as the need for a "designer economy," an evocative description of the need but difficult to put into practice, including in the United States and China, which are at the digital technology frontier.[12] Policy solutions for the technologies of the twenty-first century will need to become more adaptive and acknowledge the different characteristics of intangible assets, as compared to physical assets, to ensure meaningful public interest oversight of the way these innovations are shaping society and the economy.

This chapter sets out a framework for approaching the policy challenges. After describing briefly some key aspects of change in the structure of the global economy, it turns to the distinctive features of digital markets and some of the important strategic industrial and competition policy implications. Next, it focuses on the role of data, the fuel of the digital economy. These challenges cover only a part of the necessary landscape; the pervasive impact of digitalization implies rethinking the entire policy agenda and institutional framework. For example, one important debate concerns the implications for jobs and income distribution.[13] The chapter concludes, therefore, with some reflections on the broader economic policy landscape as affected by digital transformation.

The New Structural Context

The starting point is appreciating the extent of the transformation that has already occurred in the global economy, particularly within advanced and middle-income economies. Over the four decades since 1980, value added in economic activity has been increasingly intangible. This reflects

FIGURE 4.1. Material Footprint of the UK Economy

Source: Author's calculations based on https://circabc.europa.eu/sd/a/2e3e7aa5-3826-40dc-a6c8-2da986b30a27/UK%20material%20flows%20review%20-%20final%20report.pdf and https://www.ons.gov.uk/economy/environmentalaccounts/datasets/ukenvironmentalaccountsmaterial flowsaccountunitedkingdom.

Note: The vertical axis shows metric ton per £GDP, 1970=100. The material flow accounts show the physical exchange processes between economy, society, and nature. The estimates, which cover domestic extraction, imports, and exports, are grouped into four types of material: biomass (crops, wood, and fish); metal ores (iron and nonferrous metals); nonmetallic minerals (such as construction materials); and fossil fuels (coal, oil, and gas).

both the shift toward services, from tourism to business services to digital, and the increased servicification of manufacturing. At the same time there has been a growing appreciation of the costs economic activity has imposed on nature, such that the true (social) marginal cost of nature has increased substantially,[14] the material and energy inputs per dollar of GDP have been in secular decline in the advanced economies.[15] For example, figure 4.1 shows the long-term downward trend in the material footprint of the UK economy.

The key enablers of the structural shifts have been ICTs, with the cost of computation continuing to decline substantially.[16] As well as the progressive shift of value into intangibles (all the way from design and organizational and logistics know-how to marketing and after-sales service), the location of valued added has shifted with the creation of global supply chains. The business model phenomenon that is emblematic of this globalization of production is the multinational corporation, progressively contracting out lower value-added activities to economies in East Asia, Central and Eastern Europe, and Latin America. Among these, there has been a subsequent process of moving up the value chain and contracting elsewhere.[17] In the early phase of the rollout of digital technologies, improved communications and certain digital innovations (such as computer-aided design and computer-aided manufacturing) triggered the initial creation of these extensive global production networks.[18]

The wave of globalization after 1980 was therefore a digital as well as a trade policy and political phenomenon, enabled by new and expanding communications networks and the logistics networks these supported. The process has encompassed the phenomenon of servicification and factoryless production; by the early 2020s, almost one-fifth of production in some sectors of the US and UK economies (such as consumer electronics and pharmaceuticals) was contracted in this way.[19] Process and business model innovations have been a significant driver of economic growth, involving structural change in the economy. One metric of the extent of the digitally enabled reshaping of production since the 1980s is the upward trend in trade in intermediate goods and business services. For example, in 2021, the share of intermediates in EU goods exports had reached 49 percent, while in EU goods imports it had reached 60 percent.[20] Conversely, the share of domestic value added in exports had shown a strong decline for many countries over the period between 1970 and 2013.[21]

A more recent inflection point in the structure of the economy has been the spread beginning in 2007 of the smartphone, 3G/4G networks, and market design algorithms, enabling digital platform business models. The platform model creates a digital intermediary between suppliers and buyers able to crystallize and capture economies of scale and scope, along with the surplus created by greater variety and improved matching. In addition to the well-known consumer-facing platforms such as Uber and Airbnb, or Amazon Marketplace, there are a growing number of business-to-business platforms. Many aspiring digital platforms fail—for reasons discussed in the next section—and others run at a loss for long periods as they begin by maximizing user numbers (rather than profits or even revenues).[22] However, there are wide-ranging examples of successful use of the model. Chinese insurer Ping An, for example, has founded a number of platforms in markets ranging from health care to banking, European companies such as Siemens and Phillips have created supply chain platforms, and Walmart in the United States has founded a marketplace directly connecting its suppliers to consumers.

The digitally enabled transformation of production sits on the foundation provided by two essential enablers: sustained investment in research and development (R&D); and major infrastructure investments in wired and wireless communication networks, including under-sea cables, internet network infrastructure, and data centers. The history of the founding technologies of the internet and the US digital sector has been told in numerous accounts.[23] There are few systemic accounts of either China's digital sector or of the physical rewiring of the globe.[24] Fiber optics have greatly expanded available capacity, and there have been substantial continuing technological improvements, such as enhanced data compression and reduced latency. But demand for connectivity and computer power has continued to rise substantially, with the emergence of new generative AI applications likely to increase the requirement for computational power even further.[25] Combined with the returns to scale in the digital markets relying on the physical infrastructure, China and the United States are the two countries that host the global digital giants. Data governance and trade in data have become increasingly prominent policy issues; as discussed below, China and the United States are the world's main data importers.

This brief summary has outlined the dramatic digitally enabled shifts in economic structure during recent decades: value added is increasingly intangible, and the global distribution of its creation and capture has relocated. Although the restructuring has enabled substantial growth in trade and poverty-reduction, it has clearly also been and continues to be disruptive. For the purposes of this chapter, there are two key points. One is that the world economy is experiencing two simultaneous major transformations in the form of general-purpose technologies: in energy and communications. Such transformations are rarely smooth, and the intangible nature of value added in the digital economy poses new challenges.[26] The other point is that R&D, particularly the adoption and use of technology, have become an important differentiator between the economic fortunes of different countries and of businesses within countries.[27] To explore further some of the policy implications, I turn next to the distinctive features of digital markets and the following section considers the central role of data.

Digital Markets

Productivity, or getting more valuable economic output from the same or fewer scarce inputs, is the engine of long-term improvements in living standards. While we often focus our attention on innovation in terms of products or inventions, major productivity improvements rest on process innovations. Early examples were the American system of manufactures (introducing interchangeable parts) in the early nineteenth century, the nineteenth-century factory system, and the assembly line in the early to mid-twentieth century. A more recent example is the just-in-time manufacturing revolution of the 1970s and 1980s. The digitally enabled phenomena of production networks and platform business models described in the previous section are similarly process innovations, offering significant productivity potential. However, in contrast to previous process innovation waves, digital processes are more difficult to adopt. Like earlier technologies, they require significant organizational change.[28] There is evidence of a current "productivity J curve" due to the amount of time required to undertake such restructuring.[29]

One reason for the slow adoption of digital technologies by many firms is that an increasingly intangible-value economy requires more tacit, or hard-to-convey, knowledge than previous production restructurings. Even standard machine tools are not straightforward to use; there is learning-by-doing as experience teaches operators the ways small adjustments or tweaks can turn written guides into production practice. As Khan (2013) writes, "Owners, managers and supervisors do not know how to set up the factory, align the machinery, set up systems for quality control, reduce input wastage and product rejection, manage inventories, match order flow with production cycles, maintain after-sales services and a host of other coordination and management issues."[30] Even more tacit knowledge is involved in adopting advanced software or digital processes. James Bessen (2022) explains how the use of proprietary software and large amounts of proprietary data enable larger firms to manage complex production environments and tailor products better for customers. Business investment in internal software has increased substantially in large firms.

This has led to a pattern whereby many sectors of the economy have a small number of "superstar" firms.[31] The dominance of the big tech companies is widely noted, with antitrust authorities around the globe focusing on evidence of market power such as Google's and Meta's hold over half the digital advertising in the United States (more in some other countries) or the fact that Amazon Web Services and Microsoft account for more than half the cloud computing market. However, there is good evidence that the most productive (often among the largest) firms across the whole economy are pulling ever-further ahead of the rest in terms of productivity and profitability, and that digital use is a significant differentiator among firms.[32] For the superstars—the dominant companies in a range of sectors rather than just big tech—there seems to be positive feedback between digital adoption, productivity, wages, and skilled workers, as wage dispersion is wider within many industries (especially industries where some businesses invest more intensively in digital technologies) than across industries. Whether this remains the case given the most recent advances in generative AI remains to be seen. Although the very large models produced by leaders such as OpenAI, Google, and Microsoft have required vast computational, energy, and human resources to produce, and the market will remain concentrated at that level, the generative technology simplifies and makes more usable not only other AI applications but also many other tech-related tasks such as writing code or manipulating data. It has also already become significantly cheaper to train smaller competing models.[33]

Few countries other than the United States and China seem likely to be able to push forward the frontier of these advanced digital technologies given the existing gap and the scale of R&D and other investment required. However, there are important policy questions concerning how to diffuse the use of advanced digital technologies, how to enable wider business model and product innovation using the new platforms, what investments are needed to develop complementary capabilities and infrastructure, and how to mitigate against key risks and vulnerabilities. The policy challenges can be divided into three broad areas: skills, physical infrastructure, and supply chain risks. Details of these fall outside the scope of this chapter, but they all form part of the wide scope of economic policy challenges posed by digital transformation.

It is worth noting, though, that the EU and US debates about developing advanced chip manufacturing capabilities in the domestic market speak to the issue of tacit knowledge. For although the physical facilities are difficult and costly to develop, building the engineering practice and know-how is at least as challenging. The loss of tacit knowledge due to outsourcing to global supply chains has long been one of the concerns of the advocates of industrial policy. As Tassey (2014) points out, advanced manufacturing involves complicated system technologies, with multiple phases requiring extensive use of data and automation. Processes need to be flexible while also high quality and low cost. He adds: "Advanced manufacturing often displays important colocation synergies resulting in benefits to new product development when manufacturing firms are located close to their research and development efforts and to many of their key suppliers. These synergies arise from the fact that much of the technical knowledge developed in the early phases of the research and development cycle is tacit in nature (as opposed to being codified in, say, patents)."[34] Past efforts in Europe to reintroduce semiconductor manufacturing failed, in part because the efforts focused around creating national champions built on incumbent firms that were unable or unwilling to disrupt their existing business.[35] New efforts will need to focus on the knowledge base for manufacture as well as the physical facilities and, above all, remember the importance of the disciplining power of competition.

Competition Policy

Economic strategies need to span investment in infrastructure and physical facilities and in skills and capabilities; they must also enable the accumulation of tacit knowledge or know-how. The intangible character of value in the digital economy makes for new development challenges. The inherent difficulty of access to the market for new entrants in the face of dominant companies is a key issue, making competition policy—and its relationship to industrial policy—an area of active debate and change. Competition policy involves broader concerns than strategies for particular sectors. Digital technology is reshaping markets across the economy, and there have been specific investigations and actions taken against the big tech monopolies, in particular, ranging from the passage of new legislation regulating digital markets in the EU and the UK to the antitrust cases recently brought by the Department of Justice in the United States. Partly as a result of the specific concerns about technology markets, there is a shift under way across the advanced economies toward more active competition enforcement in general after some decades of weak enforcement. This is an important context for new industrial strategies: vigorous competition enforcement is one of the key characteristics of success for broader industrial policies.[36]

The dynamics of digital markets make such enforcement more challenging. While the big tech companies offer highly valued services, there is a strong policy concern that the lack of competition implies either concurrent harms (associated with high concentration of market power) or future harms (less innovation).[37] A suite of policy reports on the challenges of enforcing competition in digital markets have underlined their strong tendency toward superstar or winner-take-all dynamics.[38] One reason is extreme economies of scale, with a high ratio of fixed to variable costs, making the minimum efficient scale of operation very large, even global. In the extreme, when the code is written and the infrastructure in place, marginal cost may be close to zero.

A second reason is the power of network effects. These consist of direct network effects (such as those that operate in the telephone network), when each user benefits the more users there are, and indirect network effects, such that every buyer benefits from greater choice of supply and each seller benefits from a bigger potential market. Digital platforms are multisided markets, often combining different types of products and services that can benefit either from an established consumer base (for example, people looking for a plumber might also later want to hire a piano teacher) or from a set of supply capabilities (drivers who can pick up passengers or deliver meals). This strategy ("envelopment") can amplify already-powerful network effects.

A third reason is the data advantage an incumbent will generally enjoy. The more customers the platform has, the more data it can use either to generate advertising revenue or to inform improvements in the service, and with better services, it can attract more users and more data (the "data loop"). The fact that one side of the platform, usually the consumer side, is subsidized (even free) cements this loop in place.

A corollary of these dynamics is that many platforms fail.[39] To succeed, a digital platform must build both sides, users and suppliers, in an appropriate ratio to each other—known as the "chicken and egg problem." For example, a platform for booking restaurant tables needs to sign up enough restaurants to appeal to diners, but it will fail to appeal to restaurants unless it has enough diners using the app. The platform will grow slowly and lose money until it reaches a certain critical or tipping point beyond which the nonlinear network effects kick in and accelerate its growth. The need to finance a loss-making phase implies that platforms backed by successful venture capitalists are more likely to be able to get to the tipping point, itself a factor that encourages further concentration in digital markets. These characteristics of digital markets mean that competition is "for" the market rather than "in" the market, sometimes described as "Schumpeterian" competition, or competition by innovation and entrepreneurship.[40]

Policymakers have begun to recognize and respond to the challenge of how to enable continuing innovation and potential replacement of current incumbents by newcomers—just as Google overtook Yahoo as a search engine or Facebook overtook MySpace. The EU (Digital Markets Act and the Digital Services Act) and the UK (the Digital Markets Unit) have implemented new legislation to address behaviors by big tech firms that are seen as creating barriers to entry, such as the practice of promoting their own services on their websites or seeking to prevent suppliers providing better terms on their own websites compared to the big platform. The head of the Federal Trade Commission in the United States under President Biden, Lina Khan, has taken a more activist approach to big tech based on her well-known analysis of the dominance of Amazon.[41] Her critique is that what had become the standard approach to competition analysis, focused only on prices paid by final consumers, is unable to deal with the consolidation of market power in which many services may be 'free' but other consumer harms occur, for example, due to predatory pricing or the leveraging of existing market positions to dominate other markets. Across the main antitrust jurisdictions, there are emerging signs of more competition enforcement in technology markets.[42] Whether these actions will be enough to open markets such as search engines, social media, online marketplaces, and payments to significant new entry is not yet clear.

The competition policy challenges are not confined to ensuring new entry. The dynamic mode of innovation in digital markets, and the absence of substantial competition from new entrants or smaller firms, raise some important and underappreciated policy challenges, meaning that competition policy needs to be rethought for the digital age. Some of the standard analytical tools are not applicable in digital markets, for example, because of zero-priced services, or because digital platforms operate across markets leveraging their technical capabilities. As noted, the markets' winner-take-all character means that competition is "for" the market rather than "in" the market, making the potential for entry at sufficient scale the key focus of contestability. There are also new concerns about monopsony power over workers and small suppliers, after decades during which only consumer harms have been the policy focus. The previous attitude to take-overs of smaller businesses by dominant tech companies is now seen to have been unduly relaxed, with few challenged in any major jurisdiction until recently. There are also calls for break-up of the big tech companies (despite the consumer benefits of the extensive economies of scale and network effects) or, alternatively, for specific *ex ante* utility-style regulation of the tech giants.

All of these competition policy challenges have required a refresh of the analytical framework used by antitrust authorities to take better account of the dynamics of digital markets and the incumbents' market power. They also raise questions of capacity. The antitrust authorities themselves have had to acquire rapidly relevant, in-house technical expertise. In some countries, new regulatory bodies with a focus on digital markets have been established, while elsewhere there has been new legislation combined with beefed-up expertise or specialist units within existing competition bodies.[43] In most cases, there is at least an implicit recognition that *ex post* compe-tition policy such as antitrust enforcement alone is inadequate to ensure digital markets work well, necessitating the introduction of new *ex ante* regulation.

MARKET-SHAPING. Winner-take-all markets imply that competition law and its enforcement by competition authorities will determine the identity of the winner. Clearly, the less activist the approach, the more likely it will be that current incumbents remain dominant. In general, though, either action or inaction means regulatory decisions will shape the market. For example, in the case of a proposed acquisition in a nascent market (such as cloud gaming or generative AI), both allowing and barring the merger will deter-mine market structure. This may seem an obvious point as the purpose of merger policy is to shape market structure. The difference with winner-take-all digital markets, however, is that if there is, broadly speaking, only one winner, some principles for determining their identity may come into play. It will not be possible to rely only on rules of thumb guides to assess-ing consumer welfare, the standard approach to economic analysis, because the decision will involve forward-looking judgements about likely future innovation. Governments increasingly care about the nationality of domi-nant firms, having come to recognize both geopolitical and supply chain uncertainties and the importance of ensuring national capabilities in key areas. AI may prove to be one of these.

STANDARDS. One of the features of large digital platforms is that they enable greater competition on the platform. For example, Airbnb hosts many smaller and more specialized digital short-stay accommodation platforms and platforms offering services such as babysitting or tour guides. Facebook and Amazon Marketplace enable many additional suppliers to gain access to market and increase the extent of competition in many products and services. Competition authorities have some concerns, particularly about the scope for anticompetitive pricing, but there are large consumer welfare gains in terms of variety and choice.[44] Large platforms self-regulate to a large extent, for example, by setting extensive terms and conditions and potentially removing access if they are breached, or by implementing rating or escrow systems.[45] But a question that regulators face is about the level of the technology stack at which they want to enforce competition and regulatory policies, and what this implies for technical standards.

Different choices have been made with prior technologies. For example, the competition in videotape was played out in the market in the late 1970s between VHS and Sony's Betamax. The market eventually tipped to VHS, imposing costs on Betamax and on consumers who had bought the losing technology. In the case of mobile telephony, however, the industry GSM standard emerged early in the 1990s, encouraged by European governments, leading to rapid gains from economies of scale in network and consumer equipment and the consequent rapid growth of a global market with falling prices. Telecoms providers competed on the playing field of the common standard. In many digital markets, the issue is one of interoperability and whether or where—as in telecoms—this should be mandated. For example, different social media platforms have been engineered not to be interoperable; Twitter has seen its interoperability recently decrease. Others, after being acquired (such as Instagram by Facebook), have been engineered to link to each other. Telecoms markets are significantly regulated by standards and interconnect rules, so the question is should different regulatory choices have been made in digital markets, and if so, what those choices are. For example, should common technical standards and terms of service access have been enforced, or might they be in the future?

DATA. The existence of the data loop described above makes data one of the key arenas of debate about interoperability or portability of data provided (knowingly or inadvertently as data exhaust) by users. Data portability is often recommended as a potential antitrust remedy, but to be effective, it requires mandated common standards (for the classification of data records and metadata, for instance, as well as some software standards). The implementation is also challenging, as the UK experience with open banking data has shown.[46] For example, the sensitivity of personal data means that new online businesses and platforms might have to be accredited to demonstrate regulatory compliance for access to individual-level data. New entrants will also need to win customer trust by safeguarding data security and privacy. Alternatively, the level of data aggregation versus granularity (across individuals) and data timeliness necessary to enable competition while safeguarding privacy as well as security need to be decided. This is likely to vary between markets and uses of data. Data for marketing purposes can be more highly aggregated over individuals and time while helping potential competitors, whereas data for competing online transport information providers needs to be granular in time and data for health technology services needs to be granular across individuals. There is a lively policy debate about broader aspects of data governance. The digital market context serves to highlight how complex and context-specific policy decisions in this area will need to be.

The Role of Data and Data Policy

Like digital markets in general, data has some distinctive economic characteristics.[47] It is nonrival, meaning that it is not depleted by use and can be used simultaneously by many people. This makes it a public good, in the sense in which economists use that term, implying its societal value is likely to be higher than its private value. It has both negative and positive externalities. The negative ones include the fact that providing data may reveal additional information, perhaps about other people, harming their privacy.[48] The positive ones arise from the fact that linking different data records will create information that is much more useful than that provided by a single dataset. For example, aggregating individual cars' location data will provide information about congestion; a company planning a product launch will want several data types (sociodemographic data, transport data, location of competitors, etc.) to project demand. Beyond these two key features, nonrivalry and pervasive externalities, different types of data will have important depreciation features depending on use—very

Table 4.1. Characteristics Affecting the Value of Data

Economic lens	Contextual lens
Nonrival (although excludable)	Data type
Positive and negative externalities	Provenance
Increasing/decreasing marginal returns	Data subject/sensitivity
Depreciation rate	Generality (reference data)
High fixed costs	Accuracy
Complementary investments	Interoperability/accessibility

Source: Coyle et al. 2020.

slow in the case of marketing data, very rapid in the case of traffic and sensor data needed for autonomous vehicles. The former type of data will have diminishing returns to each additional data point, the latter increasing returns.

Data also has information characteristics affecting its value, such as its accuracy, timeliness, granularity, personal or commercial sensitivity, degree of generality (for example, geospatial data), or specificity (for example, personal finance data). These can also drive a wedge between private and social value. For example, proprietary standards and software will enhance private value by creating a barrier to other potential data users, whereas interoperability will increase the social value.

The key economic and informational features influencing data value, both the private value to its holders and broader social welfare value, are summarized in table 4.1.

Valuing Data

That the use of data by businesses creates economic value is clear. For example, stock markets indicate the value investors place on corporate data use. Coyle and Li (2021) describe the large gap in market valuations of organizational capital as between companies that are and are not data-intensive in the hospitality industry. Armstrong, Konchitchki, and Zhang (2023) find that companies' digital traffic such as website visitor data is a contemporaneous and leading indicator of firm profitability.

Unfortunately, there is no consensus about how to value data or data use in practice. There are few markets where data is bought and sold, and those that exist do not post prices. Market-based prices such as share prices are an alternative for some types of data. But in many cases, there are no observable prices. A recent survey enumerates many alternative methods of valuing data (figure 4.2).[49] In the case of aggregate national statistics, data valued at its cost of production and maintenance is likely to be introduced as an intangible asset when the next revision of definitions for the System of National Accounts is published in 2025.[50] This approach, although entirely reasonable when there are no observed transaction prices, will not capture the use value of data or indeed its inherent risks and optionality.[51]

The inability to value data matters mainly because attaching a zero price to an economically valuable asset will result in underinvestment. Although digital-intensive companies (which tend to be either large or digital-native) clearly understand the value of appropriately collecting, managing, and using data, many businesses do not, or even use the data assets they already hold. Governments are also likely to underinvest in data infrastructure. The nonrivalry makes data a form of public good, and underprovision by the private sector requires some government provision. Reference geospatial data, for instance, may be provided and maintained by a public body. There will be a case for government intervention in other types of data, such as data on urban transport (for socially desirable connectivity and transport planning), utilities (for network resilience or monitoring capacity and maintenance), financial markets (to monitor systemic risk), and so on. Such data types are needed for economic management and may also be desirable as open data for other providers to use. It is important to address data gaps and consequent digital exclusion due to groups without an online presence, as missing data becomes a problem when policy is increasingly based on data analysis and even algorithmic decision-making. For instance, policies to encourage fintech startups serve people who already have digital access via smartphones and mobile broadband, but this access is highly unequal. Even where countries have a data strategy, however, there is no systematic analysis or detailed mapping of what the open and/or public data infrastructure should be, nor how much should be invested in data as digital infrastructure.[52]

Data Policy and Governance

A further area needing fresh policy consideration is the legal protection around data, particularly personal data. Although there are protections in different jurisdictions, such as the EU's General Data Protection Regulation, the way control of data is framed in policy debate as "ownership" is in effect a corner solution: data is seen as wholly owned by the data

FIGURE 4.2. Alternative Methods for Valuing Data

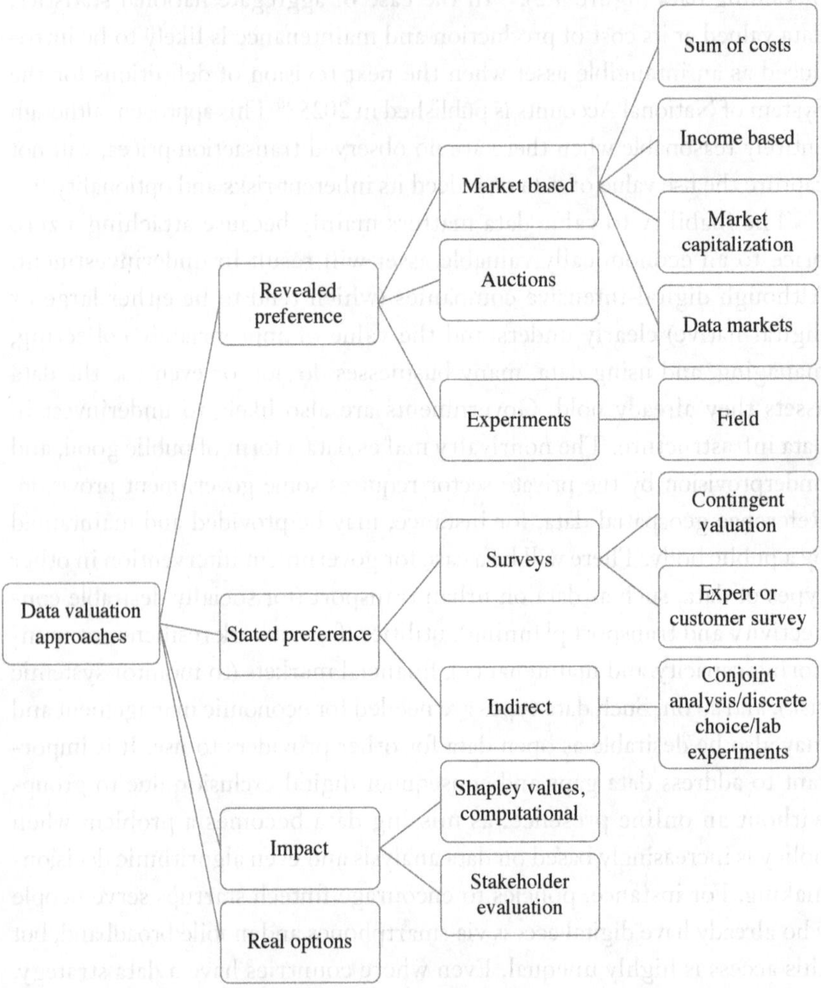

Source: Coyle and Manley 2023.

Note: The typology distinguishes four broad valuation approaches: revealed preference using market prices or behaviors; stated preference using surveys; impact on outcomes such as profits; and real options modeling.

controller, with some restrictions on use depending on permissions by the data "provider" or data subject. The legal structures allocate a disproportionate share of the rents to corporate data controllers. This all-or-nothing treatment of data online differs from the inherent physical limits on offline knowledge about people, and ignores the inherently relational character of data. This refers to the fact that data is not only useful to both data subject and data controller but is also jointly created by them: purchase record data depends on customer purchases and retailer service provision. A richer data policy debate would consider conditions and rights of access to data, and address questions such as the purpose for which data is to be used and by whom and who else has rights of access. Given that concerns about privacy loss and surveillance—carried out by both big tech companies and states— hinge on the scope for joining up data about individuals and hence gathering an uncomfortable amount of insight into each of us, these would be best addressed by a more nuanced debate about access rights and responsibilities. The concern is not that sometimes others have personal information about each of us, such as our bank knowing our financial position, but rather that a small number of powerful entities can collate different kinds of personal information.

As for nonpersonal data, the ownership and subsequent copyright framing seem bound to be challenged by the rapid spread of generative AI models that have been trained on massive amounts of data scraped online. Legal challenges to the models are now proliferating. But the issue was in the courts already given the claim by some manufacturers (such as John Deere and General Motors) that data generated by use of their vehicles is not owned by those who bought the vehicles. In other words, farmers in effect merely leased the costly equipment they had paid thousands of dollars for and could not do self-repairs without breaching the manufacturer's copyright in the data.[53] This is self-evidently unsustainable. Relational data—coproduced from the farmer's land and activities and the manufacturer's software and aggregation—requires a balance in the sharing of benefits. The economically desirable amount of protection for intellectual property, with its inherent nonrivalry, is always a matter of balance. Policy has not yet found the right balance, in data copyright or in other areas of IP protection and exclusion in the digital world.

A final area of policy challenge regarding data concerns data trade and localization policies. Data centers are so costly and energy-intensive that for the foreseeable future, not every country will have them. In any case, data flows around the internet according to network need, unless explicitly banned from leaving a nation's borders. Coyle and Li (2021) categorize countries in terms of whether they are net data importers (China and the United States) or exporters, and in terms of their domestic market scale and their digital infrastructure and skill-base. Even if data about a country's inhabitants or businesses leaves its borders for a data center elsewhere, its primary use is in the country of origin. The economic policy challenge, then, is to have adequate domestic capabilities in the form of physical networks and data infrastructure and people with appropriate skills. If these are in place, there will be opportunities for even small economies to build some more digitally intensive activities and potentially many opportunities for larger middle-income economies.[54] There might be good non-economic or civic reasons for preferring data localization, but such policies are not the most important for strategies for growth in the digital economy. The intangibles, including soft data infrastructure and human capital, are key, in addition to the physical capital such as data centers and cables.

Conclusion

The implications of the digital restructuring of the economy are wide-ranging, posing many policy challenges. This chapter has focussed on a narrow slice of the policy landscape but even so has ranged across policies relating to innovation, competition, and data, all involving substantial and demanding agendas for change. Stepping back from the detail, what are the general themes for those developing policies for the digital economy?

Investment

Significant investment will be needed in physical infrastructure, data infrastructure, innovation and R&D, and skills. Although these investments must be financed, these are not costs but opportunities for growth and productivity enhancement. Much debate about digital policy focuses on negative aspects such as potential job losses, surveillance, and even existential risk. These are important issues and must be addressed. At the same time, however, the technologies must be harnessed so they deliver widespread benefits. If governments do not play a strategic role in investing for the future of their societies, a few private actors will make all the investment and capture all the gain.

Public Goods

Digital technologies and data have the key characteristics of public goods. This underlines the need for state-shaped and enhanced investment because private sector investment will be below the social optimum. Governments must ensure that all citizens have access to the tangible and intangible infrastructures that will allow them to benefit from digitalization.

Spillovers

Another important characteristic of digitalization and data is that they inherently involve externalities, both negative and positive. Some of these, such as privacy or data bias, lie outside the domain of economic policy, although regulation in such areas will shape the economic uses of the technology. In terms of opportunities for long-term economic development, though, capturing positive externalities will be important, ranging from network effects to the enhanced information content of linked data. How to benefit from positive spillovers depends critically on the specific context: is it a specific industry supply chain, personal health data, or public transportation or urban planning? Moving from general analyses to domain-specific considerations is essential.

Competition

Competition in digital and digitalized markets poses challenges for analysis and enforcement given their winner-take-all dynamics. Concentration has risen in many markets across the developed economies, with adverse implications for future entry and innovation—and inequality. The rise in market power has prompted policy responses, but the adaptation of competition policy to the new challenges of the digital economy is a work in progress. It is not clear to what extent the new legislation and legal actions will succeed in opening concentrated markets.

Dynamics

The digital economy involves complex systems and nonlinear dynamics with tipping points for the reasons described earlier. The chicken-and-egg situation facing nascent digital platforms exists more broadly. Policies will be more effective if they can identify and take advantage of the linkages and critical points, for example, in planning infrastructure investments or developing policies for implementing new standards such as electric vehicles or data infrastructure for autonomous vehicles.

Tacit Knowledge and Skills

Humanity's codified knowledge is accessible online, but tacit knowledge, not written and recorded, is all the more valuable. Know-how has always been vital, and it is increasingly becoming the relatively scarce input to the economy. This places a focus on human-to-human communication and on economic geography, with many uncertainties given both the emerging use of new digital tools and the impact of the pandemic shock on working patterns.[55] It is also unclear what specific skills are going to be needed in the decades ahead. Will generative AI's ability to write code or do data visualisation destroy the relatively new jobs of the programmer or the data scientist? Or will it increase demand for such workers? It is impossible to be sure. This uncertainty again points to a focus on metaskills such as the ability to learn, or to learn how to learn specific tasks.

The Adjacent Possible

The new features of the digital economy do not make all existing insights about economic development redundant. Rather, they emphasise some above others. For instance, it has always been important to provide infrastructure and consider the role of tacit knowledge, but now the infrastructure priorities will differ, and know-how (and other intangibles) must be understood as complementary factors of production. Another old lesson taking on a new form is that development must take advantage of the adjacent possible. Few countries will push forward the AI frontier, but there will be AI-enabled possibilities for all others given sufficiently detailed attention to national capabilities. Complexity economics provides one tool for analyzing a country's or region's adjacent possible because it focuses on the range of products a country can produce and its trade possibilities.[56] In general, the policy challenge is a combination of sufficiently detailed mapping of existing capabilities and the political economy of encouraging a specific direction of change.

International Cooperation

Many of these policy challenges, from competition policy and data governance to technical standards for interoperability, require international coordination so as to avoid regulatory arbitrage, harmonize standards, and ultimately avoid economic conflict. The potential for conflict related to industrial policy is particularly apparent in the policy discussion of AI, and its related supply chains, in terms of strategic, geopolitical concerns. While there have been numerous statements of general principle on issues such as the regulation of AI from groups, including the OECD and the G20, much of the international policy development required will involve detailed work, including addressing questions of governance.

Although the aforesaid issues can be summarized in a few words, they imply the need for a significant step-up in policy capability. The challenges are new and difficult, the technology is evolving rapidly, and there is an important political dimension overlaid on the analysis of specific policy questions because major structural transformations involve winners and losers. However, there is no option other than to accept the challenge; the alternatives to shaping an economy that uses technological progress to deliver benefits widely to the population are economically, socially, and politically undesirable.

NOTES

I thank Zia Qureshi, Tom Wheeler, and other participants in the Conference on New Global Dynamics held at Brookings for their constructive and helpful comments. I also thank Janina Bröker for her careful reading.

1. Cherif and Hasanov (2019).
2. Juhász et al. (2022).
3. Bloom, Van Reenen, and Williams (2019).
4. Kim and Qureshi (2020).
5. Rodrik (2015).
6. Yusuf (2023).
7. Kauffman (1996).
8. Hidalgo and Hausmann (2009).
9. Besley and Persson (2010).
10. Corrado, Hulten, and Sichel (2009).
11. Yusuf (2008).
12. "A Designer Economy's primary focus is on a dynamically changing future, and it aims to produce tools to enable various actors in the economy to adapt to these changes" (Feygin and Gilman 2023).
13. Autor (2015, 2022) and Eloundou et al. (2023).
14. Dasgupta (2021).
15. Coyle (1998) and Agarwala and Martin (2022).
16. See Coyle and Hampton (2024) for estimates of declining computation costs based on different measures.
17. Baldwin (2019).
18. Carvalho and Tahbaz-Salehi (2019).
19. Coyle and Nguyen (2022).

20. https://ec.europa.eu/eurostat/statistics-explained/index.php?title= International_trade_in_goods_by_type_of_good.

21. Pahl and Timmer (2019).

22. Cusumano, Gawer, and Yoffie (2019) and Van Alstyne, Parker, and Choudary (2016).

23. For example, O'Mara (2019).

24. For one, see Greenstein (2020).

25. Sevilla et al. (2022).

26. Perez (2003).

27. World Bank (2016).

28. Hitt and Brynjolfsson (2002).

29. Brynjolfsson, Rock, and Syverson (2021).

30. Khan (2013), p. 248.

31. Autor et al. (2020) and Manyika et al. (2018).

32. Andrews, Criscuolo, and Gal (2015); Cathles, Nayyar, and Rückert (2020); Coyle et al. (2022).

33. See, for example, Patel et al. (2023).

34. Tassey (2014), p. 30.

35. Martin (1996) and Cobby (2023).

36. Cherif and Hasanov (2019).

37. Brynjolfsson et al. (2019) and Coyle and Nguyen (2020).

38. Directorate-General for Competition, European Commission (2019); Furman et al. (2019); Stigler Center (2019).

39. Cusumano, Gawer, and Yoffie (2019).

40. Aghion and Howitt (1992) and Coyle (2019).

41. Khan (2017).

42. Including China; see Zhang (2021).

43. For example, in the UK, a Digital Markets Unit has been set up with statutory status within the Competition and Markets Authority. Canada has a new Digital Enforcement and Intelligence Branch within the Competition Bureau. Japan has set up an interministry body, the Headquarters for Digital Market Competition. The European Commission is staffing up to implement the Digital Markets Act and the Digital Services Act, but not as a separate agency.

44. Waldfogel (2017).

45. Cohen and Sundararajan (2015).

46. Open Banking (2023).

47. Coyle et al. (2020).

48. Bergemann and Bonatti (2015).

49. Coyle and Manley (2023).

50. UNECE (2023); see also Goodridge, Haskel, and Edquist (2022).

51. Coyle and Gamberi (2024), forthcoming.

52. Coyle, Deshmukh, and Diepeveen (2023).
53. Carrier (2023) and Wiens (2015).
54. Yusuf (2023).
55. Bloom, Han, and Liang (2022).
56. Hidalgo and Hausmann (2009) and Mealy and Coyle (2022).

REFERENCES

Agarwala, Matthew, and Josh Martin. 2022. "Environmentally-Adjusted Productivity Measures for the UK." The Productivity Institute Working Paper 028. https://doi.org/10.2139/ssrn.4273944.

Aghion, Philippe, and Peter Howitt. 1992. "A Model of Growth through Creative Destruction." *Econometrica* 60 (2): 323–51.

Andrews, Dan, Chiara Criscuolo, and Peter Gal. 2015. "Frontier Firms, Technology Diffusion and Public Policy: Micro Evidence from OECD Countries." Organization for Economic Cooperation and Development, Paris.

Armstrong, Chris, Yaniv Konchitchki, and Biwen Zhang. 2023. "Digital Traffic, Financial Performance, and Stock Valuation." Stanford University Graduate School of Business Research Paper 4416683. https://doi.org/10.2139/ssrn.4416683.

Autor, David. 2015. "Why Are There Still So Many Jobs? The History and Future of Workplace Automation." *Journal of Economic Perspectives* 29 (3): 3–30.

———. 2022. "The Labor Market Impacts of Technological Change: From Unbridled Enthusiasm to Qualified Optimism to Vast Uncertainty." NBER Working Paper 30074. National Bureau of Economic Research, Cambridge, MA.

Autor, David, David Dorn, Lawrence Katz, Christina Patterson et al. 2020. "The Fall of the Labor Share and the Rise of Superstar Firms." *Quarterly Journal of Economics* 135 (2): 645–709.

Baldwin, Richard. 2019. *The Globotics Upheaval: Globalization, Robotics, and the Future of Work.* London: Weidenfeld & Nicolson.

Bergemann, Dirk, and Alessandro Bonatti. 2015. "Selling Cookies." *American Economic Journal: Microeconomics* 7 (3): 259–94.

Besley, Timothy, and Torsten Persson. 2010. "State Capacity, Conflict, and Development." *Econometrica* 78 (1): 1–34.

Bessen, James. 2022. *The New Goliaths.* New Haven, CT: Yale University Press.

Bloom, Nicholas, Ruobing Han, and James Liang. 2022. "How Hybrid Working from Home Works Out." NBER Working Paper 30292. National Bureau of Economic Research, Cambridge, MA.

Bloom, Nicholas, John Van Reenen, and Heidi Williams. 2019. "A Toolkit of Policies to Promote Innovation." *Journal of Economic Perspectives* 33 (3): 163–84.

Brynjolfsson, Erik, Avinash Collis, Erwin Diewert, Felix Eggers et al. 2019. "GDP-B: Accounting for the Value of New and Free Goods in the Digital Economy." NBER Working Paper 25695. National Bureau of Economic Research, Cambridge, MA.

Brynjolfsson, Erik, Daniel Rock, and Chad Syverson. 2021. "The Productivity J-Curve: How Intangibles Complement General Purpose Technologies." *American Economic Journal: Macroeconomics* 13 (1): 333–72.

Carrier, Michael. 2023. "The Right to Repair, Competition, and Intellectual Property." *Landslide* 15 (2). https://ssrn.com/abstract=4323277.

Carvalho, Vasco, and Alireza Tahbaz-Salehi. 2019. "Production Networks: A Primer." *Annual Review of Economics* 11 (1): 635–63.

Cathles, Alison, Gaurav Nayyar, and Désirée Rückert. 2020. "Digital Technologies and Firm Performance: Evidence from Europe." EIB Working Papers 2020/06. European Investment Bank, Luxembourg. https://ideas. repec.org//p/zbw/eibwps/202006.html.

Cherif, Reda, and Faud Hasanov. 2019. "The Return of the Policy That Shall Not Be Named: Principles of Industrial Policy." IMF Working Paper 2019/074. International Monetary Fund, Washington, DC.

Cobby, Roy. 2023. "The Eurochip." *Phenomenal World*, April 5. https://www. phenomenalworld.org/analysis/the-eurochip/.

Cohen, Molly, and Arun Sundararajan. 2015. "Self-Regulation and Innovation in the Peer-to-Peer Sharing Economy." *University of Chicago Law Review Online* 82 (1). https://chicagounbound.uchicago.edu/uclrev_online/vol82/iss1/8.

Corrado, Carol, Charles Hulten, and Daniel Sichel. 2009. "Intangible Capital & US Economic Growth." *Review of Income and Wealth* 55: 661–85.

Coyle, Diane. 1998. *The Weightless World: Strategies for Managing the Digital Economy.* Cambridge, MA: MIT Press.

———. 2019. "Practical Competition Policy Tools for Digital Platforms." *Antitrust Law Journal* 82 (3): 835–60.

Coyle, Diane, Sumedha Deshmukh, and Stephanie Diepeveen. 2023. "Understanding Progress in a Changing Society." Bennett Institute for Public Policy, University of Cambridge. https://www.bennettinstitute.cam.ac.uk/ wp-content/uploads/2023/04/Understanding-progress-in-a-changing-society.pdf.

Coyle, Diane, and Luca Gamberi. 2024. "Valuing Data with Real Options." Forthcoming.

Coyle, Diane, and Lucy Hampton. 2024. "Twenty-First Century Progress in Computing." *Telecommunications Policy* 48 (1). https://doi.org/10.1016/j.telpol. 2023.102649.

Coyle, Diane, and Wendy Li. 2021. "The Data Economy: Market Size and Global Trade." In *Economic Statistics Centre of Excellence (ESCoE) Discussion*

Papers. London: Economic Statistics Centre of Excellence. https://doi.org/
10.2139/ssrn.3973028.
Coyle, Diane, Kieran Lind, David Nguyen, and Manuel Tong. 2022. "Are
Digital-Using UK Firms More Productive?" In *Economic Statistics Centre of
Excellence (ESCoE) Discussion Papers*. London: Economic Statistics Centre
of Excellence. https://www.escoe.ac.uk/are-digital-using-uk-firms-more-
productive/.
Coyle, Diane, and Annabel Manley. 2023. "What Is the Value of Data? A Review
of Empirical Methods." *Journal of Economic Surveys*. https://doi.org/10.1111/
joes.12585.
Coyle, Diane, and David Nguyen. 2020. "Free Goods and Economic Welfare."
In *Economic Statistics Centre of Excellence (ESCoE) Discussion Papers*. London:
Economic Statistics Centre of Excellence. https://www.escoe.ac.uk/
publications/free-goods-and-economic-welfare-escoe-dp-2020-18/.
———. 2022. "No Plant, No Problem? Factoryless Manufacturing, Economic
Measurement and National Manufacturing Policies." *Review of International
Political Economy* 29 (1): 23–43.
Coyle, Diane, Stephanie Diepeveen, Julia Wdowin, Jeni Tennison et al. 2020.
"The Value of Data: Policy Implications." Bennett Institute for Public
Policy, University of Cambridge. https://www.bennettinstitute.cam.ac.uk/
publications/value-data-policy-implications/.
Cusumano, Michael, Annabelle Gawer, and David Yoffie. 2019. *The Business of
Platforms: Strategy in the Age of Digital Competition, Innovation, and Power*.
New York: Harper Business, an imprint of Harper Collins Publishers.
Dasgupta, Partha. 2021. "The Economics of Biodiversity: The Dasgupta Review."
London: HM Treasury. https://www.gov.uk/government/publications/final-
report-the-economics-of-biodiversity-the-dasgupta-review.
Directorate-General for Competition (European Commission), Yves-Alexandre
de Montjoye, Heike Schweitzer, and Jacques Crémer. 2019. *Competition Policy
for the Digital Era*. Publications Office of the European Union. https://data.
europa.eu/doi/10.2763/407537.
Eloundou, Tyna, Sam Manning, Pamela Mishkin, and Daniel Rock. 2023.
"GPTs Are GPTs: An Early Look at the Labor Market Impact Potential of
Large Language Models." arXiv. https://doi.org/10.48550/arXiv.2303.10130.
Feygin, Yakov and Nils Gilman. 2023. "The Designer Economy." *Noema*,
January 19. https://www.noemamag.com/the-designer-economy.
Furman, Jason, Diane Coyle, Amelia Fletcher, Philip Marsden, and Derek
McAuley. 2019. "Unlocking Digital Competition." HM Treasury Digital Com-
petition Expert Panel. https://assets.publishing.service.gov.uk/government/
uploads/system/uploads/attachment_data/file/785547/unlocking_digital_
competition_furman_review_web.pdf.

Goodridge, Peter, Jonathan Haskel, and Harald Edquist. 2022. "We See Data
Everywhere Except in the Productivity Statistics." *Review of Income and
Wealth* 68 (4): 862–94.

Greenstein, Shane. 2020. "The Basic Economics of Internet Infrastructure."
Journal of Economic Perspectives 34 (2): 192–214.

Hidalgo, César, and Ricardo Hausmann. 2009. "The Building Blocks of Economic Complexity." *Proceedings of the National Academy of Sciences* 106 (26):
10570–75. https://doi.org/10.1073/pnas.0900943106.

Hitt, Lorin, and Erik Brynjolfsson. 2002. "Information Technology, Organizational Transformation, and Business Performance." In *Productivity, Inequality,
and the Digital Economy: A Transatlantic Perspective.* Cambridge, MA: MIT
Press.

Juhász, Réka, Nathan Lane, Emily Oehlsen, and Verónica Pérez. 2022. "The
Who, What, When, and How of Industrial Policy: A Text-Based Approach."
SSRN Scholarly Paper. https://doi.org/10.2139/ssrn.4198209.

Kauffman, Stuart A. 1996. *Investigations: The Nature of Autonomous Agents and
the Worlds They Mutually Create.* Vol. 96, Issues 8–72 of SFI Working Papers.
Santa Fe, NM: Santa Fe Institute.

Khan, Lina. 2017. "Amazon's Antitrust Paradox." *Yale Law Journal* 126 (3):
710–805.

Khan, Mushtaq. 2013. "Political Settlements and the Design of Technology
Policy." In *The Industrial Policy Revolution II. Africa in the Twenty-First Cen-
tury,* edited by Joseph Stiglitz, Justin Lin Yifu, and Ebrahim Patel, 243–80.
International Economic Association Series. London: Palgrave Macmillan.

Kim, Hyeon-Wook, and Zia Qureshi. 2020. *Growth in a Time of Change: Global
and Country Perspectives on a New Agenda.* Washington, DC: Brookings Institution Press.

Manyika, James, Sree Ramaswamy, Jonathan Woetzel, Michael Birshan, and
Zubin Nagpal. 2018. "'Superstars': The Dynamics of Firms, Sectors, and
Cities Leading the Global Economy." Discussion Paper. McKinsey Global
Institute, New York. https://www.mckinsey.com/featured-insights/innovation-
and-growth/superstars-the-dynamics-of-firms-sectors-and-cities-leading-
the-global-economy.

Martin, Stephen. 1996. "Protection, Promotion and Cooperation in the
European Semiconductor Industry." *Review of Industrial Organization*
11 (5): 721–35.

Mealy, Penny, and Diane Coyle. 2022. "To Them That Hath: Economic Complexity and Local Industrial Strategy in the UK." *International Tax and Public
Finance* 29 (2): 358–77.

Olson, Mancur. 1996. "Distinguished Lecture on Economics in Government:
Big Bills Left on the Sidewalk: Why Some Nations Are Rich, and Others
Poor." *Journal of Economic Perspectives* 10 (2): 3–24.

O'Mara, Margaret. 2019. *The Code: Silicon Valley and the Remaking of America.* New York: Penguin Press.

Open Banking. 2023. Impact Report: March 2023. https://www.openbanking. org.uk/wp-content/uploads/Open-Banking-Impact-Report-4-30-March-2023.pdf.

Pahl, Stefan, and Marcel Timmer. 2019. "Patterns of Vertical Specialisation in Trade: Long-Run Evidence for 91 Countries." *Review of World Economics* 155 (3): 459–86.

Patel, Mihir, Cory Stephenson, Landan Seguin, and Austin Jacobson. 2023. "Training Stable Diffusion from Scratch for <$50k with MosaicML (Part 2)." MosaicML, April 23. https://www.mosaicml.com/blog/training-stable-diffusion-from-scratch-part-2?utm_source=substack&utm_medium=email.

Perez, Carlota. 2003. *Technological Revolutions and Financial Capital: The Dynamics of Bubbles and Golden Ages.* Cheltenham: Elgar.

Rodrik, Dani. 2015. "Premature Deindustrialization." NBER Working Paper 20935. National Bureau of Economic Research, Cambridge, MA.

Sevilla, Jaime, Lennart Heim, Anson Ho, Tamay Besiroglu et al. 2022. "Compute Trends Across Three Eras of Machine Learning." arXiv. https://doi.org/10.48550/arXiv.2202.05924.

Stigler Center for the Study of the Economy and the State. 2019. "Stigler Committee on Digital Platforms: Final Report." https://www.chicagobooth.edu/-/media/research/stigler/pdfs/digital-platforms---committee-report---stigler-center.pdf.

Tassey, Gregory. 2014. "Competing in Advanced Manufacturing: The Need for Improved Growth Models and Policies." *Journal of Economic Perspectives* 28 (1): 27–48.

UNECE. 2023. "Measuring the Value of Data." United Nations Economic Commission for Europe. https://unece.org/statistics/documents/2023/04/measuring-value-data-canada.

Van Alstyne, Marshall, Geoffrey Parker, and Sangeet Choudary. 2016. "Pipelines, Platforms, and the New Rules of Strategy." *Harvard Business Review,* April.

Waldfogel, Joel. 2017. "How Digitization Has Created a Golden Age of Music, Movies, Books, and Television." *Journal of Economic Perspectives* 31 (3): 195–214.

Wiens, Kyle. 2015. "We Can't Let John Deere Destroy the Very Idea of Ownership." *Wired,* April 21. https://www.wired.com/2015/04/dmca-ownership-john-deere/.

World Bank. 2016. *World Development Report 2016: Digital Dividends.* Washington, DC.

Yusuf, Shahid. 2008. "Intermediating Knowledge Exchange between Universities and Businesses." *Research Policy* 37 (8): 1167–74.

————. 2023. "Can Fast Growing Unicorns Revive Productivity and Economic Performance?" CGD Notes. Center for Global Development, Washington, DC. https://www.cgdev.org/publication/can-fast-growing-unicorns-revive-productivity-and-economic-performance.

Zhang, Angela Huyue. 2021. *Chinese Antitrust Exceptionalism: How the Rise of China Challenges Global Regulation*. New York: Oxford University Press.

FIVE

Double Standard

Economic Policy Is Mostly Industrial Policy

JUSTIN YIFU LIN AND CÉLESTIN MONGA

I t typically starts with a short meeting in a cozy office of a prosaic building on 19th Street or H Street in Washington DC. Participants—whose number is limited to three or four people at most—are senior managers of the International Monetary Fund (IMF) and the World Bank. They meet discreetly, mainly to decide whether and when they should send a joint team of experts to a developing country to assess macroeconomic progress. The decision to go ahead with such a trip is often based solely on their own initial assessment of how well the authorities in that country have been adhering to the IMF program (often covering a three-year period) and some World Bank project agreed upon earlier.

The trip under discussion is critical for the country in question: depending on the results of the assessment, the country would receive a tranche of an IMF loan granted to support its balance of payments, and the World Bank would follow with additional lending. In developing countries under IMF and World Bank programs, the disbursement of such funds is critical not only to provide the government with much needed cash to address urgent financing needs arising from macroeconomic imbalances but also to trigger additional financial support from bilateral aid agencies and regional development banks, as well as to favorably influence evaluations by private investors and rating agencies—all of whom rely on the IMF and World Bank macroeconomic assessments for their own policy, investment, and disbursement decisions regarding developing countries.

The initial short meeting of senior managers to authorize the kickoff of the formal process leading to the joint trip and eventually to the disbursement of precious funds is not necessarily based on a rigorous preassessment of the country's macroeconomic performance. While there is a tentative calendar of regular interactions set at the time of the approval of the three-year loan, the actual timing of the trip sometimes depends on decisions made elsewhere by influential shareholders (such as the United States or a major European country). The joint team of experts is then dispatched to the field for a review of progress against a set of predetermined performance criteria.

The operation is called a "mission" and is prepared as such. Many of the team members tapped for the mission are well-trained and well-meaning people who joined these two Bretton Woods institutions to make a difference in the world and help developing countries transform their economies. They have become part of the "donor" community that offers financing, policy advice, and technical assistance to "recipient" countries. Their thinking and recommended strategies typically embody mainstream development economics in practice.

All economies change constantly as their relative distribution of endowments (capital, labor, land, and technology) evolve to reflect market dynamics and natural developments, and these changes can be abrupt and profound in times of economic crises or structural transformation. Yet despite the pioneering work carried out on the empirics of structural transformation by Hollis Chenery, the World Bank's first chief economist, the intellectual framework underpinning the reasoning and policy advice of the Bretton Woods institutions since the 1970s has typically followed the standard neoclassical argument that markets are generally efficient and that there is little need for government to intervene in the sectoral allocation of resources.[1]

Market failures are generally significant during periods of change, however, especially in economies going through a major structural transformation. They must be corrected by well-informed state interventions, but the policy advice from IMF-World Bank missions typically goes in the opposite direction. Industrial policy, often defined as "targeted sectoral interventions" by governments, is viewed as a source of costly distortions and poor governance, and a recipe for weak economic performance. Even in the rare instances where markets are acknowledged as being inefficient, the stance often taken by the IMF and the World Bank on economic development strategies has been that government action is unlikely to improve matters. While the thinking of these institutions has evolved over time, the main lens through which they view economics and provide policy advice to developing countries has remained largely unchanged—and focused on the need to avoid "government failures."

The profound economic shocks caused by the Great Recession following the 2008 global financial crisis and by the 2020 COVID-19 pandemic, however, have led advanced economies—which also happen to be the major shareholders of these institutions—to openly question their traditional faith in market efficiency and even adopt industrial policies in various domains. Interestingly, in the case of these countries, this change in strategy and policies has been generally welcomed by them.

In this chapter, we argue that there has been a double standard in the assessment of the role of government in economic policy by mainstream economics and its proponents. Strong government interventions in advanced economies are generally accepted while such interventions in developing economies are too often dismissed. We revisit industrial policy in the context of the changing global dynamics and new thinking about economic development. We review recent developments in industrial policy in advanced economies. We also discuss evolving rationales for industrial policy, including an increasing focus on the importance of fostering knowledge and learning as an engine of economic transformation and government's role in that process. Finally, we present a new structural economics approach to rationalize and optimize industrial policy at all levels of economic development—and avoid the double standard.

Industrial Policy Battles in Unlikely Places

Starting in 2017, a series of industrial policy discussions took place in Versailles, France, and made news headlines, not only because of the symbolism of the place where they occurred and the profile of the participants but also because of the significance of the matters discussed, the positions taken, and the reaction they caused among Western advanced economies. Hosted by President Emmanuel Macron, a former investment banker who proudly defines himself as a pragmatic center-right politician, these meetings unsettled some of France's closest political allies, including the United States. All previous French presidents had publicly supported industrial policies regardless of their ideological positioning, so there was really nothing fundamentally new about Macron's support for such policies. But the significance of the Versailles meetings was brought into sharper relief in 2022 when an open rift developed between American and European governments after the US Congress passed the Inflation Reduction Act (IRA) containing $370 billion in tax credits and subsidies for green energy and US-made electric cars and batteries.

European political leaders reacted strongly to the IRA and its "Buy American" domestic production requirements, which they viewed as a threat to European jobs, especially in the energy and auto sectors. They criticized the American act as protectionist because it aimed to make companies shift investments from Europe and elsewhere to the United States and encourage customers to buy American products. European countries have launched their own European Green Deal and a carbon border adjustment mechanism that imposes an emissions tariff on imports, and it is being followed up by a European Green Deal Industrial Plan. Interest in a "Buy European Act" also has surged. For developing economies, the trade aspects of these dueling initiatives looked like "Fortress US" and "Fortress EU": rich countries responsible for the most climate-threatening emissions appeared to be locking others out of the fortresses their prosperity built.[2]

French Minister of Finance Bruno Le Maire publicly accused the United States "of pursuing a China-style industrial policy."[3] In a statement, Le Maire said: "We have entered a new globalization. China has been in this globalization for a very long time with massive state aids that are reserved exclusively for Chinese products, [but] the fact is that the U.S. has just entered this new globalization before our eyes to develop its industrial capacity on American soil. Europe must not be the last of the Mohicans."[4] He called on Europe to bring in its own substantial subsidy scheme and establish a new European industrial policy to support green industry and encourage industries to relocate to European territory.

In November 2022, France and Germany, the two largest economies in Europe, issued a joint statement vowing to explore industrial policy options to safeguard European industries from discriminatory trade measures from the United States and China. "We call for an EU [European Union] industrial policy that enables our companies to thrive in the global competition," the statement read, adding, "we want to coordinate closely a European approach to challenges such as the United States Inflation Reduction Act."[5] While the statement included a proforma clause that EU state aid measures must be in line with the World Trade Organization rules (which means they should not discriminate against foreign parties), it called on the European Commission to speed up procedures to approve subsidies under its framework of Important Projects of Common European Interest. This new industrial policy alliance between Germany and France marked an escalation of European efforts to protect home-grown manufacturing from the threat of unfair competition from abroad.

In releasing Germany's Industrial Strategy 2030, the country's Federal Ministry for Economic Affairs and Energy advocated an ambitious, long-term EU industrial strategy with specific measures to support European companies. The strategy identified industries and sectors that should benefit from lower levels of taxation, limited social insurance contributions, more flexible labor market regulations, secure and affordable energy costs, and financial support from a Future Fund to improve financing possibilities for game-changing technologies.[6]

Earlier, in 2017, UK Prime Minister Theresa May, who defined herself as a conservative on economic matters, wrote: "one of my first actions as Prime Minister was to begin the development of a modern Industrial Strategy that would help businesses to create high-quality, well-paid jobs right across the country. . . . At its heart it epitomizes my belief in a strong and strategic state that intervenes decisively wherever it can make a difference."[7] Policy measures to implement the UK's industrial strategy were quite diverse and included increases in research and development (R&D) funding and tax credits, funding for infrastructure to boost the construction of electric vehicles by private firms, and the establishment of a government investment fund to finance innovative and high potential businesses. In 2022, another conservative UK government issued a new Plan for Growth, which included many features of industrial policy such as government interventions in the energy market, tax incentives, and new investment zones.[8]

In 2017, the EU's Competitiveness Council called on the European Commission to provide a holistic EU industrial policy strategy, with particular attention to support to small and medium-size businesses and start-ups,

R&D and innovation, digital transformation, tackling unfair commercial practices, and sustainable and affordable energy sources.[9] After the COVID-19 pandemic, the EU identified fourteen industrial ecosystems deserving special attention and support.[10]

Europe's official public discourse on industrial policy has been largely consistent over time, reflecting a belief that governments must be interventionist not only in setting the rules and regulatory frameworks for economic activity but also in identifying upfront those sectors, industries, and firms that are viewed as strategically important for growth and economic transformation.[11] Even so, the EU has intensified its focus on industrial policy in recent years. In fact, governments in practically all advanced economies have been revamping their industrial policies.[12]

What is particularly noteworthy is that the United States, for so long the bastion of a philosophy of free markets with limited government intervention, has recently emerged as a proponent of a "new Washington Consensus" favoring industrial policy. As stated by White House National Security Adviser Jake Sullivan, "When President Biden came into office. . . . America's industrial base had been hollowed out. The vision of public investment that had energized the American project . . . had faded. It had given way to a set of ideas that championed tax cutting and deregulation, privatization over public action, and trade liberalization as an end in itself. There was one assumption at the heart of all of this policy: that markets always allocate capital productively and efficiently. . . . A modern American industrial strategy identifies specific sectors that are foundational to economic growth, strategic from a national security perspective, and where private industry on its own isn't poised to make the investments needed to secure our national ambitions. It deploys targeted public investments in these areas."[13]

This statement by a top US government official was welcomed by the Bretton Woods institutions. But leaders from developing countries making the same arguments for government intervention in economic matters typically received strong criticism for advocating industrial policies aimed at picking winners. Viewing some features of the global free trade system as a disadvantage in the race to lead the world in technology, the United States has deployed a whole set of industrial policy instruments of a protectionist nature, including tariffs, sanctions, blacklists, export and import controls, investment restrictions, visa bans, and technology transaction rules.[14] It has imposed restrictions limiting China's ability to acquire advanced semiconductors and the technology to make them.[15] The CHIPS and Science Act enacted in 2022 provides for major government support to revitalize the US semiconductor industry.[16]

Industrial Policy: Fuzzy Semantics and New Rationale

What exactly is industrial policy, and what is its most compelling justification? The policy shifts that have occurred across ideological lines in the Western world and revealed tensions among long-time allies are not simply quarrels about trade strategies. After all, most of these countries have domestic markets large enough to withstand shocks in external trade. Domestic demand is their main engine of growth: while trade brings substantial economic benefits to a country such as the United States or Germany or Japan, their large domestic markets and high incomes allow them to withstand some declines in external demand. The raging debate on trade more fundamentally reflects a reassessment of national strategies for growth, economic transformation, and inclusion, which sees what is labeled industrial policy more broadly as economic policy at large. This section discusses the semantic fuzziness and false dichotomies about industrial policy, its evolving rationale, and the new thinking about what may be its key justification—knowledge and learning.

Despite the debates and controversies over the pertinence, scope, instruments, and conditions for the effectiveness of industrial policy, economic literature has not offered a rigorous definition of precisely what it is and what distinguishes it from other government economic policies. The first US secretary of the treasury, Alexander Hamilton, stated in his famous report on the subject of manufactures in 1791 that in order to bring about "the desirable changes as early as may be expedient," industries needed "the incitement and patronage of government," and ever since then, industrial policy focused on boosting manufacturing has generated strong intellectual interest and differing views.[17] From influential thinkers in the nineteenth century, such as Friedrich List (1841), who supported Hamilton's view, to today's generation of scholars, the literature has tended to see industrial policy as state intervention in the economy but without providing a clear delineation of the unique features and scope of such policy in comparison to other government policies in the realm of economic development.

Over the past half-century, the rise of Asian economies has spurred burgeoning new literature on industrial policy, either to explain their economic success in terms of their use of industrial policy and recommend that other countries follow similar strategies, or to warn against such strategies. Without defining it formally, Becker (1985) states emphatically that "the best industrial policy is none at all." In contrast, Reich (1982) notes that "industrial policy, which is better known in Japan and Europe than in America, is more concerned with capital allocation than with aggregate capital formation. Industrial policy focuses on the most productive *pattern* of investment, and thus it favors business segments that promise to be strong international competitors while helping to develop the industrial infrastructure (highways, ports, sewers) and skilled work force needed to support those segments."

While also limiting industrial policy to the industry sector, Pinder (1982) makes a strong case for a broader definition, which includes all policies designed to support that sector. He points out that fiscal and monetary incentives for investment, direct public investment and public procurement programs, incentives for investment in R&D, and policies to support small and medium enterprises are all part of the toolkit to boost industrial competitiveness. The same reasoning applies to other government interventions, such as support for the improvement of physical infrastructure and social infrastructure (institutions), skill development, trade policy, and competition policy.

Others highlight the selective nature of industrial policy, viewing it as government activities that aim to support the development of certain industries in a national economy to maintain international competitiveness,[18] as state interventions that discriminate and select among industries, sectors, and agents,[19] or as government actions to enhance production and technological capacity in industries considered strategic for national development.[20] While such reasoning helps to clarify conceptually which particular policy can be considered "industrial," in practice, the separation of policies between selective and nonselective can be rather arbitrary.

Pack (2000) offers a narrower definition, which has influenced much of the recent literature, stating that industrial policies comprise a variety of actions designed to target specific sectors to increase their productivity and their relative importance within the *manufacturing* sector. Sectoral classifications inherited from the early research on structural change may have been appropriate prior to the technological transformation of recent decades, but in today's global economy and the Fourth Industrial Revolution, the boundaries between sectors such as industry and services are fuzzy.[21] In their survey of arguments for and against industrial policy, Pack and Saggi (2006) no longer restrict the scope to manufacturing but define industrial policy more generally as any type of selective government intervention or policy that attempts to alter the structure of production in favor of sectors that are expected to offer better prospects for economic growth in a way that would not occur in the absence of such intervention.

The quest for precision and intellectual coherence has led some to a new conceptual framing of policies that separates narrow "vertical" government policies that favor specific industries or sectors from broad "horizontal" policies that aim at improving the business environment and boosting the prospects of an economy more generally.[22] The vertical-versus-horizontal framing of the debate about industrial policy has been embraced by the World Bank and the IMF. After decades of opposition to state interventions in the economy and the promotion of the Washington Consensus (which championed privatization, deregulation, and free trade), a new generation of researchers in these institutions have acknowledged that market mechanisms do not always deliver growth and welfare. They have become less skeptical of industrial policy and more inclined to embrace some of its elements.

For example, World Bank researchers Hevia, Loayza, and Meza-Cuadra (2023) define industrial policies as consisting of selective government interventions to promote certain economic sectors with the aim of increasing their productivity and spreading positive externalities throughout the economy. They add that industrial policies can vary in a range that goes from vertical policies that favor specific firms or narrow sectors to horizontal policies that target broad sectors by improving the business environment, and that the more horizontal these policies are, the more they approach characterization as public goods. They note that providing public goods is likely to dominate industrial policies when government capacity to formulate and implement narrower interventions is low. Such research on industrial policy options is an important departure from past World Bank research on industrial policy, which concluded unequivocally that "attempts to guide resource allocation with nonmarket mechanisms have generally failed to improve economic performance.[23]

IMF researchers also have recently joined the debate and, surprisingly, embraced the idea of industrial policy. Against the traditional narrative of their own institution, Cherif and Hasanov (2019) contend that standard growth policy prescriptions are not sufficient for economic prosperity and that the important role of industrial policy in the success of the Asian Miracle economies cannot be ignored. They state that much can be learned from their development strategies, based on three pillars that constitute "True Industrial Policy": government intervention to fix market failures that preclude the emergence of domestic producers in sophisticated industries, beyond the initial comparative advantage; export orientation, in contrast to the typical failed policies of the 1960s and 1970s that mostly favored import substitution; and the pursuit of fierce competition, both abroad and domestically, with strict accountability. In a subsequent IMF paper, Cherif et al. (2022) also define industrial policy as targeted sectoral interventions.[24] They recommend focusing on the market failures that justify targeted sectoral interventions, subjecting such interventions to a cost-benefit test, analyzing potential government failures stemming from weak governance that can undermine these interventions, and finding ways to mitigate the risks associated with weak governance.

The intellectual evolution of research at the World Bank and IMF from a rejection of nonmarket allocative mechanisms to a willingness to study their appropriateness is welcome. Their new research has helped bring the fundamental issues of economic transformation and inclusive development back to the global agenda. Their definitions and theoretical and empirical analyses of industrial policy, however, rely heavily on false dichotomies: the distinctions between "sectoral" and "economy-wide" policies and between "vertical" and "horizontal" government interventions are conceptually elegant but erroneous in practice. The claims that sectoral/vertical measures (called industrial policy) are particularly prone to causing distortions and require much greater government capacity and expertise than economy-wide/horizontal measures (called economic or broad public policy) are not well founded.

Almost all economic policies directly or indirectly affect economic structure.[25] Disentangling broad and sector-specific policy and market failures and their relative impacts carries the risk of uncovering more noise than signal. Sector-specific or industry-specific policies can have economy-wide repercussions, which can either be in the form of direct and observable impacts on other sectors or industries not specifically targeted, or in the form of opportunity costs to other economic agents in various activities. It is unrealistic to posit, for instance, that the effects of (sectoral) industrial policy can be detached from broad macroeconomic or regulatory policies and studied in isolation. Tariffs and quotas, often viewed as typical indicators of industrial policy, illustrate the semantic fuzziness of the classifications. Empirical studies using tariffs and quotas to assess the effectiveness of industrial policy in any given country often neglect the fact that they are not used simply to protect noncompetitive or infant domestic industries. They also often help generate additional fiscal revenue or pursue some macroeconomic terms of trade goals.[26] Therefore, analyses of public policies in isolation run the risk of confusing the relationships between policy measures labeled industrial policy and the broader macroeconomic and development dynamics.[27]

Perhaps to circumvent this problem, Juhász et al. (2023) use a definition that focuses on the goals of policy: "Industrial policy is a goal-oriented state action. The purpose is to shape the composition of economic activity. Specifically: industrial policy seeks to change the relative prices across sectors or direct resources toward certain selectively targeted activities (for example, exporting, R&D), with the purpose of shifting the long-run composition of economic activity."[28] Again, many governmental economic policy interventions would meet such criteria. To measure industrial policy, Juhász et al. (2023) take politicians at their word and adopt a language-based approach in their empirical analysis, focusing on the stated intentions of policymakers and the announced descriptions of policies. They develop a classification algorithm and use machine learning to automatically determine which tariff and nontariff measures fit the label "industrial." It is an original approach and a valiant effort, yet even with the sophistication of machine learning, reliance solely on public policy pronouncements is an inadequate basis for policy classification and analysis.

Virtually every item in budget bills adopted annually by parliaments around the world are pieces of industrial policy, as they implicitly or explicitly favor specific industries, sectors, regions, cities, or firms. Even many so-called "neutral" macro/financial policy measures often presented as the antithesis of industrial policy are not entirely neutral. For example, exchange-rate policies have industrial policy aspects because they favor some sectors and industries relative to others. Policies such as financial sector regulation or social safety nets are not advertised as tools for changing economic structure, but they always imply winners and losers, often in specific geographic areas or social groups, which can be identified *ex ante* or *ex post*. Public expenditure reviews and incidence analyses carried out around the world by the World Bank for many decades often bring out important distributional issues in terms of who benefits from expenditures and who does not.[29]

Moreover, policies have indirect effects and interconnections. For instance, in countries with limited fiscal space, well-meaning social programs presented as broad and neutral, and important cross-cutting projects (not aimed at favoring specific industries, regions, or groups), could still change the structure of the economy eventually if their costs pose public debt and macroeconomic risks—which hurt some sections of the economy and population disproportionately.[30]

To sum up, despite extensive debate over a long period, industrial policy still means different things to different people.[31] Our view aligns mostly with the definition of industrial policy by Rodrik (2009) as a strategic collaboration between the private and public sectors—and civil society, we might add—with the primary goal of promoting areas of an economy where it has comparative advantage and with all parties benefiting from the information and other externalities not otherwise available to them.

New thinking on industrial policy goes beyond traditional rationales based on market failures and externalities to focus on the unique role that only governments can play to foster knowledge and learning as a driver of economic growth and societal well-being.[32] Early economists such as Adam Smith and Thomas Malthus thought, erroneously, that the determinants of the prosperity of nations were to be found in physical objects and capital. Their analyses of the process of wealth creation were, therefore, dominated by notions of scarcity. While economists quickly recognized that other factors besides physical resources were important—such as ideas, new knowledge, and ways to rearrange physical resources to make them more valuable—they did not have the analytical tools to integrate them into a full-fledged growth framework. The easy solution was to lump together all these other elements and refer to them as "technological change" and treat them as exogenous—coming from outside the economic system. Not enough attention was paid to the underlying process of technological change.

Addressing Knowledge Deficits and Learning Failures: New Structural Economics

Addressing knowledge deficits and learning failures, and identifying latent economic opportunities and translating them into comparative advantage, are key drivers of prosperity. But knowledge generation and diffusion is not a linear process. It often involves trial and error and can be costly, especially for developing countries with big knowledge deficits and limited R&D resources. For them, identifying and using the right idea (to help the economy exploit its latent comparative advantages) can be particularly challenging in the absence of a good framework for search and implementation. New Structural Economics (NSE) aims to provide a conceptual and policy framework to help countries navigate this process.

Endogenous growth theory has shed light on the sources of improvements in material well-being in advanced economies. It focuses on the effects of technological change on the economy, the structural details of the innovation process, and the various ways in which laws, policies and institutions, and customs affect peoples' incentive and ability to create new knowledge and profit from it.[33] NSE aims at fostering knowledge accumulation and application for economic transformation for countries at all levels of development. It offers strategies to ensure that learning externalities are captured within and beyond individual firms and to build capabilities to adapt and evolve in line with the needs of industrial upgrading.

Structural Change and Industrial Policy

The theoretical framework of the NSE draws on some key tenets of early structuralism, as its name suggests, and on the virtues of market mechanisms as advocated by neoclassical economics. It offers an *aggiornamento* of key lessons learned from development thinking and practice and aims to enrich it with new insights on the dynamics of economic change, the role of the state, and implications for public policies and institutions.

NSE posits that the economic system in an economy consists of a set of interrelated structures, such as the endowment structure (factors such as capital, labor, and land and other natural resources), the production structure (industries and technologies), physical infrastructure, and institutional superstructure.[34] The production structure in an economy is endogenous to the structure of its endowments, which are the most basic elements for initiating any economic activity. They are given at any point in time but changeable over time. The endowment structure determines the economy's latent comparative advantages and thus the appropriate technologies and industries—those that will make the economy competitive if infrastructure and superstructure also are appropriate for the production structure.[35] The optimal industrial structure in an economy reflects its endowment structure. Development strategies and industrial policy that are consistent with the comparative advantage of the endowment structure are more likely to successfully address knowledge deficits and learning failures.

The optimality of the industrial structure is defined by the consistency of its industries with comparative advantage. Empirically, this is analyzed, for example, by documenting the capital-intensity of firms while accounting for limited substitutability between labor and capital in the production function (for some industries). Recent empirical work in low-income countries has shown that once firms have adopted capital-intensive technology, the ability of the economy to increase output (and generate employment) in response to new opportunities is often reduced.[36] That is because the cost curve of the new technology is steeper: due to the scarcity of capital and complementary inputs (skills, infrastructure), potential expansion of output and employment is choked off by rising costs. Not only is the comparative advantage of the economy in those industries undermined but its supply curve becomes less responsive. This partly explains the inability of manufacturing in Africa and in other lagging regions to scale up.

The structural transformation process is not unidirectional. There is also reverse causality because changes in sectoral and industrial patterns also impact income and relative prices, and there is simultaneity, as changes in structural transformation and changes in income/relative prices can occur simultaneously and affect each other constantly. Consequently, industrial structures often determine sectoral allocation, and changes in sectoral allocation also impact and alter industrial structures. These fluctuating dynamics and two-way relationships have important implications for modeling economic growth and structural transformation.[37]

Policy Framework for Knowledge Diffusion and Continuous Learning

The knowledge and capacity requirements for industrial policy are not much different from what is needed for economic policy in general. It is misleading to suggest that developing countries typically lack the expertise needed for industrial policy while they have adequate capacity for macroeconomic and other policies such as in infrastructure and education.

The key requirement for success is the ability to generate or borrow good ideas and integrate them into growth and development strategies. There is a need to rethink the role of all stakeholders—government, the private sector, civil society, and international financial institutions—in the facilitation of access to relevant knowledge and its use.

Successful industrial development also depends on building institutions to facilitate the dynamic process of the emergence of sectors and industries that are competitive because they are consistent with the economy's comparative advantage. Trying to engineer industrial upgrading by looking at the wrong reference-economy to emulate and copying ideas not consistent with the comparative advantage of the economy is bound to be costly and ultimately unsustainable. That is why the choice of the reference-economy, the types of industries to encourage, and the policies used must all be consistent with the dynamics of the economy's endowment structure. What is crucial is the generation, borrowing, and use of ideas that are relevant to the economy in these fundamental dimensions.

The requirement of "good" institutions as a precondition for effective industrial policy (or economic policy in general) and successful development must be seen in context. Historical analyses tend to indicate a strong correlation between (subjective) measures of institutional development and economic growth.[38] Yet today's high-income and good-governance countries generally had poor-governance environments at lower levels of income.[39] Moreover, many of today's most successful emerging economies still exhibit suboptimal governance indicators because they are still building the widely accepted political settlements needed to sustain societal activities.[40]

NSE proposes knowledge and learning strategies reflective of the specific dynamics of the economy's endowment.[41] The success of industrial policy—and all economic policy—ultimately depends on the relevance of knowledge underlying public policy. In developing economies, such knowledge cannot be wholesale imports of ideas in vogue in advanced economies and derived from their high level of industrial sophistication. To the contrary, policies for structural transformation should be consistent with the unique needs, endowment structures, and comparative advantages of developing economies.

The NSE policy framework addresses some of the most pervasive knowledge deficits and learning failures that have constrained developing economies—especially those with industries furthest from the technological frontier—in their industrial development. It stresses the need to go back to a key principle of economics: allocating scarce resources to sectors and industries with the highest possible payoffs. Inevitably, this requires rigor in selecting where to devote the limited financial resources and institutional capacity available in developing economies and being thoughtful in targeting reform efforts. As Hausmann, Rodrik, and Velasco (2008) have shown, not all constraints are equal—or deserve the same degree of attention from policymakers.

Critics of industrial policy object to strong government intervention in markets, which they liken to "picking winners and losers." True, the record of most activist governments is mixed. They generally used limited public resources to pursue unsustainable import-substitution policies in nonviable sectors and industries selected to modernize the economy. In many cases, governments invested large amounts of financial resources in the creation of "white elephants"—investment projects with negative social surplus— or favored the emergence of public enterprises in sectors with no comparative advantage.[42] To reduce the burden of public subsidies, activist governments sometimes resorted to measures such as granting the nonviable enterprises in priority industries market monopoly, suppressing interest rates, manipulating the domestic currency, and controlling the prices of raw materials. Such interventions introduced further distortions. Preferential access to credit deprived others of resources. There was a high opportunity cost. While industrial policies were often blamed for these disappointing outcomes, failures in macroeconomic policies and governance often played a bigger role.[43]

Still, in contrast to conventional wisdom, NSE advocates picking winners but doing so following a rigorous and collaborative process—an improvement over what all governments in the world do constantly but rather randomly and without transparency. The emergence of new and viable industries and sectors (consistent with the economy's latent comparative advantage) requires state action to reduce transaction costs and improve physical infrastructure and regulations so that businesses can become competitive and prosper in domestic and global markets. The state may also provide some incentives to first movers in new industries to compensate for the externalities they generate. It can do so by providing tax holidays, facilitating access to finance, and subsidizing skills development without distorting prices or granting monopolies. Governments can work closely with the private sector and civil society (such as academic institutions, think tanks, and business organizations) to pick winners openly and through a transparent process, as well as identify potential losers so that policies are in place to mitigate losses and social costs of major failures.

Successful industrial (and economic) policy also requires a knowledge and learning strategy to address the inability of firms, especially in developing economies, to build innovation capabilities and improve access to new technologies, which may be constrained by several factors, including intellectual property rights barriers.[44] In most developing economies, the limited use of new technology and new knowledge is not simply a reflection of low levels of R&D budgets. It is also due to the shortage of research expertise and capabilities within most firms. In such circumstances, increasing government subsidies in support of R&D by private firms—which is costly and risky even in the best of circumstances—may not necessarily lead to substantial improvements in technology adoption and the creation of new goods and services by the private sector. In most low- and middle-income economies, the optimal policy could be for governments to facilitate the borrowing of knowledge from advanced economies. Technological innovation and industrial upgrading can rely on the adoption and adaptation of technology that is new to a developing economy but mature elsewhere in the world and available at an affordable cost. That latecomer advantage can be substantial.[45]

To mitigate the small-size constraints of many developing country firms, NSE recommends drawing lessons from the successful economic transformation experiences of countries such as China, Costa Rica, and Vietnam, where governments facilitated the sharing of knowledge, expertise, and resources and addressed collective action problems by promoting an aggregation of their production to reach a critical mass. Economists have known since Adam Smith that the division of labor, which is an essential feature of prosperous industrial clusters, is often limited by the size of the market. International trade agreements negotiated by well-informed governments can help increase demand exponentially. On the supply side, public goods provision is equally important: governments can implement industrial policy at the local level to foster the building of clusters. This can include providing infrastructure and business information services, subsidizing product development in competitive sectors, encouraging the establishment of trade associations, and helping to attract processing firms with expertise and technology not yet available locally, among others.[46]

Industrial policy (and economic policy in general) should aim to help industries find their latent comparative advantages and transform them into actual comparative advantages. How can governments identify industries with latent comparative advantage? Economic theory and practice offer many lessons about what to do and what to avoid. Lin (2017) suggests a framework for thinking about different types of industries and the policy measures that can be considered in relation to them.

CATCH-UP INDUSTRIES. As a first step, countries can identify catch-up industries for tradable goods and services, and these are usually labor-intensive activities, where other countries are likely to lose comparative advantage as their wages rise after decades of growth and capital accumulation. The next step is to prioritize, among these industries, those in which the country can be potentially competitive and which some domestic firms have already entered. Bottlenecks holding back firm performance in these industries should be identified. In these industries, efforts can be made to attract investors from other countries, including those that are losing their comparative advantage. At the same time, the entry of more domestic firms can be catalyzed, including through incubation programs. In addition to these industries, technology can open up new catch-up opportunities. Governments can support firms in discovering and capturing such opportunities.

Countries with poor infrastructure, an unfriendly business environment, and budget and capacity constraints, can provide improved infrastructure to select, potentially competitive industries, especially if they are located in geographical areas that allow costs to be minimized and economies of scale in production to be maximized, and remove bottlenecks in the business environment. Governments should liaise with private investors and partner with development finance institutions in these efforts, including building special economic zones and industrial parks. Learning opportunities among firms (even as they compete against each other) and knowledge dissemination in clusters are among the most important Marshallian externalities.

Governments can also provide limited incentives to pioneering domestic or foreign firms to compensate them for the public knowledge created by their investments, such as tax holidays, priority access to credit (in countries with financial repression), or priority access to foreign exchange for importing key equipment (in countries with capital controls). Such incentives should be limited in time because the targeted industries should have a latent comparative advantage that enables them to become competitive in domestic and foreign markets. To minimize the risks of rent-seeking and political capture, or distorting markets, the incentives need to be carefully designed and monitored and should not be in the form of monopoly rents, high tariffs, or other such distortions.

LEADING-EDGE INDUSTRIES. Some developing economies, especially middle-income ones, can acquire leading technologies and successfully penetrate industries in which high-income economies, previously dominant, are losing the competitive edge and exiting the market due to diminishing value addition. This requires, among other needs, more investment in R&D to innovate and develop new products. Such R&D is costly and risky, and individual firms may have weak incentives to undertake it, especially where it involves research of a more basic, public-good nature. Governments can help by boosting public R&D programs and encouraging more cooperation between research and training institutions supported by public funds and firms seeking to develop new products by adopting or adapting new, higher-end technologies. They can also consider other supportive measures where appropriate, such as using public procurement to help firms scale up production, reduce unit costs, and increase competitiveness.

INDUSTRIES LOSING COMPARATIVE ADVANTAGE. Wages are a major component of production cost in labor-intensive industries. Fast-growing developing economies that initially rely on such industries eventually find themselves losing comparative advantage in them. In such situations, some firms may be able to maintain their competitive edge by altering their production technologies and upgrading their activities in the value chain. Others may have to relocate their production to countries with lower wages, taking advantage of and disseminating their knowledge in technology, management, and marketing while their production still counts in their country's gross national product (as distinguished from gross domestic product). Governments can support these firms by helping them with technological upgrading and moving up the value chain (for example, through actions relating to R&D and value-chain logistics) or by facilitating their relocation abroad. In the latter case, firms can be helped through measures such as the provision of information on host countries, training of personnel needed for overseas operations, and the establishment of export processing zones together with the host governments to provide adequate infrastructure and conducive business environments for the firms.

LANE-CHANGING INDUSTRIES. The information age has brought both challenges and opportunities for developing economies. On the one hand, it has worsened the digital divide by enlarging the gap between advanced economies, with their strong human capital needed to work with the new technologies, and developing economies, where much of the youth has not benefited from high-quality education and training. On the other hand, the information age brings new knowledge and economic opportunities to developing economies, especially middle-income and upper-middle-income economies, in some industries—notably software production, where innovations depend mainly on human capital and the innovation cycle is relatively short.[47]

The dynamics of industrial upgrading and the pursuit of new opportunities in the global economy are not really comparable to a car race, but a metaphor from race car driving helps make the point on competition among economies at different levels of development. Race car drivers can change lanes to overtake competitors, but they must do so only after careful consideration of the speed of their car and that of the competitor. Changing lanes successfully requires a good awareness of traffic at a specific point in the race and the ability to stay in one's lane while picking a good gap to overtake a speeding competitor.

Innovations in industries such as medicine or aviation are capital-intensive and require time, and advanced economies are best placed to lead such technology races. But thanks to the information age, innovations in software industries require only talented and creative engineers and limited amounts of capital. As in a car race, a developing economy can quickly overtake an advanced economy competitor by changing lanes—that is, quickly entering an industry where the leading players are advanced economies.

In industries such as the production of electric vehicles, upper-middle-income economies and advanced economies compete from roughly the same starting line. However, an upper-middle-income economy such as China, which is well endowed with human capital and has also built strong digital infrastructure, can outperform an advanced economy because of the size of its market. Therefore, it may have comparative advantage over much richer countries and overtake these competitors by entering quickly into the market ("changing lanes"). Digitalization and the Fourth Industrial Revolution have opened up such new possibilities for countries in short-cycle industries. Governments can support such overtaking strategies through a range of measures, such as investing in education to accumulate the needed human capital, strengthening digital infrastructure, setting up incubators, encouraging venture capital and facilitating start-ups, and providing tax incentives.

STRATEGIC INDUSTRIES. An old rationale for industrial policy now being articulated more forcefully by political leaders in advanced economies is the need for governments to build sectors and even firms to protect their national security. Notably, statements from the Biden administration envision an American industrial strategy that identifies specific sectors and industries that are strategic from a national security perspective and deploys targeted public investments and incentives for the private sector to promote them.[48] Actions taken in pursuance of this strategy have focused, in particular, on high-tech industries considered vital for US technological leadership and defense.

National defense is typically a major motivation for government support of strategic industries. True, every country needs national defense. National defense industries are usually highly capital-intensive and require long R&D cycles. For developing economies, such industries generally are not compatible with their comparative advantage. Public expenditures devoted to them may not be assessed simply using traditional internal rates of return rules. Firms in such industries may not be viable in an open, competitive market. Subsidies, R&D grants, public procurement, and other support from government may be indispensable. The rationale for building defense industries cannot be assessed solely on economic grounds, but with the government's limited fiscal capacity in developing economies, the choice of strategic industries should be very selective and their number kept small. Governments should focus on those industries deemed truly essential for national defense and, preferably, that also generate positive externalities for nondefense industries.

Conclusion

For decades, international financial institutions such as the IMF and the World Bank (and the mainstream economic community in general) have advised developing economies to rely on market mechanisms and liberal economic policies as their guiding principles and compass for economic growth and transformation. This implied avoiding state interventions in the economy, except in very narrowly defined circumstances, namely, well-identified market failures and externalities. As a result, industrial policy—often defined inconsistently in economic literature—was viewed as a source of distortions. But as advanced economies faced economic shocks and geopolitical challenges in recent years and openly embraced industrial policy, the Bretton Woods institutions reacted approvingly to such policies that had been denied to developing economies. The implicit rationale was that advanced economies had the fiscal space, financial resources, and the administrative capacity and governance frameworks to design and implement such policies successfully.

We have pointed out this double standard in this chapter and sought to dispel some of the myths that have clouded the debate over industrial policy. We have highlighted the arbitrary distinctions between policies to change the structure of the economy and other policies, and the inconsistencies of attempting to distinguish between vertical and horizontal policies. In fact, most economic policy by governments can be deemed industrial policy in some way. The key question is not whether developing economies (and other economies) should engage in industrial policy but how to do it right—that is, how economies at different levels of development can mobilize human, capital, and technological resources and promote knowledge and learning to facilitate the emergence and scaling up of the most productive and competitive sectors and industries.

Beyond the traditional rationales for industrial policy based on market failures and externalities, we have emphasized the importance of fostering and disseminating new and relevant ideas and the government's role in that process. Industrial policy (and economic policy generally) should aim to identify industries with latent comparative advantage and design and implement state interventions to help turn these potential engines of growth into competitive sources of growth. Knowledge diffusion and continuous learning are essential ingredients for success. The dynamics of economic growth and structural transformation require an active and benevolent state working collaboratively with the private sector to identify and prioritize activities with the highest potential returns and channel limited resources toward them. In addition to effective market mechanisms, governments must play a key and carefully codified role. In particular, their role as an engaged facilitator in generating, borrowing, using, and disseminating ideas consistent with an economy's comparative advantage and development goals is crucial.

Finally, it is important to distinguish industrial policy from protectionism. Industrial policy actions taken by countries are often protectionist, but they don't have to be. For example, subsidies or tax credits for buying electric vehicles can be justified as industrial policy, especially given the environmental externalities involved, but limiting those incentives to vehicles manufactured or assembled domestically (or in selected other countries considered "friendly") goes beyond industrial policy and into protectionism. Protectionist actions—not only traditional border measures but an increasing array of behind-the border measures—and discriminatory regionalism are on the rise. There is much concern today about the risks of global economic fragmentation, but these risks arise not from a resurgence of interest in industrial policy per se but rather from a resurgence of protectionism in a more contested world marked by increased geopolitical tensions.

NOTES

1. See Chenery (1969, 1971) and Chenery and Syrquin (1986).
2. Woods (2023).
3. Quoted by Horobin and Delfs (2002).
4. Quoted by Von der Burchard and Leali (2022).
5. Ministère de l'Economie, des Finances et de la Souveraineté Industriel et Numérique (2022).
6. Federal Ministry for Economic Affairs and Energy (2019).
7. HM Government (1917, p. 4).
8. HM Treasury (2022).
9. Council of the European Union (2017).
10. European Commission (2021).
11. Tagliapietra and Veugelers (2020).
12. Haraguchi, Cheng, and Smeets (2017); Aiginger and Rodrik (2020); Rodrik (2021); Mazzucato (2013, 2024).
13. Sullivan (2023)
14. Woods (2023).
15. Sheehan (2023).
16. More than 90 percent of advanced chips, crucial for defense and artificial intelligence (AI), come from Taiwan Province of China, which raises concerns about US industry vulnerability to supply shock. The US government is allocating $39 billion in funding from the $280 billion CHIPS and Science Act to support the development of advanced semiconductor manufacturing capability. Funding recipients also face extensive conditions, such as a ten-year ban on expanding advanced chip capacity in China. This action comes on top of the $370 billion in IRA subsidies for clean energy. Meanwhile, Japan is providing subsidies worth more than $500 million to fifty-seven companies to encourage them to invest domestically, part of its efforts to reduce reliance on China. The European Union is setting aside €160 billion of its COVID-19 recovery fund for digital innovations such as chips, batteries, and climate adaptation (Agarwal 2023).
17. Hamilton (1791). See Juhász and Steinwender (2023) for a review of the literature on industrial policy since the nineteenth century.

18. Johnson (1984).

19. Landesmann (1992).

20. Chang (1994). See Peres and Primi (2009) for a detailed comparative analysis.

21. The traditional boundaries of manufacturing as an economic activity are defined by the International Standard Industrial Classification of All Economic Activities (ISIC) recommended by the United Nations Statistical Commission. For a technical critique of the manufacturing value-added methodology, see Monga (2024).

22. Rodrik (2002) and Warwick (2013).

23. World Bank (1993).

24. Another recent paper by IMF staff defines industrial policy as "government efforts to shape the economy by targeting specific industries, firms, or economic activities" (Agarwal 2023).

25. Stiglitz, Lin, and Monga (2013) and Stiglitz et al. (2013).

26. See Broda and Weinstein (2004) or Cagé and Gadenne (2018). It should also be noted that since the end of World War II, global tariffs have generally declined, while protection has increasingly been carried out through a variety of nontariff measures, many of which are difficult to quantify and are not captured in empirical analyses of industrial policy. See UNCTAD (2022).

27. Rodrik (2012) and Harrison and Rodriguez-Clare (2010).

28. Juhász et al. (2023, p. 9).

29. See, for instance, World Bank (2022a) on Egypt's public expenditure review.

30. World Bank (2022b) highlights such issues in the public expenditure review of Tajikistan.

31. Evenett (2003).

32. Stiglitz (2001, 2014) and Greenwald and Stiglitz (2013). See also Acemoglu (2023) on the role of government in supporting and directing technological change toward societal goals.

33. Aghion and Howitt (1997).

34. In new institutional economics, these institutions include formal ones, such as laws, rules, and economic, social, and political institutions, and informal ones, such as behavior patterns, traditions, beliefs, values, and ideology.

35. Lin (2011).

36. Diao et al. (2021).

37. Lin, Liu, and Zhang (2023); Lin et al. (2021); Ju, Lin, and Wang (2015); Lin and Monga (2011).

38. Acemoglu and Robinson (2012).

39. Glaeser and Goldin (2008) and Teachout (2016).

40. Khan (2018).

41. Lin (2013, 2014, 2016) and Lin and Monga (2017).
42. Lin (2009); Robinson and Torvik (2005); World Bank (1995).
43. Monga (2006, 2017, 2019).
44. Lee (2019).
45. Lin (2017) and Lin and Monga (2013, 2014).
46. Zhang and Hu (2014) and Rodriguez-Clare (2007).
47. Lee (2013).
48. Sullivan (2023).

REFERENCES

Acemoglu, D. 2023. "Distorted Innovation: Does the Market Get the Direction of Technology Right?" *AEA Papers and Proceedings* 113: 1–28.

Acemoglu, D., and J. Robinson. 2012. *Why Nations Fail: The Origins of Power, Prosperity, and Poverty*. New York: Crown Business.

Agarwal, R. 2023. "Industrial Policy and the Growth Strategy Dilemma." *Finance and Development* 60 (3): 50–53.

Aghion, P., and P. Howitt. 1997. *Endogenous Growth Theory*. New York: Penguin Random House.

Aiginger, K., and D. Rodrik. 2020. "Rebirth of Industrial Policy and an Agenda for the Twenty-First Century." *Journal of Industry, Competition and Trade* 20: 189–207.

Becker, G. 1985. "The Best Industrial Policy Is None at All." *Business Week*, August 26.

Broda, C., and D. Weinstein. 2004. "Variety Growth and World Welfare." *American Economic Review* 94 (2): 139–44.

Cagé, J., and L. Gadenne. 2018. "Tax Revenues and the Fiscal Cost of Trade Liberalization, 1792–2006." *Explorations in Economic History* 70: 1–24.

Chang, H.-J. 1994. *The Political Economy of Industrial Policy*. Basingstoke: Macmillan.

Chenery, H. 1969. "The Process of Industrialization." Economic Development Report no. 146, Harvard University Center for International Affairs, Cambridge, MA.

———. 1971. "Growth and Structural Change." *Finance and Development* 8 (3): 16–27.

Chenery, H., and M. Syrquin. 1986. "Typical Patterns of Transformation." In *Industrialization and Growth: A Comparative Study*, edited by H. Chenery, S. Robinson, and M. Syrquin. New York: Oxford University Press.

Cherif, R., and F. Hasanov. 2019. "The Return of the Policy That Shall Not Be Named: Principles of Industrial Policy." IMF Working Paper 19/74. International Monetary Fund, Washington, DC.

Cherif, R., F. Hasanov, and N. Spatafora et al. 2022. "Industrial Policy for Growth and Diversification: A Conceptual Framework." Departmental Paper 2022/017. International Monetary Fund, Washington, DC.

Council of the European Union. 2017. "Outcome of the Council Meeting: Competitiveness (Internal Market, Industry, Research and Space)." 3544th Council Meeting, Brussels, May 29–30.

Diao, X., M. Ellis, M. McMillan, and D. Rodrik. 2021. "Africa's Manufacturing Puzzle: Evidence from Tanzanian and Ethiopian Firms." NBER Working Paper 28344. National Bureau of Economic Research, Cambridge, MA.

Evenett, S. 2003. *Study on Issues Related to a Possible Multilateral Framework on Competition Policy.* WT/WGTCP/W228. World Trade Organization, Geneva.

European Commission, 2021. *Updating the 2020 New Industrial Strategy: Building a Stronger Single Market for Europe's Recovery.* Brussels. May.

Federal Ministry for Economic Affairs and Energy. 2019. *Made in Germany— Industrial Strategy 2030: Guidelines for a German and European Industrial Policy.* Berlin.

Glaeser, E., and C. Goldin, eds. 2008. *Corruption and Reform: Lessons from America's Economic History.* Chicago: University of Chicago Press.

Greenwald, B., and J. Stiglitz. 2013. "Industrial Policies, the Creation of a Learning Society, and Economic Development." In *The Industrial Policy Revolution I*, edited by J. Stiglitz and J. Y. Lin. International Economic Association Series. London: Palgrave Macmillan.

Hamilton, A. 1791. "Alexander Hamilton's Final Version of the Report on the Subject of Manufactures." National Archives and Records Administration. Philadelphia, December 5.

Haraguchi, N., C. Cheng, and E. Smeets. 2017. "The Importance of Manufacturing in Economic Development: Has this Changed?" *World Development* 93 (C): 293–315.

Harrison, A., and A. Rodriguez-Clare. 2010. "Trade, Foreign Investment, and Industrial Policy for Developing Countries." In *Handbooks in Economics*, edited by D. Rodrik and M. Rosenzweig, vol. 5. New York: Elsevier.

Hausmann, R., D. Rodrik, and A. Velasco. 2008. "Growth Diagnostics." In *The Washington Consensus Reconsidered: Towards a New Global Governance*, edited by J. Stiglitz and N. Serra. Oxford: Oxford University Press.

Hevia, C., N. Loayza, and C. Meza-Cuadra. 2023. "Industrial Policies vs. Public Goods under Asymmetric Information." *Economia* 46 (91): 39–52.

HM Government. 2017. *Industrial Strategy: Building a Britain Fit for the Future.* London: Prime Minister's Office.

HM Treasury. 2022. *The Growth Plan 2022.* London: HM Treasury.

Horobin, W., and A. Delfs. 2022. "France Accuses US of Pursuing China-Style Industrial Policy." *Bloomberg*, November 27.

Johnson, C. 1984. "The Industrial Policy Debate Re-examined." *California Management Review* 27 (1): 71–89.

Ju, J., J. Y. Lin, and Y. Wang. 2015. "Endowment Structures, Industrial Dynamics, and Economic Growth." *Journal of Monetary Economics* 76 (C): 244–63.

Juhász, R., N. Lane, E. Oehlsen, and V. Pérez. 2023. "The Who, What, When, and How of Industrial Policy: A Text-Based Approach." STEG Working Paper. Centre for Economic Policy Research, London.

Juhász, R., and C. Steinwender. 2023. "Industrial Policy and the Great Divergence." NBER Working Paper 31736. National Bureau of Economic Research, Cambridge, MA.

Khan, M. 2018. "Political Settlements and the Analysis of Institutions." *African Affairs* 117 (469): 636–55.

Landesmann, M. 1992. "Industrial Restructuring and East-West Trade Integration." Department of Applied Economics Working Paper 9213. University of Cambridge.

Lee, K. 2013. *Schumpeterian Analysis of Economic Catch-up: Knowledge, Path Creation, and the Middle-Income Trap.* Cambridge: Cambridge University Press.

———. 2019. *The Art of Economic Catch-Up: Barriers, Detours, and Leapfrogging in Innovation Systems.* New York: Cambridge University Press.

Lin, J. Y. 2009. *Economic Development and Transition: Thought, Strategy and Viability* (Marshall Lectures). New York: Cambridge University Press.

———. 2011. "New Structural Economics: A Framework for Rethinking Development." *World Bank Research Observer* 26 (2): 193–221.

———. 2013. *Against the Consensus: Reflections on the Great Recession.* Cambridge: Cambridge University Press.

———. 2014. *The Quest for Prosperity: How Developing Economies Can Take Off*—Updated Edition. Princeton, NJ: Princeton University Press.

———. 2016. "The Latecomer Advantages and Disadvantages: A New Structural Economics Perspective." In *Diverse Development Paths and Structural Transformation in Escape from Poverty*, edited by M. Andersson and T. Axelsson. Cambridge: Cambridge University Press.

———. 2017. "Industrial Policies for Avoiding the Middle-Income Trap: A New Structural Economics Perspective." *Journal of Chinese Economic and Business Studies* 15 (1): 5–18.

Lin, J. Y., Z. Liu, and B. Zhang. 2023. "Endowment, Technology Choice, and Industrial Upgrading." *Structural Change and Economic Dynamics* 65 (2023): 364–81.

Lin, J. Y., and C. Monga. 2011. "Growth Identification and Facilitation: The Role of the State in the Dynamics of Structural Change." *Development Policy Review* 29 (3): 264–90.

———. 2013. "Comparative Advantage: The Silver Bullet of Industrial Policy." In *The Industrial Policy Revolution I: The Role of Government Beyond Ideology*, edited by J. Stiglitz and J. Y. Lin. New York: Palgrave Macmillan.

———. 2014. "The Evolving Paradigms of Structural Change." In *International Development: Ideas, Experience, and Prospects*, edited by B. Currie Adler, R. Kanbur, D. Malone, and R. Medhora. New York: Oxford University Press.

———. 2017. *Beating the Odds: Jump-Starting Developing Countries*. Princeton, NJ: Princeton University Press.

Lin, J. Y., Y. Wang, Y. Wen, and Y. Xu. 2021. *Endowment Structure and Role of State in Industrialization*. Peking University Institute of New Structural Economics, unpublished manuscript.

List, F. 1841. *The National System of Political Economy*. London: Longmans, Green, and Company.

Mazzucato, M. 2013. *The Entrepreneurial State: Debunking Public vs. Private Sector Myths*. London: Anthem Press.

———. 2024. "Governing the Economics of the Common Good: From Correcting Market Failures to Shaping Collective Goals." *Journal of Economic Policy Reform* 27 (1): 1–24.

Ministère de l'Economie, des Finances et de la Souveraineté Industriel et Numérique. 2022. *Joint Statement by Bruno Le Maire and Robert Habeck: "We call for a renewed impetus in European industrial policy."* Paris, November 22.

Monga, C. 2006. "Commodities, Mercedes-Benz, and Adjustment: An Episode in West African History." In *Themes in West Africa's History*, edited by E. Akyeampong. Oxford: James Currey.

———. 2017. "Industrialization: A Primer." In *Industrialize Africa: Strategies, Policies, Institutions, and Financing*. Abidjan: AFDB Group.

———. 2019. "Truth is the Safest Lie: A Reassessment of Development Economics." In *The Oxford Handbook of Structural Transformation*, edited by C. Monga and J. Y. Lin. New York: Oxford University Press.

———. 2024. "Manufacturing: Dead or Alive?" Growth Lab Working Paper. Harvard Kennedy School, Cambridge, MA.

Pack, H. 2000. "Industrial Policy: Growth Elixir or Poison?" *World Bank Research Observer* 15 (1): 47–67.

Pack, H., and K. Saggi. 2006. "Is There a Case for Industrial Policy: A Critical Survey." *World Bank Research Observer* 21 (2): 267–97.

Peres, W., and A. Primi. 2009. "Theory and Practice of Industrial Policy: Evidence from the Latin American Experience." Production Development Policy Series 187. Economic Commission for Latin America and the Caribbean, Santiago.

Pinder, J., ed. 1982. *National Industrial Strategies and the World Economy*. London: Routledge.

Reich, R. 1982. "Why the U.S. Needs Industrial Policy." *Harvard Business Review* 60 (1): 74–81.

Robinson, J., and R. Torvik. 2005. "White Elephants." *Journal of Public Economics* 89 (2–3): 197–210.

Rodriguez-Clare, A. 2007. "Clusters and Comparative Advantage: Implications for Industrial Policy." *Journal of Development Economics* 82 (1): 43–57.

Rodrik, D. 2008. "Industrial Policy: Don't Ask Why, Ask How." *Middle East Development Journal* 1 (1): 1–29.

———. 2009. *One Economics, Many Recipes: Globalization, Institutions, and Economic Growth*. Princeton, NJ: Princeton University Press.

———. 2012. "Why We Learn Nothing from Regressing Economic Growth on Policies." *Seoul Journal of Economics* 25 (2):137–51.

———. 2021. "The Future of Economic Development Strategies." Lecture at the Centre for Economic Performance, London School of Economics and Political Science, Stockholm, March 18.

Sheehan, M. 2023. "Biden's Unprecedented Semiconductor Bet." Carnegie Endowment for International Peace, Washington, DC.

Stiglitz, J. 2001. "Information and the Change in the Paradigm in Economics." Nobel Lecture, December 8.

———. 2014. "Why Learning Matters in an Innovation Economy." *The Guardian*, June 9.

Stiglitz, J., J. Y. Lin, and C. Monga. 2013. "Rejuvenation of Industrial Policy." In *The Industrial Policy Revolution I: The Role of Government Beyond Ideology*, edited by J. Stiglitz and J. Y. Lin. New York: Palgrave Macmillan.

Stiglitz, J., J. Y. Lin, C. Monga, and E. Patel. 2013. "Industrial Policy in the African Context." In *The Industrial Policy Revolution II: Africa in the 21st Century*, edited by J. Stiglitz, J. Y. Lin, and E. Patel. New York: Palgrave Macmillan.

Sullivan, J. 2023. "Remarks by National Security Advisor Jake Sullivan on Renewing American Economic Leadership." Brookings Institution, Washington, DC, April 27.

Tagliapietra, S., and R. Veugelers. 2020. *A Green Industrial Policy for Europe*. Brussels: Bruegel.

Teachout, Z. 2016. *Corruption in America: From Benjamin Franklin's Snuff Box to Citizens United*. Cambridge, MA: Harvard University Press.

UNCTAD. 2022. "Non-Tariff Measures from A to Z." United Nations Conference on Trade and Development, Geneva.

Von der Burchard, H., and G. Leali. 2022. "Germany and France Join Forces against Biden in Subsidy Battle." *Politico*, November 22.

Warwick, K. 2013. "Beyond Industrial Policy: Emerging Issues and New Trends." OECD Science, Technology, and Industry Policy Papers 2. Organization for Economic Cooperation and Development, Paris.

Woods, N. 2023. "Superpowers Are Forsaking Free Trade." *Finance and Development* 60 (2): 44–47.

World Bank. 1993. *The East Asian Miracle: Economic Growth and Public Policy.* New York: Oxford University Press.

———. 1995. *Bureaucrats in Business: The Economics and Politics of Government Ownership.* New York: Oxford University Press.

———. 2022a. *Egypt Public Expenditure Review for Human Development Sectors.* Washington, DC: World Bank.

———. 2022b. *Tajikistan—Public Expenditure Review: Strategic Issues for the Medium-Term Reform Agenda.* Washington, DC: World Bank.

Zhang, X., and D. Hu. 2014. "Overcoming Successive Bottlenecks: The Evolution of a Potato Cluster in China." *World Development* 63: 102–12.

PART III

New Trade Dynamics

SIX

Digital Trade Policies
and International Cooperation

BERNARD HOEKMAN

Digital trade is a rapidly growing part of the world economy, accounting
for 12 to 22 percent of world trade, depending on the definition of digital
goods and services that is used.[1] Growth rates of digital-based services
associated with cross-border data flows over online networks have been
outpacing all other types of trade.[2] Such trade is subject to regulation,
such as protectionist trade policies that explicitly discriminate against foreign suppliers motivated by industrial policy objectives, prohibitions on
the use of certain types of digital products or business practices to safeguard national security or societal values such as labor standards and
human rights, and more general (nondiscriminatory) regulation that seeks
to address market failures. As is true for trade more broadly, where regulation of production is becoming a more prominent element of trade policy
by conditioning imports of goods and services on *how* they were produced,
as opposed to compliance with technical and safety norms reflected in specific product standards, the production processes used by companies in the

area of digital trade, notably the extent to which data are transferred across borders and are protected to ensure privacy of individuals, are an important element of the policy framework that governs digital trade flows.

In this chapter, we review the state of play regarding policies affecting trade in digital products and current efforts by governments to facilitate digital trade through international cooperation. Geopolitical tensions and differences in interests and priorities across major countries have had negative repercussions for multilateral cooperation on international trade, including efforts to agree on rules of the road for digital trade. Repeated failures to conclude the World Trade Organization (WTO) Doha Round negotiations, launched in 2001, have led many countries to devote greater effort to negotiate bilateral or regional trade agreements that include provisions on e-commerce, digital trade, and data flows. As a result, regional arrangements have become a test bed for international cooperation on digital trade. Such arrangements go beyond traditional trade agreements that center on reciprocal liberalization of trade in general to span domain-specific initiatives that cover cross-border digital transactions. These initiatives provide a basis for learning from experience and informing the long-running WTO talks on e-commerce.

The chapter is organized as follows. The next section presents available information on digital trade policies and research on their effects on trade. The pattern of digital policies and analysis of their effects suggest that there are significant potential gains for countries to reduce associated trade costs through cooperation. The following section then discusses the main forms such cooperation has taken, including bilateral mutual recognition arrangements (MRAs), extension of preferential trade agreements to encompass digital policies, domain-specific digital agreements, and plurilateral negotiations at the WTO. We then draw some implications from the experience to date regarding the scope for international cooperation on digital policies. Differences in societal values and noneconomic objectives that motivate digital policies are likely to preclude broad multilateral agreement on politically sensitive areas of digital regulation, suggesting that digital policy cooperation will be issue-specific and comprise a mix of bilateral, plurilateral, and multilateral cooperation. Given that national regulatory regimes will continue to differ and the likelihood of a proliferation of bilateral and plurilateral digital initiatives, there is a strong case for multilateral scrutiny and analysis of the effects and effectiveness of regulatory regimes to inform policy reform, identify good regulatory practices, and evaluate both the domestic implications of regulatory measures and their spillover effects. The final section provides some concluding observations.

Digital Trade and Digital Trade Policies

There is no generally accepted definition of digital trade. The IMF-OECD-UN-WTO Handbook on Measuring Digital Trade defines digital trade as all international trade that is digitally ordered or digitally delivered.[3] The former includes goods and services, while the latter includes only services, defined to include all services except those closely tied to goods trade (transport, maintenance and repair of goods, construction) or cross-border travel by natural persons. Digitally ordered trade includes transactions that are intermediated through e-commerce platforms ("computer networks").

Ferracane and van der Marel (2021) use the sectoral ratio of software to labor costs to define digital/data intensive trade. Sectors with the highest ratios include telecommunications, computer services, information services, finance, and insurance. Another approach is to define digital trade based on the sectoral composition of companies that self-certify and register under the EU-US Privacy Shield Framework, which accords firms committing to conform with specific data privacy and security standards the ability to transfer data across the Atlantic. The list of such companies (maintained by the US Department of Commerce) suggests that business services, health care, publishing, audio-visual and broadcasting activities, media and entertainment, education, and travel services should be included in any definition of sectors engaging in digital trade.[4] Ultimately, which sectors and activities rely more on cross-border flows of data and services is an empirical question that will change over time as a function of the adoption and use of digital technologies.

Whatever the specific definition used, digital trade has been expanding rapidly. Global trade in digitally delivered services stood at $3.8 trillion in 2022, accounting for around 55 percent of the $6.8 trillion in world trade in services.[5] Digitally delivered services increased fourfold between 2005 and 2022, an average increase of 8.1 percent per year, compared to average annual growth of 5.6 percent for merchandise and 4.2 percent for other services exports.[6] It is more difficult to assess the magnitude and growth of digitally ordered trade. Data on the share of digitally intermediated transactions in purchases by firms and by consumers in retail outlets are scarce.[7]

Granular analyses that focus on the role of specific technologies such as internet platforms document large positive effects on international sales of especially small firms as a result of reductions in search and information-related trade costs.[8] The prospects are for even faster growth in digital trade and digital globalization in the future as digital technologies, automation, and artificial intelligence advance, further enhancing the international tradability of goods and services.[9]

Digital Trade Policies

A broad range of policies and regulations affect the ability to engage in digital trade and the costs associated with digital trade. In part, these are familiar trade policies, involving restrictions on market access and discriminatory treatment of foreign suppliers. The OECD Services Trade Restrictiveness Indicators (STRI) provides information on trade policies in services sectors. Figure 6.1 summarizes the state of policy for sectors that are more intensive in data flows and digital provision for selected OECD and non-OECD countries. High-income OECD countries tend to have lower restrictiveness indicators than emerging economies, but the data reveal significant variation across sectors within countries and across countries. Professional services such as legal and accounting tend to be the most restricted in a number of high-income and emerging economies. Courier services (important for digitally ordered trade) often have above average levels of restrictiveness, while computer services (important for digital trade in services) are among the least restricted services.

The significant heterogeneity across countries in services trade restrictiveness reflects a mix of discriminatory and protectionist trade policies and domestic regulations, the latter including measures to protect consumers and address market failures. Such measures help explain why the restrictiveness indicators vary across members of the European Union (EU), which is a customs union with a common external commercial policy. Some measures affecting services trade that are regulatory in nature are not governed by a common EU regime.[10]

The focus of the STRI is on measures that affect services trade. It does not specifically assess digital trade policy. The regulation of digital activity has been increasing in scope and intensity. The Digital Policy Alert, which was initiated in 2020 as a complement to the longer-running Global Trade Alert, compiles information on new policy activity affecting the production, consumption, or trade in digital products around the globe. As of the

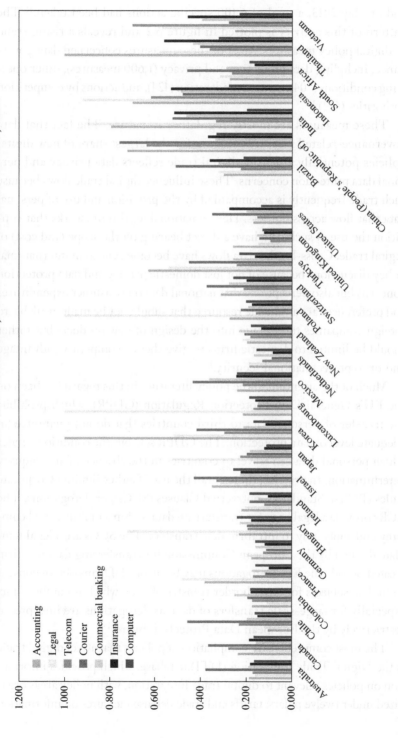

FIGURE 6.1. Services Trade Restrictiveness Indicators, Selected Countries and Sectors, 2022

Source: OECD STRI database.

end of May 2023, a total of 6,100 specific actions had been taken.[11] The pattern of this activity is plotted in figure 6.2 and reveals a rising trend in digital policy measures. Most of these measures concerned data governance, including data protection and privacy (1,600 measures), other operating conditions (704), content moderation (424), and actions by competition authorities (422).[12]

These measures are mostly regulatory in nature. The fact that data governance-related measures account for the largest share of new digital policies potentially affecting digital trade reflects data privacy and personal data protection concerns. These influence digital trade flows because such trade frequently is accompanied by the provision and use of personal data that flow across borders. Hence, national legal frameworks that condition the use of such data have a direct bearing on the scope (and cost) of digital trade. Cross-border data flows have become central in international policy discussions because of not just domestic privacy and data protection concerns but also perceptions that national data on consumer expenditures and preferences are a valuable resource that should not be made available to foreign companies to leverage into the design of new products but rather should be limited to domestic firms to give them a competitive advantage and/or to protect national security.[13]

Much of the attention in the policy literature in this regard has been on the EU's General Data Protection Regulation (GDPR), which prohibits the transfer of personal data to third countries that do not guarantee an adequate level of data protection. The GDPR sets out the conditions under which personal data can travel to countries in the absence of an adequacy determination. In practice, these entail the use of either Binding Corporate Rules (BCRs), Standard Contractual Clauses (SCCs), or derogations. The BCRs provide a legal basis for transferring data within a multinational company and apply only to intrafirm data transfers. The SCCs are a legal template defined by the European Commission for transferring data to a firm located outside the EU. Derogations may be invoked if firms obtain consent from data subjects for cross-border transfer of data, which is cumbersome, especially for large-scale transfers of data, as derogations are interpreted restrictively by the European Data Protection Board.[14]

The most comprehensive compilation of policies that affect digital trade is the Digital Trade Integration (DTI) database, which provides information on policies relevant to digital trade integration, with policy areas organized under twelve pillars: tariffs and trade defense measures on information

FIGURE 6.2. Digital Policy Activity since January 2020 (Number of Monthly Observations)

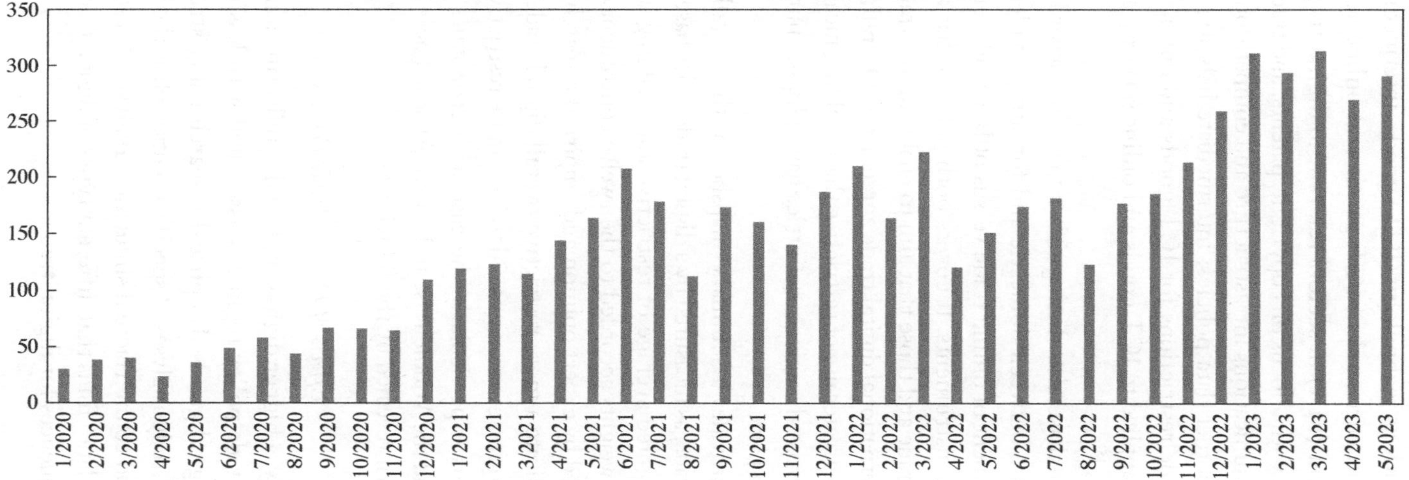

Source: Digital Policy Alert (https://digitalpolicyalert.org).

and communications technology (ICT) goods, intermediate goods, and inputs; public procurement of ICT goods and online services; foreign direct investment (FDI) in sectors relevant to digital trade; intellectual property rights, with a focus on copyright, patents, and trade secrets regulation; telecommunications infrastructure and competition; domestic data policies; cross-border data policies; intermediate liability; content access; quantitative trade restrictions for ICT goods and online services; technical standards applied to ICT goods and online services; and online sales and transactions.[15]

The DTI database also distinguishes measures according to whether they differentiate between domestic and foreign providers, imply more restrictive treatment of online trade versus offline trade, and entail use of trade-distortive instruments. It covers both policies that are expected to restrict digital trade and those that aim to enable digital trade, such as participation in international digital trade agreements. Overall, policy regimes tend to display a greater use of restrictive than enabling measures, as shown in figure 6.3. Across all regions, countries have a higher number of restrictive measures in place.

Figure 6.4 provides a summary snapshot of the overall policy regime toward digital trade, as measured by a digital trade index based on the DTI.[16] It reflects a weighted average of restrictive and enabling measures across countries, with weights accorded to the twelve constituent elements of the index determined by expert opinion and empirical research. Higher values of the index indicate a more restrictive overall digital trade policy regime. In general, emerging economies tend to have more restrictive digital policy regimes, and this is particularly the case with economies in South Asia, Central Asia, and the Middle East and North Africa. These results are similar to the pattern revealed by the STRI data.

Effects of Digital Trade Policies

Not surprisingly, a higher digital trade index reflecting a more restrictive overall digital trade policy regime is associated with less digital trade in services and digital goods. Empirical research using structural gravity models,[17] event study analyses of specific events such as the introduction of the GDPR,[18] and counterfactual simulation analysis of restrictions on the use of personal data[19] finds that different types of digital trade barriers have negative consequences for digital trade.

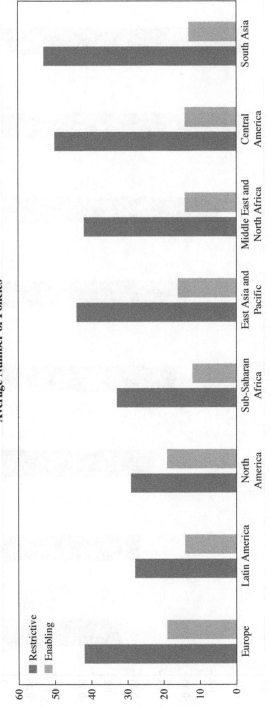

FIGURE 6.3. **Restrictive vs. Enabling Digital Trade Policies (Number, 2022)**

Average Number of Policies

Source: DTI database (Ferracane et al. 2023).

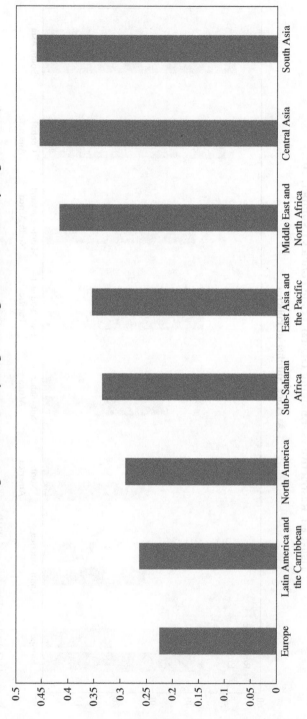

FIGURE 6.4. Overall Digital Trade Policy Regime (Digital Trade Index by Region, 2022)

Source: Ferracane (2022).

Ferracane and van der Marel (2021) assess whether global regulatory models of cross-border transfers and domestic processing of personal data have a bearing on digital services exports. They find positive correlations between exports and data models open to cross-border transfers of personal data, as well as for data models offering a high-level of protection to personal data at the domestic level. The latter finding is explained by the facilitating effect of data protection and the associated trust on the part of consumers when engaging in digital trade.[20] Schulze and van der Marel (2021) find that higher taxation of digital services is associated with lower competitiveness in digital services. A negative relationship between restrictive digital trade policies and ICT exports is found by Gupta, Ghosh, and Sridhar (2022).

Jiang, Liu, and Zhang (2023) use Chinese Customs data from 2014 to 2018 to assess the impacts of OECD members' digital trade policies, using the OECD's DSTRI. They find that Chinese exports of manufactured goods dropped by 2.3 percent, or $30.9 billion, because of a rise in digital trade barriers during the sample period. Ma, Shen, and Fang (2024) use information on digital trade provisions in preferential trade agreements (PTAs)[21] to analyze the effects of PTAs that embody relatively open cross-border data flow regimes and find that these are positively associated with trade in both goods and services, with a greater impact on trade in services. Wu, Luo, and Wood (2023) find that PTAs that include provisions on facilitating data flows or more broadly e-commerce support greater trade in digital products. These findings are consistent with the recent literature estimating the impact of services PTAs on trade in services: for example, Borchert and Di Ubaldo (2021) find that ambitious provisions to promote services trade are associated with 15 to 65 percent higher bilateral trade.

Sun et al. (2023) analyze the impact of data regulation on e-commerce using a random sample of 555,800 customers on the Alibaba platform. This sample is divided into treatment and control groups, with the former subjected to a ban on the use of personal data by the homepage recommendation algorithm that matches users to merchants. Relative to the control group, they observe a sharp decrease in matching outcomes as measured by customer engagement and purchases, with the latter falling by more than 70 percent. The decline is concentrated in smaller, less well-known merchants, consistent with findings by Johnson, Shriver, and Goldberg (2023) that the implementation of the GDPR resulted in an increase in the relative concentration of the website vendor market.[22] This unintended consequence of the GDPR does not imply an argument against such regulation, which is aimed at ensuring personal data protection in line with what European law regards as a fundamental human right. But this effect of the GDPR points to a need to consider potential distributional consequences in the design of data protection regulation, including issues related to firm size and prevailing market structure. Another implication is a need to complement data protection and digital trade policies with effective competition policy.

Levels of trade restrictions are only one factor affecting digital trade. Also important is variation in regulatory policies across countries. Regulatory heterogeneity is a distinct source of trade costs, given that idiosyncratic regulations imply that companies engaging in cross-border digital transactions must demonstrate compliance with regulatory requirements in each market they operate in.[23] Related to the concern about increasing trade costs for individual digital trade businesses arising from regulatory heterogeneity, differences across jurisdictions may also be "strategic" in the sense of reflecting foreign policy or industrial policy objectives. If regulation is deliberately designed and implemented in a way to control digital trade as opposed to doing so inadvertently as an unintended consequence of domestic preferences and priorities, it increases the potential for splintering the World Wide Web and the risks of geoeconomic fragmentation.[24]

Regulatory heterogeneity costs are augmented by policy uncertainty and frequent digital policy changes. As illustrated by the data compiled by the Digital Policy Alert, regulation of the digital economy is highly dynamic.[25] These features of the policy landscape drive calls by international businesses for efforts to agree on rules of the road for digital trade policies and to facilitate digital trade. Such efforts are being pursued actively by many states, as discussed below. Agreements on the equivalence of data protection regimes have been found to have a positive effect on digital trade.[26]

There is a close link between trade and competition policies in the digital domain. Technology platforms operated by big multinational enterprises can give rise to potential abuse of their dominant positions in markets, which may be reflected in anticompetitive practices that disadvantage other suppliers of goods and services. These include preventing business users from accessing data that they generate on a platform, not permitting third parties to inter-operate with the platform's own services, and discriminating against third-party product by ranking them below those offered by the platform owner. Research has found that dominant internet platforms are associated with increasing supplier concentration and worse matching between consumer demand and available supply.[27]

Many large jurisdictions are using competition policy instruments more actively, complemented by new regulations that define the responsibilities of the owners of dominant technology platforms regarding consumer protection, quality of service, and competition. The EU has been a leader in this respect, adopting a set of regulations in 2022 in a legislative package comprising the Digital Services Act (DSA) and the Digital Markets Act (DMA).[28] These regulations seek to protect the fundamental rights of the users of digital platforms and services and to provide a level playing field for businesses. The DSA pertains to a broad range of online providers, for example, online marketplaces, social networks, content-sharing platforms, app stores, and online travel and lodging platforms. The DMA focuses on big gatekeeper platforms that play a systemic role and act as intermediaries between companies providing digital services and users. These regulations also seek to limit the scope to provide illegal products and content, combat the spread of disinformation, and provide transparency regarding content moderation policies and paid content. Noncompliance with these regulations may result in fines or other remedial actions.

The potential for trade conflicts associated with this type of regulation of the digital economy is significant, given that many operators of dominant digital platforms in any given national market tend to be foreign owned. More generally, international cooperation is needed to agree on common principles, develop standards and good regulatory practices, and resolve potential disputes.

International Cooperation on Digital Trade Policies

International cooperation is being pursued through various channels, including PTAs, multilateral trade agreements, and plurilateral initiatives that center on the adoption of common regulatory practices and mutual recognition of the equivalence of regulatory regimes.

Preferential Trade Agreements

Many recent PTAs include dedicated chapters on e-commerce, provisions pertaining to taxation of electronic transmissions, regulation of cross-border data flows, and the processing or local storage of personal data. PTAs and digital trade agreements are heterogeneous in terms of coverage and nature of provisions (binding, enforceable commitments versus soft provisions). The extent to which PTAs liberalize or seek to maintain an open trade regime for digital trade varies substantially, depending on the countries involved and their underlying approaches to the regulation of the digital economy.

The Regional Comprehensive Economic Partnership (RCEP) between the Association of Southeast Asian Nations (ASEAN) and five regional partner countries (Australia, China, Japan, Korea, and New Zealand), for example, includes disciplines on digital trade and associated cross-border data flows but permits wide scope for parties to restrict such flows if deemed necessary to satisfy national noneconomic objectives such as national security. The Comprehensive and Progressive Agreement for Trans-Pacific Partnership (CPTPP), the United States-Mexico-Canada Agreement (USMCA), and recent bilateral trade agreements negotiated by the UK with Singapore and Australia ban local data processing requirements and embody commitments by parties to allow data to flow freely across borders.[29] Such commitments are conditioned by exceptions provisions that may be invoked by parties to defend national security interests or public morals and safety.

Multilateral Trade Cooperation

Cooperation is also being pursued at the multilateral level in the WTO. At the December 2017 Ministerial Conference, groups of WTO members abandoned the long-standing working practice based on consensus and launched several "joint statement initiatives" (JSIs) on issues including e-commerce, domestic regulation of services, and investment facilitation.[30] This shift to plurilateral engagement offered an alternative to embedding regulatory cooperation in large and comprehensive trade agreements. One of these JSIs has resulted in a new plurilateral Services Domestic Regulation agreement. Signatories span some seventy WTO members who will add the agreement to their commitments under the General Agreement on Trade in Services (GATS), using a provision in the GATS that allows for additional commitments (Art. 18 GATS). The provisions of the agreement center on matters associated with the authorization and certification of foreign services providers (licensing, qualification, and technical standards) rather than on the substance of regulations. The aim is to reduce the trade-impeding effects of domestic regulation by enhancing the transparency of policies; establishing good practice timeframes for processing of applications; promoting the acceptance of electronic applications by service providers; ensuring that national authorizing bodies are independent and impartial; and providing mechanisms for foreign providers to request domestic review of decisions.

Of particular relevance to digital trade are e-commerce talks. These currently involve eighty-nine WTO members, mostly middle- and high-income nations. The WTO Work Programme on Electronic Commerce defines e-commerce as the production, distribution, marketing, sale, or delivery of goods and services by electronic means. The focus of negotiations, led by Australia, Japan, and Singapore, is to agree on new rules for governing e-commerce, building on existing WTO agreements. The talks center on a mix of trade restrictive policies, such as the regulation of cross-border data flows and data localization requirements, and measures to facilitate digital trade, such as the use and acceptance of electronic invoicing/signature/payment and cooperation on consumer protection (for example, combatting fraud).

A consolidated draft negotiating text of the Joint Initiative on E-commerce is organized around six main issue areas: (i) enabling electronic commerce by facilitating electronic transactions (electronic authentication and e-signatures; electronic contracts, invoicing and payment services); (ii) non-discriminatory treatment of digital products, including cross-border data flows, location of computing facilities, imposition of duties (tariffs) on electronic transmissions, and principles on access to and use of the internet for e-commerce and digital trade; (iii) consumer protection and trust (regulation of spam, personal data protection, cybersecurity, use of cryptography); (iv) transparency of domestic regulation, capacity building, and technical assistance; (v) updating the WTO Reference Paper on telecommunications services, e-commerce-related network equipment and products; and (vi) market access for e-commerce-related goods and services, including temporary entry of electronic commerce-related personnel.[31]

As of mid-2023, there was agreed text on the regulation of spam, use of electronic signatures, authentication, e-contracts, online consumer protection, and open government data, and there are good prospects that parties will be able to make progress on e-invoicing, cybersecurity, and customs duties on electronic transmissions. Some of the latter areas are opposed by nonparticipants. India, for example, does not support making the moratorium on customs duties on electronic transmissions permanent.[32] The ability of nonparticipants to block an eventual agreement will depend on whether it will be applied on a nondiscriminatory basis.

Plurilateral Initiatives Outside the WTO

Outside the WTO, groups of countries have gone beyond what is being discussed in the e-commerce JSI as well as PTAs such as the CPTPP and the RCEP by entering into digital economy partnership agreements.[33] These often address many more specific digital trade-related policies and issues than the trade agreements that incorporate digital provisions. Examples include the Digital Economy Partnership Agreement (DEPA) between Chile, New Zealand, and Singapore[34] and the Japan-US Agreement on Digital Trade.[35] Singapore has negotiated three digital economy agreements in addition to the DEPA—with Australia, the UK, and Korea.[36] ASEAN members are negotiating a Digital Economy Framework Agreement, building on an ASEAN Agreement on Electronic Commerce signed in 2019.

Such initiatives aim to support cross-border data flows and build a trusted and secure digital environment for businesses and consumers. They often build on existing trade agreements but are an alternative to expanding trade agreements to include a greater focus on digital policies. In addition to addressing matters such as cross-border transfer of data and data localization, they deal with issues such as the protection of source code, cooperation on compatible e-invoicing and e-payment frameworks, location of computer facilities for financial services, open government data, digital identity, digital standards, artificial intelligence (AI) and fintech, and establish benchmarks (focal points) for regulatory reforms to support the digital economy, greater inclusion, and associated governance frameworks.[37]

The e-commerce JSI talks and the non-WTO, non-PTA initiatives that go beyond bilateral cooperation are examples of plurilateral initiatives and may take the form of an open plurilateral agreement (OPA).[38] An example of an OPA is the DEPA negotiated by Chile, New Zealand, and Singapore—all signatories to the CPTPP—in June 2020 and which went into effect in January 2021. It is designed to be open to new accession and comprises a series of modules that can be used by nonparties in their trade agreements or that could be used as a basis for new disciplines in the WTO. Korea became the first country to accede to the DEPA, concluding accession talks in June 2023.[39] Other countries that have applied for accession so far include Canada, China, Costa Rica, and Peru. China submitted a request seeking accession in November 2021, and an accession working group was formed in August 2022. Negotiations with China are ongoing on a range of subjects covered by the DEPA, including paperless trade, e-invoicing, e-payments, and mutual recognition of digital certificates, electronic contracts, and electronic documents.[40]

Almost one-third of the DEPA text concerns dispute settlement and administrative implementation procedures, reflecting a recognition that the DEPA comprises a mix of hard and soft law, with cooperation and learning constituting an important objective.[41] This also applies to other digital agreements. The Singapore-Australia Digital Economy Agreement, for example, includes eight areas that are covered by separate MOUs providing a basis for cooperation to operationalize modules, including through collaboration projects (for example, artificial intelligence, electronic invoicing, digital identity, personal data protection, data innovation, and electronic certification).

OPAs differ from "standard" trade agreements in at least four ways.[42] First, they are open: any country able to satisfy the membership conditions can participate, in contrast to trade agreements that generally are not open to accession by additional countries. Second, they do not lend themselves to quid pro quo exchange of concessions because of their focus on good regulatory practice, limiting regulatory heterogeneity. Third, because they are domain specific, they are limited to commitments for the issue or class of goods and services covered. Fourth, insofar as an OPA requires only equivalent performance—not identical procedures or institutions—they permit members to produce the required outcome through their own regulatory regimes and institutions, subject to reciprocal review of existing regulatory policies and their implementation and joint evaluation of potential adaptation to changes in circumstances.

Mutual Recognition of Regulatory Regimes

In addition to efforts to devise agreements on international standards and common principles for the regulation of the digital economy, the costs associated with satisfying conditions for cross-border digital trade can be reduced through mutual recognition of regulatory regimes that govern digital activity. A prominent example is data adequacy determinations, under which data protection regimes prevailing in two or more countries are assessed for their equivalence. The EU is an important focal point for such efforts, given its strong legal disciplines governing cross-border transmission of personal data and the framework that has been put in place in the GDPR by the European Commission to determine whether partner countries have data protection regimes that are "essentially equivalent" to that of the EU. While the most common form of international agreements dealing with digital trade-related policies are PTAs, often through provisions embedded in e-commerce chapters,[43] cooperation on digital policies need not take the form of a trade agreement. International regulatory cooperation, including international standardization, coordination of the activities of national regulators, and initiatives to assess and agree on the equivalence of national regulatory systems are examples of cooperation that may complement or substitute for trade agreements.

Between 2000 and 2023, the EU granted adequacy to fifteen states or territories.[44] While for all other decisions the European Commission certifies if the data protection regime of the trading partner is overall essentially equivalent to that of the EU, those pertaining to the United States certify the adequacy of a specific framework put in place to govern data flows, with adequacy status accorded only to companies that certified compliance with the applicable standards. Decisions pertaining to the United States represented an exception, as a country-wide adequacy determination was not possible given the absence of data privacy legislation in the United States[45]

If adequacy is granted to a country, personal data can flow freely from the EU (and Norway, Lichtenstein, and Iceland) to that country, akin to intra-EU data flows. Absent an adequacy decision, companies that want to process data outside the EU are required to rely on (often-expensive) mechanisms such as Binding Corporate Rules (BCRs) and Standard Contractual Clauses (SCCs), or exceptionally on derogations for instances when consent is obtained from data subjects for every cross-border transfer of personal data. SCCs are company-specific legal instruments that have been established by the EU as a mechanism to ensure that firms satisfy the GDPR requirements. They are widely used by companies to transfer personal data in and out of the EU[46] but are relatively costly for firms because of burdensome procedures for approval.[47]

The costs associated with SCCs and BCRs are both fixed and variable. Aside from the contractual arrangement that the data exporter needs to fulfill to use these model documents, firms may need to hire data specialists and consultancy firms to provide data mapping, management, and third-party auditing services. The costs will depend on the number of countries, type of data transfer, and the processing activities involved. New SCCs must be drafted every time personal data processing activities change.[48] In the case of BCRs, the Data Protection Authority (DPA) of each EU member state where the firm or a subsidiary is located must approve the data transfer. The relative burden of the fixed costs of using these legal templates will be larger for small- and medium-size enterprises (SMEs), with likely implications for cross-border digital trade given that firms trading services tend to be relatively small.[49] SCCs are not a guarantee, as their use can be contested. A finding that SCCs were not implemented appropriately, resulting in a violation of the GDPR, was the basis for a record €1.2 billion fine imposed on Meta Platforms Ireland Inc. in 2023 by the Irish Data Protection Commission.[50]

A major motivation for seeking to negotiate adequacy decisions is to avoid the company-specific costs of using SCCs. The two specific types of adequacy decisions the United States received from the EU, first under the Safe Harbor and subsequently under the Privacy Shield framework, were both struck down by the Court of Justice of the European Union (CJEU), ruling that the schemes did not sufficiently limit the potential for US authorities to access EU citizens' personal data and, therefore, did not guarantee the protection of the EU fundamental right of privacy.[51]

A new Transatlantic Data Privacy Framework (sometimes called Privacy Shield 2.0) to allow personal data to flow between the EU and the United States was agreed upon in 2022, and it continues to rely on self-certification by US entities given the absence of a national data privacy protection law in the United States. It was implemented in the United States through a presidential executive order that introduces new binding limitations and safeguards on access to personal data by US intelligence agencies and establishes an independent redress mechanism within the Department of Justice to handle and resolve complaints from EU citizens regarding the collection of their data for national security purposes. The requirements companies must abide by pertain to matters such as purpose limitation, data retention, and specific obligations concerning data security and sharing of data with third parties.[52] This framework was questioned by the European Data Protection Board, which raised several concerns,[53] and was rejected in a vote of the European Parliament. While neither is binding on the European Commission, if the EU Council endorses the framework and it is implemented, it is very likely that it will be challenged before the CJEU.[54]

Ferracane et al. (2023) assess the trade effects of EU adequacy decisions and show that they enhance digital trade between the EU and third countries. They find that transatlantic digital flows are significantly influenced by bilateral data adequacy frameworks, increasing digital trade by up to 16 percent relative to a situation where companies must use SCCs or process and store EU-sourced data locally in the EU. Beyond the two transatlantic partners, other adequacy-receiving countries appear to have benefitted indirectly from the adequacy decisions granted to the United States. Their digital exports to the US market started to grow as soon as a transatlantic data deal was put in place—an "adequacy club effect." This may reflect the fact that global supply chains in digital goods and services are spread across many countries. If US firms outsource their data-based activities to third countries with an adequacy determination, the trade cost of doing so is lower because no additional safeguards are required.

Ferracane et al. (2023) find that the adequacy decisions agreed on between the EU and the United States had an impact on the composition of digital trade within supply chains: about 7 percent of digital value-added trade shifted toward the network of countries with adequacy, away from being previously sourced from countries without adequacy (or from the domestic market). A synthetic control estimation of the potential effects of data adequacy, which compares countries that obtain EU adequacy decisions with a synthetically constructed control group that does not, supports the conclusion that bilateral adequacy can give rise to club effects. This is illustrated in their finding for Argentina, shown in figure 6.5. In 2003, Argentina became one of two Spanish-speaking countries granted adequacy by the EU. Using other Spanish-speaking countries to simulate Argentina's digital trade performance had the country not received adequacy, the synthetic control analysis shows that the adequacy decision had a significant positive impact on Argentina's digital trade with other countries that also have adequacy status, particularly the United States.

Thus, adequacy decisions have implications for digital trade that go beyond flows between the country pair covered by an agreement. If other countries have an EU adequacy framework, that may also facilitate digital trade with them. This is plausible given that their regulatory and legal frameworks presumably are similar, as otherwise they would not have been granted adequacy by the EU. While bilateral digital trade will be governed by national legal frameworks, Saluste (2021) notes that Argentina, Israel, Switzerland, the UK, and Uruguay leverage EU adequacy to also accord each other equivalence, creating a de facto plurilaterization of adequacy.[55] Such club effects may involve trade diversion if they give a competitive

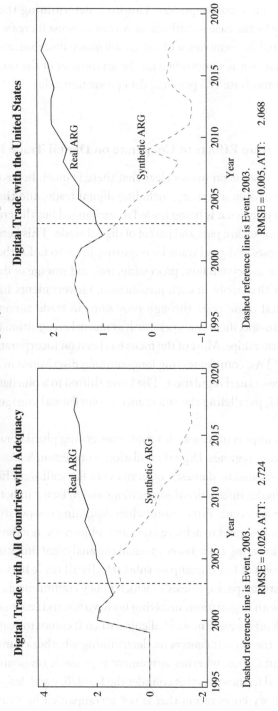

FIGURE 6.5. Effects of EU Data Adequacy: The Case of Argentina

Digital Trade with the United States

Real ARG

Synthetic ARG

Dashed reference line is Event, 2003.
RMSE = 0.005, ATT: 2.068

Digital Trade with All Countries with Adequacy

Real ARG

Synthetic ARG

Dashed reference line is Event, 2003.
RMSE = 0.026, ATT: 2.724

Source: Ferracane et al. (2023).

Note: Y-axis: $ million (log scale); RMSE: root mean square error; ATT: average treatment effect on the treated.

advantage to higher-cost suppliers. However, determining the extent to which this may be the case is difficult, as part of any cost increase relative to providers located in countries without an adequacy determination may be desirable insofar as it is associated with the attainment of the noneconomic objectives that motivate EU personal data protection rules.

Takeaways from Efforts to Cooperate on Digital Trade Policies

The foregoing discussion makes clear that there is much heterogeneity in the regulation of digital activity, including digital trade, and that much of it concerns not only what is being traded or exchanged but the cross-border data flows that often are part and parcel of digital trade. This heterogeneity increases the costs of digital trade by requiring firms to tailor the supply of services and the associated flow, processing, use, and storage of data to meet the conditions that apply in each jurisdiction. Governments have sought to reduce digital trade costs through provisions in trade agreements and through domain-specific frameworks such as mutual recognition (adequacy) and digital partnerships. Most of the focus has been on incorporating digital provisions in PTAs, complementing long-running discussions in the WTO on e-commerce-related regulation. The latter shifted to a plurilateral mode starting in 2017, paralleling the emergence of plurilateral engagement outside the WTO.[56]

There is an important research agenda concerning plurilateral cooperation on regulatory regimes. Digital regulation is one example. As regulation is generally motivated by domestic objectives but has spillover effects, there is a need to consider international implications and to factor in both the economic and noneconomic dimensions when designing cooperation. Trade agreements are designed to achieve economic objectives, notably to reduce distortions by lowering trade barriers—and the analytical literature focuses on this dimension. They encompass substantially all trade between signatories and constitute package deals in which policy commitments are linked to each other, with negotiations involving both within and cross-issue trade-offs. Such tradeoffs present more challenges when it comes to domestic regulation, where the agenda centers on determining whether countries share similar goals and, if so, whether agreement is possible on common standards. Analytical frameworks that consider the feasibility and design of issue-specific regulatory cooperation that is not accompanied by market access commitments are not well-developed, making it difficult to assess the relationship between stand-alone cooperation on digital regulation and traditional trade agreements. Many digital partnership agreements encompass countries that have concluded trade agreements. But major digital players such as the EU, the United States, China, and India do not have deep trade agreements with each other. An important question is to what extent binding market access trade commitments are needed to support cooperation on digital regulatory regimes.

In principle, the scope for broad participation is much greater for OPAs than trade agreements, and this is reflected in the number of countries participating in the WTO plurilateral e-commerce negotiations. Expanding membership over time is also easier in an OPA context, while it is a major constraint of trade agreements (most do not even have an accession provisions). Although broader participation can limit the scope of issues that can be addressed, a focus on what constitutes equivalence and on the pursuit of MRAs does not require trade agreements.

The various approaches toward cooperation to reduce digital trade costs reveal many areas where there is potential for agreement on good practices and convergence on either common standards or mutual recognition of the adequacy of regulatory regimes. They also make clear that, in some dimensions, there are fundamental differences in regulatory objectives and/or approaches to attain them that hinder cooperation.

The saga of EU-US efforts to create an adequacy framework for transatlantic flows of personal data illustrates that differences in views on state access to personal data for security purposes may be impossible to overcome, even for close allies. It is not obvious what more the United States can do to assuage the CJEU and EU privacy advocates without changing its domestic legal framework to mirror that of the EU. That will not happen, nor should it, given sovereignty and the right of countries to determine how they wish to approach such matters. The result may be that, in practice, conditional-flow regimes (EU) may end up being somewhat similar in effect to a strict control model of regulation (China) insofar as firms may have to employ local data storage and data processing, even if for very different reasons. Whether this will be an exception or the rule remains to be seen. What it does suggest is that free flow of data with trust may only be possible between countries with similar social and regulatory preferences—which may or may not correlate strongly with political or economic systems. Friends may not be like-minded when it comes to the regulation of the digital economy. Insofar as this is the case, multilateral agreements on binding rules will be extremely difficult to achieve.

This implies that firms will continue to confront both policy and judicial uncertainty, and consumers may face higher costs, less choice, and lower-quality digital supply. The WTO moratorium on customs duties on electronic transmissions is an example of the prevailing policy uncertainty. While it has been extended repeatedly since 1998, most recently for another two years at the 13th WTO ministerial in 2024, there is no assurance that it will continue to be extended in the future. The recurring judicial shocks to the regulatory framework governing transatlantic data flows are another example of policy uncertainty. Such uncertainty is augmented by geopolitical tensions and the increasing concern of many governments to safeguard national security. Large economies are imposing measures on national or economic security grounds that ban foreign companies from providing services and associated digital products. Examples include bans on the use of numerous Chinese apps by India on national security grounds (Sherman 2023), bans on the use of specific apps such as TikTok by employees of municipal and central governments (for example, New York City, the European Commission, the UK, Australia),[57] and a reported prohibition on the use of foreign-branded mobile devices by government officials in China.[58] This results in greater use of quantitative restrictions for certain types of digital trade, limiting the access of businesses and consumers to digital inputs and services.

Whether deeper cooperation will be feasible, the scope for further agreements and frameworks for regulatory equivalence and associated conformity assessment procedures, and the potential for convergence on technical standards, are all matters about which there is much uncertainty. The wide-ranging experimentation and efforts by governments to facilitate and improve the regulation of digital activities is a positive feature in the current international policy landscape.

What could usefully be considered by governments and stakeholders is to increase the transparency of the many different processes and initiatives that are being pursued. We need to learn more about the effects and effectiveness of regulatory frameworks and requirements that are motivated by noneconomic objectives. We need better assessment of the relative restrictiveness of the many elements of regulation that affect digital trade. The scope for comparative cross-country analysis of the effects of digital policies on trade and investment as well as on the noneconomic objectives that often motivate them has increased with recent and ongoing efforts to map prevailing digital policies. This provides a basis for governments to monitor and evaluate the effects of policy interventions and learn from both own and others' experience in implementing digital policies and cooperating across jurisdictions. Such analysis-based learning is a key input into the identification of opportunities to improve policies and to expand cooperation to include more countries through plurilateral clubs or multilateral agreements.

Greater transparency and better communication are first steps to reduce uncertainty. If policy regimes will continue to differ, firms will invest accordingly. Whether restrictive regimes are protectionist becomes a second-order question if regulation reflects societal or political values of a jurisdiction: the associated economic efficiency costs are not a flaw but a feature. In practice, this may imply that for some types of digital activities, it is necessary to "become local." This has long been the case for some economic activities. Public procurement is an example. Notwithstanding constructive efforts among countries to cooperate in identifying good regulatory practices such as open competitive bidding and nondiscrimination against foreign bidders through bodies such as the United Nations Center for International Trade Law, in practice, companies often will need to establish a commercial presence to be able to bid on contracts.[59] What is important is to understand the effects of a policy that implies a need to be local, including possible unintended consequences, such as disproportionately impacting SMEs that are less able to become local in foreign markets than large firms.

The WTO offers a potential venue for advancing progress in developing cooperative frameworks governing digital trade. Ongoing discussions on WTO reform include a focus on using the institution to engage in more effective deliberation and policy dialogue among members. Greater use of the specific trade concerns mechanism that has been developed in the WTO Committee on Technical Barriers to Trade and is beginning to be used in other policy areas offers a way to support constructive deliberations.[60] It allows members to raise questions regarding trading partner policies. It can readily be used to address questions regarding digital regulations but is currently not a feature of WTO bodies dealing with digital trade issues. The mechanism also offers an alternative to formal dispute settlement to address potential spillover effects of regulatory measures.

Another area where the WTO can play a constructive role is to support the expansion of digital domain MRAs. As noted previously, many of the countries deemed to have adequate personal data protection regimes by the EU have accorded each other equivalence status. The EU has not notified any data adequacy agreements to the WTO.[61] This has meant an absence of discussion among the broader WTO membership to understand how such agreements work and whether this approach can be emulated and extended to a plurilateral framework to govern efforts to establish equivalence of regulatory regimes.

The opportunities go well beyond joint action to reduce digital trade barriers, extending to the regulation of digital platforms, digital services, and artificial intelligence that is being implemented by major markets such as the EU. The increasing overlap between digital economy regulation and competition law and the rapid growth in industrial subsidies for digital sectors (for example, semiconductors) suggest that WTO members may also want to revisit the extant rules on subsidies[62] and the decision taken in 2004 to cease discussions on the possible design of cooperation on trade and competition policy.[63]

Conclusion

Digital trade offers significant opportunities as well as policy challenges. Harnessing the opportunities calls for investment in ICT and network infrastructure and effective regulation to ensure firms and consumers have digital access at reasonable cost and to safeguard consumers and market competition. Digital trade can be supported by international cooperation to reduce digital trade barriers, agree on regulatory standards, and assess the equivalence of domestic regulation. Instruments for such cooperation include not only traditional PTAs and multilateral agreements but also issue-specific plurilateral initiatives. Countries have begun to pursue the latter option to cooperate on digital trade-related policies, both in and outside the WTO. This is a new development for the trading system, as cooperation previously had mostly taken the form of trade agreements, preferential or multilateral.

Given the importance of domestic regulation as a source of international trade costs for digital products, the type of quid pro quo negotiations to reduce trade barriers that has been the staple of trade agreements is of only limited utility in digital trade, if it can be applied at all. The main implication for the WTO is that international cooperation on digital trade policies must involve a major focus on the goals and substance of domestic regulation and efforts to agree on what constitutes good practice and on the use of international standards. The WTO has already begun to go down this path in the e-commerce talks and in the 2021 Agreement on Services Domestic Regulation. The latter is a plurilateral agreement that binds only signatories. The e-commerce talks are also likely to result in a plurilateral agreement.

The WTO membership can play a more effective role in the development and implementation of new disciplines governing digital trade by accepting that in some areas of digital trade regulation, all members will not be able to agree on common rules. In such cases, subsets of the membership that can agree to move forward should be accommodated by the WTO. If this approach is rejected by countries that oppose plurilateral agreements in the WTO, digital globalization can lead to a further erosion of the role of the WTO as more and more of the policy action and efforts by countries to cooperate occur outside the WTO. Whatever emerges in terms of agreements, the heterogeneity of national digital regulations provides an important potential role for the WTO to assist its membership in assessing their effectiveness in realizing the underlying policy objectives and their effects on international trade and competition.

NOTES

I am grateful to Janina Curtis Bröker, Diane Coyle, Nadia Rocha, and Zia Qureshi for comments and suggestions.
  1. Ferracane et al. (2023).
  2. World Trade Organization (WTO) (2023).
  3. IMF et al. (2023). The handbook defines digitally delivered trade as cross-border services transactions using any form of digital delivery.
  4. Some 4,500 (5,300) firms registered under Safe Harbor (Privacy Shield), respectively, many of which are services companies. See https://www.privacyshield.gov/welcome.
  5. WTO (2023).
  6. WTO (2023).
  7. González, Sorescu, and Kaynak (2023) proxy for digitally ordered trade by measuring the value of digital inputs used in nondigital sectors. This measure grew fivefold between 1995 and 2018.
  8. Carballo et al. (2022).
  9. Jones (2023) and Baldwin and Forslid (2023).
  10. Fournier et al. (2015) and Bauer and Erixon (2016).
  11. The monitoring exercise covers the following policy areas: competition policy, taxation, content moderation, data governance, foreign direct

investment, international trade, public procurement, registration and licensing, other operating conditions, subsidies and industrial policy. See https://digitalpolicyalert.org/policy-area.

12. https://digitalpolicyalert.org/activity-tracker?offset=0&limit=10&period=2020-01-01,2023-06-25, accessed on June 25, 2023.

13. An example is India, which has put in place national digital identity, payment, and data-management systems and has imposed local data storage and processing requirements (Matthan and Ramann 2022).

14. Saluste (2021). EDPB Guidelines 2/2018 on derogations of Article 49 under Regulation 2016/679, May 25, 2018, accessed at https://edpb.europa.eu/our-work-tools/our-documents/guidelines/guidelines-22018-derogations-article-49-under-regulation_en.

15. Ferracane (2022).

16. A parallel exercise to compile a Digital STRI (DSTRI) by the OECD has less broad coverage of measures deemed to potentially affect digital trade. Analogous to the STRI data discussed above, the OECD DSTRI show that emerging economies maintain more restrictive policy stances toward digital trade in services.

17. For example, van der Marel and Ferracane (2021).

18. Johnson, Shriver, and Goldberg (2023).

19. Sun et al. (2023).

20. On the importance of trust for digital trade and implications for trade policy, see, for example, Aaronson (2023).

21. The Trade Agreements Provisions on Electronic Commerce and Data (TAPED) database, https://www.unilu.ch/en/faculties/faculty-of-law/professorships/burri-mira/research/taped/.

22. See also Frey and Presidente (2022).

23. Kox and Lejour 2006; van der Marel and Shepherd 2013; Crozet, Milet, and Mirza 2016; Nordås and Rouzet 2017.

24. Malcomson (2016); Evenett and Fritz (2022); Aiyar, Presbitero, and Ruta (2023).

25. Fritz and Giardini (2023).

26. Spiezia and Tscheke (2020) and Ferracane et al. (2023).

27. Sun et al. (2022) and Johnson, Shriver, and Goldberg (2023).

28. https://digital-strategy.ec.europa.eu/en/policies/digital-services-act-package.

29. See Mitchell and Gyanchandani (2023) and Burri (2023) for comparative analyses of CPTPP, RCEP, and EU trade agreements.

30. https://www.wto.org/english/news_e/news17_e/minis_13dec17_e.htm.

31. https://wtoplurilaterals.info/plural_initiative/e-commerce/.

32. The moratorium was established in 1998. See Wunsch-Vincent (2006).

33. See, for example, Honey (2021); Elms and Agnew (2022); Propp (2023).

34. https://www.mti.gov.sg/Trade/Digital-Economy-Agreements/The-Digital-Economy-Partnership-Agreement.

35. The agreement bans data localization, barriers to cross-border data flows, and the conditioning of access to market on the transfer of source code or algorithms, and covers financial services. See https://ustr.gov/sites/default/files/files/agreements/japan/Agreement_between_the_United_States_and_Japan_concerning_Digital_Trade.pdf.

36. https://www.mti.gov.sg/Trade/Digital-Economy-Agreements.

37. See, for example, Elms and Agnew (2022).

38. Hoekman and Sabel (2021).

39. https://www.mfat.govt.nz/en/media-and-resources/joint-press-release-on-the-accession-of-the-republic-of-korea-to-the-digital-economy-partnership-agreement/?m=918737#search:Y2hpbmEgZGVwYQ==.

40. Article 7 of a separate document entitled Digital Economy Partnership Agreement (DEPA) Accession Process lays out two benchmarks for acceding countries, stating that: "Aspirant economies must: (a) demonstrate the means by which they will comply with all of the existing provisions contained in the DEPA; and (b) undertake to embark on meaningful collaborations and projects with some or all DEPA Parties. These collaborations and projects will deliver commercially-meaningful outcomes that facilitate business-to-business connectivity in the digital age or address new issues intrinsic to the digital realm. The collaborations and projects will be mutually decided with the aspirant economy, on a case-by-case basis." See https://www.mti.gov.sg/Trade/Digital-Economy-Agreements/The-Digital-Economy-Partnership-Agreement.

41. Annex I of the Agreement states that Article 3.3 (Non-Discriminatory Treatment of Digital Products), Article 3.4 (Information and Communication Technology Products that Use Cryptography), Article 4.3 (Cross-Border Transfer of Information by Electronic Means), and Article 4.4 (Location of Computing Facilities) do not create any rights or obligations between or among the Parties under this Agreement. A consequence, stated explicitly in Annex 14-A, is that dispute settlement provisions do not apply to these provisions.

42. Hoekman and Sabel (2021).

43. More than ninety-five of the PTAs currently in force include dedicated e-commerce chapters (Burri and Polanco 2020).

44. See https://commission.europa.eu/law/law-topic/data-protection/international-dimension-data-protection/adequacy-decisions_en.

45. In the case of Canada, there are provisions conditioning adequacy for commercial operators on the adoption of equivalent regulation (legislation) at the provincial level when the provinces have jurisdiction.

46. IAPP-EY (2019) and Business Europe (2020).

47. Cory, Castro, and Dick (2020a, 2020b).

48. Chivot and Cory (2020).

49. Breinlich and Criscuolo (2011) and Bento and Restuccia (2021). Data flows based on SCCs often involve business-to-business transactions. An implication of that is these data flows are not dominated by the large platforms providing business-to-consumer-facing services, which tend to feature more in debates on cross-border data flows.

50. The Data Protection Commission found that data transfers were made by Meta in circumstances that failed to guarantee a level of protection to data subjects that is essentially equivalent to that provided by EU law and infringed Article 46(1) of the GDPR. Meta was asked to cease unlawful processing and storage of personal data of European Economic Area users in the United States. See https://edpb.europa.eu/our-work-tools/consistency-findings/register-decisions/2023/decision-data-protection-commission_en.

51. Meltzer (2021).

52. The executive order introduces the concepts of necessity and proportionality with regard to US intelligence-gathering and provides for binding safeguards that limit access to data by the US intelligence authorities to what is necessary and proportionate to protect national security; provides for enhanced oversight of activities by the US intelligence services to ensure compliance with limitations on surveillance activities; and establishes a new two-layer redress mechanism, with independent and binding authority, including the ability of EU individuals to lodge a complaint regarding access to personal data by the US national security authorities with the Civil Liberties Protection Officer of the US intelligence community and to appeal decisions to a new Data Protection Review Court. This court will have powers to investigate complaints from EU individuals, including obtaining relevant information from the intelligence agencies, and will be able to take binding remedial decisions. See https://ec.europa.eu/commission/presscorner/detail/es/qanda_22_7632.

53. See https://edpb.europa.eu/news/news/2023/edpb-welcomes-improvements-under-eu-us-data-privacy-framework-concerns-remain_en.

54. With associated knock-on effects for the UK and Switzerland, given the large cross-border data flows between these two states and the EU.

55. Two countries that have an EU adequacy decision have not (yet) extended such equivalence determinations to other members of the "adequacy club": New Zealand and Canada. To date, New Zealand has not formally designated any country as providing equivalent data protection, although it is an active proponent of digital economy partnership agreements that include provisions on data flows (Honey 2021). Digital trade between New Zealand and other EU adequacy-granted countries may nonetheless increase because of EU adequacy as any services traded that contain data on EU citizens and thus are governed by the GDPR will satisfy EU protection standards. Canada does not have privacy legislation that provides for the possibility to use adequacy decisions as a tool to support international data transfers.

56. Hoekman and Sabel (2021).
57. See https://www.nytimes.com/article/tiktok-ban.html#:~:text=Other%20 countries%20and%20government%20bodies,the%20app%20from%20official %20devices.
58. The existence of a formal ban has been contested by China. See https:// www.nytimes.com/2023/09/13/business/china-apple-iphone-ban.html.
59. Hoekman (2018).
60. Hoekman, Mavroidis, and Nelson (2023).
61. Saluste (2021).
62. Hoekman and Nelson (2020).
63. On trade and competition policy in the WTO, see, for example, Hoekman and Saggi (2006) and Bradford (2010).

REFERENCES

Aaronson, S. 2023. "Building Trust in Digital Trade Will Require a Rethink of Trade Policy-making." *Oxford Review of Economic Policy* 39 (1): 98–109.
Aiyar, S., A. Presbitero, and M. Ruta, eds. 2023. *Geoeconomic Fragmentation: The Economic Risks from a Fractured World Economy.* Washington, DC: CEPR Press and IMF.
Baldwin, R., and R. Forslid. 2023. "Globotics and Development: When Manufacturing Is Jobless and Services are Tradeable." *World Trade Review* 22 (3–4): 302–11.
Bauer, M., and F. Erixon. 2016. "Competition, Growth and Regulatory Heterogeneity in Europe's Digital Economy." European Centre for Political Economy Working Paper. https://ecipe.org/wp-content/uploads/2016/04/ PR-F5-0315.pdf.
Bento, P., and D. Restuccia. 2021. "On Average Establishment Size across Sectors and Countries." *Journal of Monetary Economics* 117: 220–42.
Borchert, I., and M. Di Ubaldo. 2021. "Deep Services Trade Agreements and their Effect on Trade and Value Added." World Bank Policy Research Working Paper 9608. World Bank, Washington, DC.
Bradford, A. 2010. "When the WTO Works, and How It Fails." *Virginia Journal of International Law* 51: 1–56.
Breinlich, H., and C. Criscuolo. 2011. "International Trade in Services: A Portrait of Importers and Exporters." *Journal of International Economics* 84 (2): 188–206.
Burri, M. 2023. "Digital Trade Rulemaking in Free Trade Agreements." In *Handbook on Digital Trade*, edited by D. Collins and M. Geist. Cheltenham: Edward Elgar.
Burri, M., and R. Polanco. 2020. "Digital Trade Provisions in Preferential Trade Agreements: Introducing a New Dataset." *Journal of International Economic Law* 23 (1): 187–220.

Business Europe. 2020. *Schrems II: Impact Survey Report*. Brussels: Business Europe, Digital Europe, ERT, and ACEA.

Carballo, J., M. Chatruc, C. Santa, and C. Volpe. 2022. "Online Business Platforms and International Trade." *Journal of International Economics* 137: 103599.

Chivot, E., and N. Cory. 2020. *Response to European Commission Consultation on Transfers of Personal Data to Third Countries and Cooperation between Data Protection Authorities*. Information Technology and Innovation Foundation Report, Washington, DC.

Cory, N., D. Castro, and E. Dick. 2020a. *Schrems II: What Invalidating the EU-U.S. Privacy Shield Means for Transatlantic Trade and Innovation*. Information Technology and Innovation Foundation Report, Washington, DC.

———. 2020b. *The Role and Value of Standard Contractual Clauses in EU-U.S. Digital Trade*. Information Technology and Innovation Foundation Report, Washington, DC.

Crozet, M., E. Milet, and D. Mirza. 2016. "The Impact of Domestic Regulations on International Trade in Services: Evidence from Firm-Level Data." *Journal of Comparative Economics* 44 (3): 585–607.

Elms, D., and N. Agnew. 2022. "Digital Trade in Asia." Robert Schuman Centre for Advanced Studies Research Paper 2022/51. European University Institute, Fiesole, Italy.

Evenett, S., and J. Fritz. 2022. *Emergent Digital Fragmentation: The Perils of Unilateralism*. A Joint Report of the Digital Policy Alert and Global Trade Alert. CEPR Press, London.

Ferracane, M. 2022. "The Digital Trade Integration Database: Description of Pillars and Indicators." Robert Schuman Centre for Advanced Studies Research Paper 2022/70. European University Institute, Fiesole, Italy.

Ferracane, M., and E. van der Marel. 2021. "Regulating Personal Data: Data Models and Digital Services Trade." World Bank Policy Research Working Paper 9596. World Bank, Washington, DC.

Ferracane, M., B. Hoekman, E. van der Marel, and F. Santi. 2023. "Digital Trade, Data Protection and EU Adequacy Decisions." Robert Schuman Centre for Advanced Studies Working Paper 2023/37. European University Institute, Fiesole, Italy.

Fournier, J., A. Domps, Y. Gorin, X. Guillet et al. 2015. "Implicit Regulatory Barriers in the EU Single Market: New Empirical Evidence from Gravity Models." Economics Department Working Paper 1181. Organization for Economic Cooperation and Development, Paris.

Frey, C., and G. Presidente. 2022. "The GDPR Effect: How Data Privacy Regulation Shaped Firm Performance Globally." VoxEU, March 10.

Fritz, J., and T. Giardini. 2023. "Data Governance Regulation in the G20: A Systematic Comparison of Rules and Their Effect on Digital Fragmentation." Digital Policy Alert. https://digitalpolicyalert.org/report/fragmentation-risk-in-g20-data-governance-regulation.

González, J., S. Sorescu, and P. Kaynak. 2023. *Of Bytes and Trade: Quantifying the Impact of Digitalisation on Trade.* Paris: OECD.

Gupta, S., P. Ghosh, and V. Sridhar. 2022. "Impact of Data Trade Restrictions on IT Services Export: A Cross-Country Analysis." *Telecommunications Policy* 46 (9): 102403.

Hoekman, B. 2018. "Reducing Home Bias in Public Procurement: Trade Agreements and Good Governance." *Global Governance* 24 (2): 249–65.

Hoekman, B., and D. Nelson. 2020. "Rethinking International Subsidy Rules." *The World Economy* 43 (12): 3104–32.

Hoekman, B., and K. Saggi. 2006. "International Cooperation on Domestic Policies: Lessons from the WTO Competition Policy Debate." In *Economic Development and Multilateral Trade Cooperation*, edited by S. Evenett and B. Hoekman. New York: Palgrave and World Bank.

Hoekman, B., and C. Sabel. 2021. "Plurilateral Cooperation as an Alternative to Trade Agreements: Innovating One Domain at a Time." *Global Policy* 12 (S3): 49–60.

Hoekman, B., P. Mavroidis, and D. Nelson. 2023. "Geopolitical Competition, Globalization and WTO Reform." *The World Economy* 46 (5): 1163–88.

Honey, S. 2021. "Enabling Trust, Trade Flows, and Innovation: the DEPA at Work," Hinrich Foundation Working Paper. https://www.hinrichfoundation. com/research/article/digital/enabling-trust-trade-flows-and-innovation-depa-at-work/.

IAPP-EY. 2019. *Annual Governance Report 2019.* Brussels: International Association of Privacy Professionals & Ernst and Young.

IMF, OECD, UN, and WTO. 2023. *Handbook on Measuring Digital Trade.* Second edition. https://www.imf.org/en/Publications/Books/Issues/2023/ 08/17/Handbook-on-Measuring-Digital-Trade-Second-edition-537466.

Jiang, L., S. Liu, and G. Zhang. 2022. "Digital Trade Barriers and Export Performance: Evidence from China." *Southern Economic Journal* 88 (4): 1401–30.

Johnson, G., S. Shriver, and S. Goldberg. 2023. "Privacy and Market Concentration: Intended and Unintended Consequences of the GDPR." *Management Science* 69: 5695–721.

Jones, E. 2023. "Digital Disruption: Artificial Intelligence and International Trade Policy." *Oxford Review of Economic Policy* 39 (1): 70–84.

Kox, H., and A. Lejour. 2006. "The Effects of the Services Directive on Intra-EU trade and FDI." *Revue économique* 574 (4): 747–69.

Ma, S., Y. Shen, and C. Fang. 2024. "Can Data Flow Provisions Facilitate Trade in Goods and Services? Analysis Based on the TAPED database." *Journal of International Trade & Economic Development*, 33 (3): 343–68.

Malcomson, S. 2016. *Splinternet: How Geopolitics and Commerce Are Fragmenting the World Wide Web* New York: OR Books.

Matthan, R., and S. Ramann. 2022. "India's Approach to Data Governance." In *Data Governance, Asian Alternatives: How India and Korea Are Creating New*

Models and Policies, edited by E. Feigenbaum and M. Nelson. Washington, DC: Carnegie Endowment for International Peace.

Meltzer, J. 2021. "Case Note: After Schrems II: The Need for a US-EU Agreement Balancing Privacy and National Security Goals." *Global Privacy Law Review* 2 (1): 83–89.

Mitchell, A., and V. Gyanchandani. 2023. "Convergence & Divergence in Digital Trade Regulation: A Comparative Analysis of CPTPP, RCEP, and e-JSI." *South Carolina Journal of International Law and Business* 19 (2): 98–150.

Nordås, H., and D. Rouzet. 2017. "The Impact of Services Trade Restrictiveness on Trade Flows." *The World Economy* 40 (6): 1155–83.

Propp, K. 2023. "More Than Adequate: New Directions in International Data Transfer Governance." Issue Brief. Atlantic Council, New York.

Saluste, M. 2021. "Adequacy Decisions: An Opportunity for Regulatory Cooperation on Data Protection?" EUI Working Paper. European University Institute, Fiesole, Italy. https://respect.eui.eu/saluste_adequacy-decisions-jan18-2021_respect_final/

Schulze, P., and E. Van der Marel. 2021. "Taxing Digital Services – Compensating for the Loss of Competitiveness." European Centre for International Political Economy, Brussels.

Sherman, J. 2023. "The Problem with India's App Bans." Atlantic Council, New York, March 27.

Spiezia, V., and J. Tscheke. 2020. "International Agreements on Cross-Border Data Flows and International Trade: A Statistical Analysis." OECD Science, Technology, and Industry Working Paper 2020/09. Organization for Economic Cooperation and Development, Paris.

Sun, T., Z. Yuan, C. Li, K. Zhang, and J. Xu. 2023. "The Value of Personal Data in Internet Commerce: A High-Stakes Field Experiment on Data Regulation Policy." *Management Science* 70 (4). https://doi.org/10.1287/mnsc.2023.4828.

Van der Marel, E., and M. Ferracane. 2021. "Do Data Policy Restrictions Inhibit Trade in Services?" *Review of World Economics* 157 (4): 727–76.

Van der Marel, E., and B. Shepherd. 2013. "Services Trade, Regulation and Regional Integration: Evidence from Sectoral Data." *The World Economy* 36 (11): 1393–405.

WTO. 2023. *Global Trade Outlook and Statistics*. Geneva: WTO.

Wu, J., Z. Luo, and J. Wood. 2023 "How Do Digital Trade Rules affect Global Value Chain Trade in Services? Analysis of Preferential Trade Agreements." *The World Economy* 46 (10): 3026–47.

Wunsch-Vincent, S. 2006. *The WTO, the Internet, and Trade in Digital Products: EC-US Perspectives*. New York: Bloomsbury Publishing.

SEVEN

Global Value Chains in a Changing World

SIWOOK LEE

International trade has grown dramatically in recent decades due to increasing globalization, trade and investment liberalization around the world, and the rapid development of transportation and communication technologies. The concurrent expansion of global value chains (GVCs) during this period has brought substantial benefits to the global economy by reducing production costs, stabilizing prices, and increasing productivity.[1] Developing countries have been among the main beneficiaries of GVC-related trade, which has boosted their growth and spurred global economic convergence. As a result, income inequality between countries in the global economy has declined for the first time since the nineteenth century.[2]

Against this background, the global economy currently is facing important changes due to the spread of protectionism, the US-China rivalry, the Russia-Ukraine war, the impact of COVID-19, rapid digital transformation, and climate change. These disruptions pose major new challenges to the international trading system and the long-term prospects of the global economy.

191

Free trade flourishes only in an environment where countries follow international norms in good faith. It has become much more challenging to safeguard free trade in the current situation where trade policies are increasingly intertwined with countries' political and security interests and strategies. Many countries have recently justified unilateral trade measures on security grounds, as well as on the grounds of promoting their values, ranging from labor rights to the environment. In reality, however, the line between values-based trade policies and protectionism aimed at promoting domestic industries is quite blurred.[3]

There is a great need today for countries to work together to address global issues such as climate change and the digital divide. International cooperation is vital to preserve an open, rules-based world trading system and secure the flexibility and viability of GVCs. Recently, however, such cooperation has been lacking. Instead, policy developments point to a growing threat of protectionism and fragmentation of global trade into allied blocs.

This chapter looks at the changing patterns of GVCs, analyzes how factors such as geopolitical changes and technology may affect GVCs in the coming years, and discusses implications for policy and international cooperation. The next section examines recent trends in GVC-related trade. We note that the recent decline in the share of GVC-related trade is due importantly to the recession and slower growth following the global financial crisis of 2008–2009 and to changes in relative prices between intermediate goods and final goods. China's domestic demand growth and the servicification of manufacturing are other demand-side factors in the changing patterns of GVCs. Meanwhile, supply shocks such as the pandemic, the U.S.-China hegemonic rivalry, the spread of protectionism, and regional conflicts have increased the likelihood of further GVC disruptions.

We then examine how these and other supply-side factors, such as digital transformation and climate change, are likely to drive structural shifts in GVCs. We analyze recent cross-border flows to show that the global economy is still in a process of "*de facto* globalization." At the same time, however, the pattern and pace of globalization are being influenced by changes in policy and institutional settings. So the process of globalization as shaped by policies and institutions, often referred to as "*de jure* globalization," needs to be carefully scrutinized. We argue that the future direction of globalization will be greatly affected by a combination of geopolitical, geoeconomic, and technopolitical factors, especially the hegemonic rivalry between the United States and China. However, given the hyper-connectedness of the global economy, a complete GVC decoupling is unlikely. A more likely outcome is a selective decoupling of some strategic industries such as semiconductors, vehicle batteries, and critical minerals.

The information and communication technology (ICT) revolution has enabled firms to unbundle production processes and engage in GVCs. But the nature of technological change in the era of digital transformation is more far-reaching, and its impact on supply chains could be quite different from previous technological advances. The full impact of digital transformation on GVCs, however, is still uncertain. Moreover, as the main energy sources are shifting from fossil fuels to renewables, there is a risk that countries may resort to "weaponizing" key minerals, such as lithium, nickel, graphite, copper, and cobalt, through strategic export controls. As a result, GVCs in industries heavily dependent on these minerals could face more disruption. We conclude the chapter by summarizing key findings and drawing some policy implications.

Recent Trends in Global Value Chains

Since the early 1990s, accelerating globalization, worldwide trade and investment liberalization, and advances in transportation and ICT technologies have led to a proliferation of GVCs in which all stages of a product's value chain, from design to production to distribution, increasingly span multiple countries and regions. The share of GVC-related trade in world trade increased by 9.5 percentage points over the 1995–2008 period, rising from 32 percent to 41.5 percent.[4]

As expected, the lion's share of GVC–related trade is trade in intermediate inputs used in the production of exports. Over the 1995–2008 period, GVC-related trade in intermediate inputs increased from 24 percent to 32.5 percent of total trade. This contrasts sharply with the share of traditional trade in intermediate goods, which remained virtually unchanged at 30–32 percent over the same period (figure 7.1).

On the other hand, the period since the global financial crisis has seen a gradual decline in the share of GVC-related trade relative to total trade due to a variety of factors, including a prolonged economic downturn and rising

FIGURE 7.1. **GVC-Related Trade and Trade in Intermediate Goods at the Global Level**

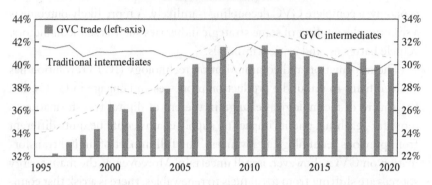

Source: Author's calculations based on the OECD Trade in Value Added (TiVA) database.

Note: The figures shown are percent of total global exports.

FIGURE 7.2. **Shares of GVC-Related Trade: OECD vs. Non-OECD Countries**

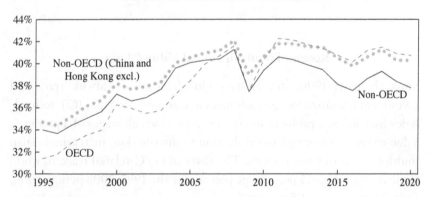

Source: Author's calculations based on the OECD TiVA database.

Note: The figures shown are percentages of total exports of the respective country group.

protectionism. The share of GVC-related trade peaked at 41.7 percent of total trade in 2011 and has been on a downward trend since then, falling to 39.7 percent in 2020.

Figure 7.2 compares the evolution of the share of GVC-related trade of thirty-eight member countries of the Organization for Economic Cooperation and Development (OECD) with that of non-OECD countries. During the period from 1995 to 2008, the GVC-related trade share of OECD countries increased faster than that of non-OECD countries, rising from 31.4 percent to 41.6 percent. Since then, it has stagnated at 40 to 42 percent, while the share of non-OECD countries has declined by 3.4 percentage points, from 41.2 percent in 2008 to 37.8 percent by 2020. However, if China is excluded from the non-OECD group, the data show a relatively similar trend between OECD and non-OECD countries.

GVC-related trade can be categorized into two types of trade participation: the first is "backward GVC participation," in which a country imports intermediate goods to produce its own exports; the second is "forward GVC participation," in which a country exports domestically produced inputs to trading partners that they use in the production of their exports. As suggested by Borin, Mancini, and Taglioni (2021), the higher the degree of forward (backward) GVC participation, the greater the exposure to demand (supply) shocks emanating from downstream (upstream) sectors. Backward GVC participation is measured, using international input-output tables, as the share of the import content embodied in gross exports, while forward GVC participation is the ratio of the domestic value added sent to third countries to the economy's total exports.[5]

The degree of backward and forward GVC participation varies across countries, depending on their economic characteristics. Most importantly, a country's sectoral specialization shapes the relative extent of backward and forward GVC participation. Countries with an abundance of natural resources such as oil, minerals, and agricultural products tend to have relatively high levels of forward GVC participation, but with a limited extent of backward participation. Countries with a comparative advantage in advanced manufacturing and services tend to depend more on imported inputs for their exports and thus engage more actively in backward GVC participation.

Figure 7.3 shows the evolution of backward and forward GVC participation for OECD and non-OECD countries over the period from 1995 to 2020. For OECD countries, the evolution of forward and backward GVC participation has been relatively similar over the period, with both growing in the 1995–2008 period and then stagnating or declining after the global financial crisis. For non-OECD countries, backward GVC participation is somewhat lower in the postcrisis period than in the precrisis period, but the difference does not seem to be significant. Forward GVC participation, on the other hand, shows a very steep increase before the crisis, followed by a rapid decline after. These results suggest that the recent

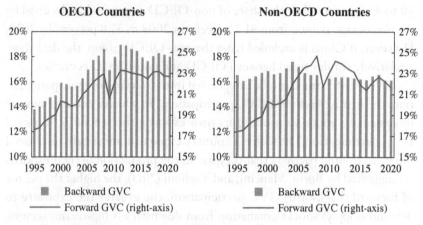

FIGURE 7.3. Backward GVC vs. Forward GVC Participation:
OECD vs. Non-OECD Countries

Source: Author's calculations based on the OECD TiVA database.

Note: The figures shown are percent of total exports.

decline in GVC-related trade has been driven by sluggish import demand following the economic downturn in advanced economies, which led to lower forward GVC participation by developing economies.

Figure 7.4 depicts the evolution of non-OECD countries' participation in forward and backward GVCs excluding China and Hong Kong. Compared to the case of non-OECD countries including China and Hong Kong shown in the right panel of figure 7.3, forward GVC participation shows a similar trend, while backward participation reveals a different pattern. The latter increased by 1.4 percentage points over the 2011–2020 period when China and Hong Kong are excluded from the sample compared to a small decline when they are included. This suggests an important role for developments in China in the observed decline in backward GVC participation in this period. We examine China's GVC transformation in more detail below.

China and GVC Transformation

Since China's accession to the World Trade Organization (WTO) in 2001, many global companies have set up their main manufacturing operations in China and engage in trade with their home country and third countries from there, leading to a sharp increase in GVC-related trade. China's active

FIGURE 7.4. GVC-Related Trade of Non-OECD Countries (China and Hong Kong Excluded)

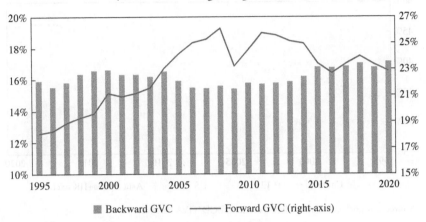

■ Backward GVC   ——— Forward GVC (right-axis)

Source: Author's calculations based on the OECD TiVA database.

Note: The figures shown are percent of total exports.

participation in GVCs has been pivotal to the rapid expansion of international trade. As shown in figure 7.5, China's GVC participation increased quite rapidly within a relatively short period of time after its WTO accession. But its share of GVC-related trade started to decline gradually after the global financial crisis. While other major exporters such as the United States and the European Union (EU) also saw their shares of GVC-related trade decline or stagnate in the postcrisis period, China's decline has been more dramatic.

Figure 7.6 reports changes in GVC participation of China and the Asian Factory 6 countries from 1995 to 2020.[6] The Asian Factory 6 countries experienced a similar decline (5.8 percentage points) in their GVC-related trade share as China did (5.6 percentage points) over the 2008–2020 period. The figure shows that the decline in China's GVC-related trade was due entirely to a decline in backward GVC participation, as China's participation in forward GVCs actually continued to increase, which implies that China is becoming less dependent on intermediate inputs from the rest of the world while continuing to increase its exports of intermediate goods for other countries' export production.

While China and the Asian Factory 6 countries share a common trend of declining backward GVC participation in recent years, there are notable

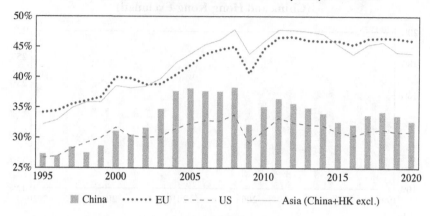

FIGURE 7.5. Shares of GVC-Related Trade by Major Traders

Source: Author's calculations based on the OECD TiVA database.

Note: The figures show percentages of total exports of each country/region.

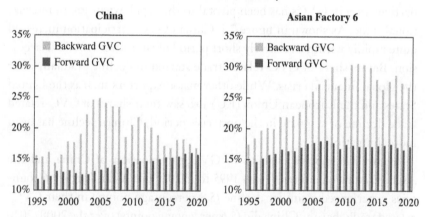

FIGURE 7.6. Decomposition of GVC-Related Trade:
China and Asian Factory 6

Source: Author's calculations based on the OECD TiVA database.

Note: The figures shown are percent of total exports of each country/region.

differences in the timing and magnitude of the decline. In the case of China, its backward GVC participation peaked at 24.8 percent in 2005 and then declined rapidly to 16.9 percent in 2020. In contrast, backward GVC participation in Asian Factory 6 countries remained high for some time after the global financial crisis and began to decline in the mid-2010s. Moreover, the magnitude of the decline has been relatively modest compared to China's.

FIGURE 7.7. China's GDP Composition by Sector

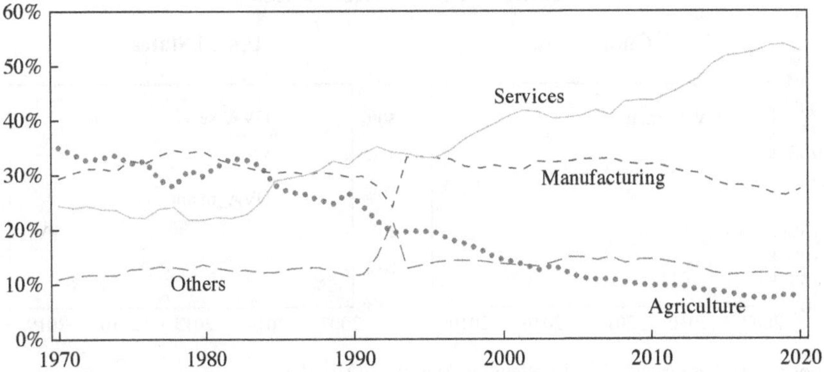

Source: Author's calculations based on the United Nations Conference on Trade and Development (UNCTAD) database.

Note: The figures show percent of GDP.

The existing literature links China's declining participation in backward GVCs primarily to the growth of its domestic market and the increasing competitiveness of Chinese domestic firms in providing manufacturing inputs for exports. For example, using Chinese micro-level data, Kee and Tang (2016) present evidence on the substitution of domestic for imported intermediates by processing exporters, leading to an increase in China's domestic content in exports from 65 percent to 70 percent from 2000 to 2007. They argue that this substitution was induced largely by China's trade and foreign direct investment (FDI) liberalization, which deepened its participation in GVCs and led to a greater variety of domestically produced materials becoming available at a lower prices.

The higher share of domestic value added in China's manufacturing exports may also be related to the expansion of its service sector. As shown in figure 7.7, China's rapid economic development has been accompanied by a process of "tertiarization"—a shift in industrial structure from the primary and/or manufacturing sectors to the service sector. Since the mid-1990s, the share of services in China's GDP has been growing, and this trend accelerated in the 2010s.

With the development of the domestic service sector, it is likely that China's manufacturing production, including exports, will become increasingly service-oriented, with a higher proportion of domestically produced services used as intermediate inputs than in the past. This phenomenon is

FIGURE 7.8. **Decomposition of Value Added of Manufacturing Exports: China vs. the United States**

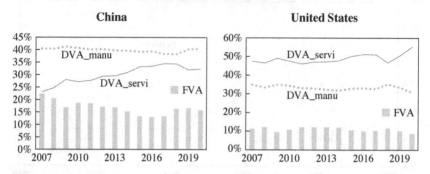

Source: Author's calculations based on the ADB-MRIO database.

Note: FVA is foreign value added embodied in gross exports; DVA_manu is domestic content of manufacturing inputs in gross exports; and DVA_servi is domestic content of services in gross exports.

often referred to as servicification of manufacturing: manufacturers increasingly expand their use of service inputs in the production process and/or increasingly sell services bundled with their products.[7]

To examine this phenomenon, we decompose and analyze the value-added content of China's manufacturing exports. As shown in figure 7.8, most of the increase in the domestic content of China's exports comes from service inputs. The value-added share of domestic service inputs in China's manufacturing exports increased from 23.1 percent in 2007 to 32.3 percent in 2020. We also find that, contrary to the microfindings of Kee and Tang (2016), the value-added contribution of domestically produced manufacturing inputs to China's exports changed little, hovering around 40 percent. Over the same period, the value-added share of foreign manufacturing and service intermediates in China's exports fell by 3.5 and 2.2 percentage points, respectively. The servicification of manufacturing in China appears to be related mainly to changes in the domestic service sector.

For comparison purposes, the change in the value-added composition of US manufacturing exports over the same period is also shown in figure 7.8. In the United States, nearly half of the value added in manufacturing exports comes from domestically produced service intermediates, and this proportion has been relatively stable. However, in 2020, the year COVID-19 struck, the share of domestic value added in services increased by 4.7 percentage points from the previous year.

FIGURE 7.9. **Composition of Domestic Service Inputs in Manufacturing Exports in Value Added**

China

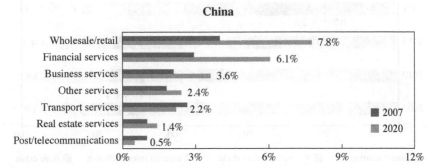

United States

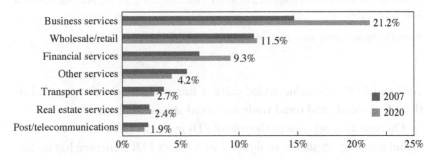

Source: Author's calculations based on the ADB-MRIO database.

Note: The figures show the value-added share in percent of each service category in gross manufacturing exports.

Figure 7.9 shows in more detail the value-added share of domestically produced service inputs in the manufacturing exports of China and the United States. In China, wholesale and retail trade accounted for 7.8 percent of total manufacturing export value added in 2020, followed by financial services (6.1 percent) and business services (3.6 percent). These are also the services that experienced the largest increases in value added between 2007 and 2020. The servicification of manufacturing in China so far has centered on the development of these three sectors. In the United States, on the other hand, business services accounted for 21.2 percent of value added in 2020, followed by wholesale and retail trade (11.5 percent) and financial services (9.3 percent). Of these, the contribution of business services, which are more knowledge-intensive, grew the most between

FIGURE 7.10. Composition of FDI Inflows into China

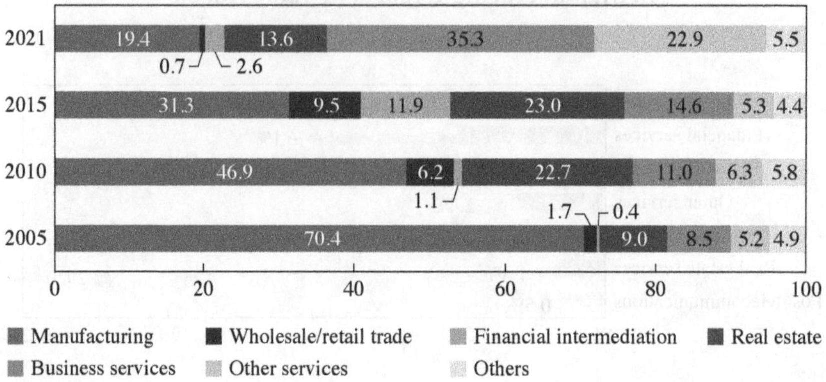

| | Manufacturing | | | | | | |

2021 | 19.4 | 0.7 2.6 | 13.6 | 35.3 | 22.9 | 5.5 |

2015 | 31.3 | 9.5 | 11.9 | 23.0 | 14.6 | 5.3 4.4 |

2010 | 46.9 | 1.1 6.2 | 22.7 | 11.0 | 6.3 5.8 |

2005 | 70.4 | 1.7 0.4 9.0 | 8.5 | 5.2 4.9 |

0   20   40   60   80   100

■ Manufacturing   ■ Wholesale/retail trade   ■ Financial intermediation   ■ Real estate
■ Business services   ■ Other services   ■ Others

Source: Author's calculations based on data from China Statistical Yearbook, National Bureau of Statistics of China.

Note: The figures shown are percent of total FDI inflows.

2007 and 2020. The value-added share of financial services also grew, while that of wholesale and retail trade remained almost unchanged.

One question pertains to the role of FDI in the servicification of Chinese manufacturing. As shown in figure 7.10, China's FDI structure has undergone a large shift. In 2005, investment into the manufacturing sector accounted for more than 70 percent of total FDI, but it has since declined rapidly to less than 20 percent as of 2021. In contrast, the share of FDI in services expanded from about a quarter to three quarters. The share of FDI in sectors that have been driving servicification, such as wholesale and retail trade, financial services, and business services, grew rapidly until the mid-2010s. While these observations do not provide direct evidence on whether FDI has contributed to the servicification of manufacturing in China, they at least suggest the possibility. More systematic analysis. particularly using firm-level data, is needed to better understand the linkages and implications for GVCs.

Data also show that FDI flows into business services, related to engineering, design, marketing, and professional consulting, have picked up sharply since the late 2010s, when tensions between the United States and China began to escalate. This suggests that the further servicification of manufacturing in China could revolve around these high-value services, which could have an important bearing on the future structure of China's GVCs.

FIGURE 7.11. **Global Real GDP Growth vs. Export Volume Growth**

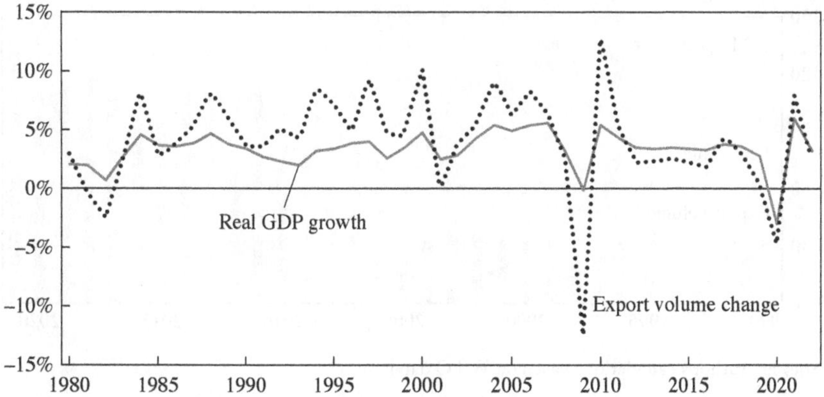

Source: Author's calculations based on IMF and WTO databases.

Why Is Trade in Intermediate Goods Stagnating?

As shown in figure 7.1, the decline in the share of intermediate goods trade in world trade in the 2010s was greater than that of GVC-related trade. Not only did the share of GVC-related intermediate goods trade decline, but the share of traditional forms of intermediate goods trade also fell. The question arises as to why the share of intermediate goods trade has declined more than the share of final trade.

For most of the period since the mid-1980s, international trade volumes have grown faster than GDP growth (figure 7.11). The period following the global financial crisis was somewhat exceptional, with export volume growth averaging 1.9 percent per year from 2009 to 2020, below the GDP growth rate of 2.3 percent. This phenomenon is similar to that observed in the mid-1970s to early 1980s, when the global economy experienced a pro-longed downturn due to the oil shock. The decades following that saw very robust trade growth, driven by global trade and investment liberalization, the integration of transition economies such as China and Russia into world markets, and the expansion of GVCs.

From the early 2000s until just before the global financial crisis, the value of international trade grew strongly in nominal terms, as export volumes expanded on the back of robust growth in global import demand, while export prices also rose, especially for intermediate goods and con-sumer durables, as shown in figure 7.12. In the aftermath of the global

FIGURE 7.12. **Global Exports: Value, Volume, and Unit Value**

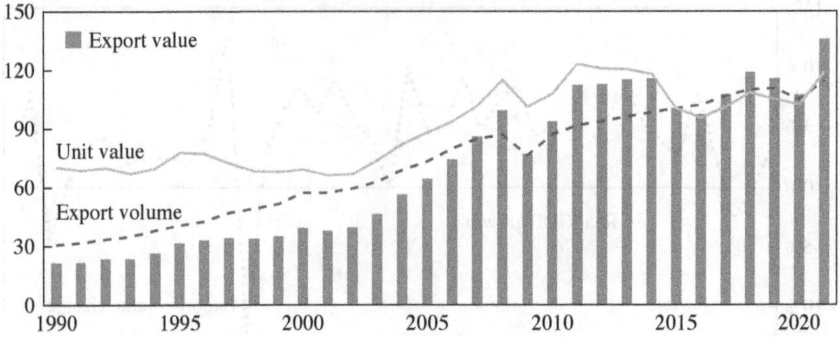

Source: Author's calculations based on WTO database.

Note: Merchandise export value fixed-base indices (2015 = 100).

financial crisis, over the 2011–2020 period, export volume growth remained relatively robust, although somewhat weaker than before, but export prices displayed a downward trend. Therefore, it is possible that some of the stagnation in global exports observed since the 2010s is attributable to the decline in export unit prices, especially of raw materials and intermediate goods.

As the bulk of GVC-related trade consists of intermediate goods that are needed to produce exports, the share of GVC-related trade in nominal gross trade can vary depending on changes in the relative prices of intermediate and final goods. Other things being equal, a fall in the price of intermediate goods relative to final goods can lead to a lower share of GVC-related trade.

As shown in figure 7.13, intermediate goods prices rose rapidly after the early 2000s but were flat or declining after the early 2010s until recently. In contrast, the prices of capital and consumer goods, which are final goods, grew steadily over the period. Given these trends, part of the decline in GVC-related trade in the 2010s, measured in nominal terms, can be explained by changes in relative export prices.

Also, the lack of a significant decline in the share of GVC-related trade since 2020, despite the disruptions caused by the COVID-19 pandemic and heightened geopolitical tensions, may be related to the sharp rise in raw materials and intermediate goods prices over this period. In any case, to better analyze structural changes in GVC-related trade, it is essential to develop and use trade statistics in real terms rather than rely on nominal data, as is often the case.

FIGURE 7.13. **Changes in US Producer Prices by Type of Goods**

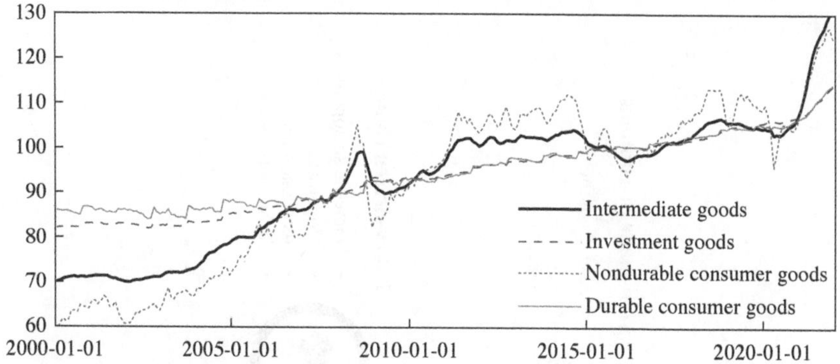

Source: Federal Reserve Economic Data.

Note: Monthly data (not seasonally adjusted) of US producer price index (2015 = 100).

In summary, the recent slowdown in GVCs is due importantly to demand shocks following the global financial crisis. Historically, the elasticity of exports to GDP tends to decline during economic downturns.[8] However, the decline in GVC-related trade also appears to be partly due to changes in relative prices between intermediate and final goods. In addition, the growth of China's domestic demand and the servicification of manufacturing are notable factors in the changing structure of GVCs. More recently, supply shocks such as the pandemic, geopolitical developments including the US-China competition and regional conflicts, and the rise of protectionism have generated strains that could lead to a further contraction of GVCs. In what follows, we examine the role of these and other supply-side factors that are likely to drive structural shifts in GVCs.

Driving Forces of GVC Transformation

GVC dynamics are affected by a range of factors, such as technological innovation, changes in consumer preferences, macroeconomic conditions, the political and policy environment, regional conflicts, and natural disasters (figure 7.14). GVCs contain risk factors inherent in their geographic dispersion and organizational fragmentation. They can exhibit changes and cycles as a result of demand/supply shocks to parts of the value chain, shifts in international norms and architecture surrounding the value chain, and systemic risks arising from internal operations.[9]

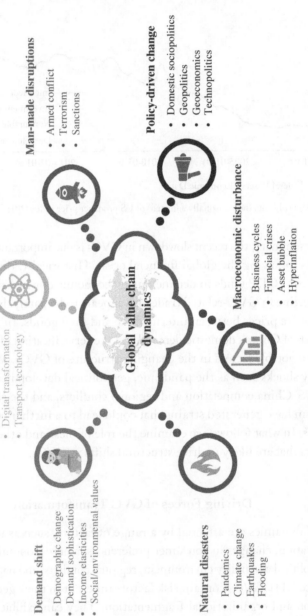

FIGURE 7.14. Sources of Risk for GVCs

Technological change
- Industry 4.0
- Digital transformation
- Transport technology

Demand shift
- Demographic change
- Demand sophistication
- Income elasticities
- Social/environmental values

Natural disasters
- Pandemics
- Climate change
- Earthquakes
- Flooding

Man-made disruptions
- Armed conflict
- Terrorism
- Sanctions

Policy-driven change
- Domestic sociopolitics
- Geopolitics
- Geoeconomics
- Technopolitics

Macroeconomic disturbance
- Business cycles
- Financial crises
- Asset bubble
- Hyperinflation

Global value chain dynamics

Source: Author's modification based on Lessard (2013).

GVCs expanded rapidly from 1990 to 2008, supported by international trade and investment liberalization and technological advances that improved global connectivity. One key factor in the expansion of GVCs has been a rules-based international system in which countries engaged in international trade and investment in accordance with the GATT/WTO multilateral norms in good faith. And the ICT revolution made it possible to coordinate complex production management across borders, which enabled firms to unbundle their production processes across GVCs. Global trade and investment expanded, generating a positive stimulus for global economic growth.

At the same time, however, the expansion of GVCs has been accompanied by stagnant middle-class incomes and rising inequality in developed countries, broad concerns that neoliberal policies are failing to deliver desired economic outcomes (including in developing regions such as Africa and Latin America), the rise of the Chinese economy and the associated global competitive tensions, and the onset of the global financial crisis, all of which have led to a backlash against globalization. The strains faced by the EU, a major testing ground for greater international integration, and challenges to the multilateral trading system of the WTO have also been part of the backdrop for a surge in protectionism.

Today, the global economy is undergoing potentially transformative change due to a variety of factors ranging from protectionism and geopolitical shifts to disruptive new technologies to climate change. They will affect offshoring patterns and GVCs and create new challenges for the growth and resilience of supply chains.

An Era of Deglobalization?

There is currently an active debate about whether the world has entered an era of deglobalization. The slowdown in international trade and direct investment since the global financial crisis has led some to argue that the global economy is de-globalizing. The COVID-19 pandemic and the war in Ukraine have exposed the vulnerability of GVCs to shocks and added fuel to the fire of those who claim that globalization has gone too far.

Globalization refers to the process of increasing integration and interdependence between countries. It is a multifaceted phenomenon spanning economic, social, and political aspects. Claims that globalization is in retreat that are based solely on the slowdown in international trade and investment miss the other dimensions of globalization.[10] From an economic perspective alone, globalization encompasses not only the expansion of trade in goods and services but also the increased international movement of labor, capital, and technological knowledge. In fact, with rapid digital transformation, the pattern of cross-border transactions is gradually shifting from traditional trade in goods to trade in digital services, data, and knowledge. Digital trade and cross-border data flows have been growing rapidly, giving globalization an increasingly digital character.

The number of internet users worldwide grew from about 1 billion in 2005 to 5.3 billion in 2022 (figure 7.15), and about two-thirds of the world's population now uses the internet. As of 2022, social media users worldwide numbered 4.6 billion.[11] The number of e-commerce users purchasing goods and services from overseas companies had already exceeded 3.8 billion in 2018.[12]

The growing demand for digital services in areas such as online streaming video, music, education, sports, and games has led to a dramatic increase in the amount of data flowing across borders. Global data bandwidth is estimated to have grown from about 155 terabytes in 2015 to 1,227 terabytes in 2022. The growth in data bandwidth is particularly significant in developing countries, where it increased 11.6 times over the 2015–2022 period, outpacing the 6.7-fold increase in developed countries.

In terms of international labor flows, the share of migrants in the global population increased from 2.9 percent in 2005 to 3.6 percent in 2020, with faster growth in the period since the global financial crisis than before (figure 7.16). Global tourist arrivals also increased sharply from the early 2010s up to the time of the COVID-19 outbreak.

Further evidence that globalization is not in retreat can be found in the degree of cross-country convergence of price levels. O'Rourke and Williamson (2002) argue that the only irrefutable evidence that globalization is taking place is a decline in the international dispersion of commodity prices, or what might be called commodity price convergence. The law of one price holds that market integration induces convergence in prices of the same goods. On the other hand, price dispersion persists when trade barriers are high and markets are fragmented.

In figure 7.17, we present data on convergence of price levels across countries, using OECD's comparative price level data. Comparative price level indices are the ratios of purchasing power parities for private final consumption expenditure to market exchange rates. They provide measures of differences in price levels between countries. We use two measures of convergence: the coefficient of variation and the standard deviation.

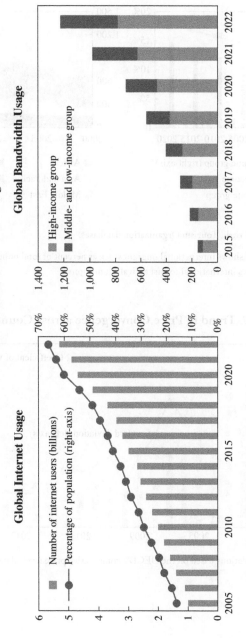

FIGURE 7.15. Trends in International ICT Usage

Global Internet Usage

Global Bandwidth Usage

High-income group

Middle- and low-income group

Number of internet users (billions)

Percentage of population (right-axis)

Source: International Telecommunication Union database.

Note: Global bandwidth usage is in terabytes.

FIGURE 7.16. Trends in International Labor and Tourist Movement

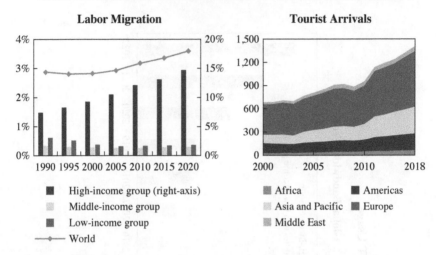

Source: UN and UN World Tourism Organization databases.

Note: Left-hand panel shows international migrant stock as percent of total population. Right-hand panel shows international tourist arrivals in millions.

FIGURE 7.17. Trend in Price Convergence across Countries

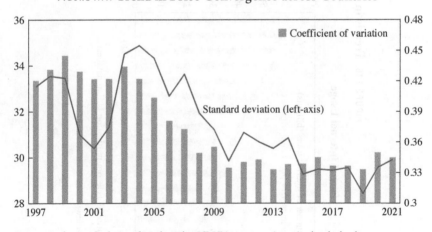

Source: Author's calculations based on the OECD's comparative price levels database.

The former is measured as the standard deviation of prices divided by the mean price and can be used to track convergence relative to the mean price. The standard deviation measure can be used to track absolute convergence of prices.[13]

As shown in the figure, price convergence proceeded at a rapid pace in the 2000s but stalled somewhat in the 2010s, as measured by the coefficient of variation. However, in terms of absolute convergence (measured by the standard deviation), we see that price convergence continued in the latter period. Overall, the evidence on price convergence seems to suggest a continuing process of globalization.

So far, we have analyzed actual developments in international flows and prices to show that the global economy is still in a process of de facto globalization. However, the picture with respect to de jure globalization, that is, developments in policies and conditions that shape globalization and will affect its future course, is more worrisome. Protectionism has been on the rise in recent years, with countries resorting to various types of explicit or disguised barriers to trade. There has been a surge in the use of nationalist industrial policies, especially in sectors related to more advanced technologies. The COVID-19 pandemic and the Russia-Ukraine war have revealed the exposure of GVCs to risks of disruption, prompting countries to consider alternative supply chains (near-shoring, friend-shoring, reshoring) to safeguard their economic security. The rise of economic power rivalry between the United States and China casts a big shadow over the world trade and investment system. Today, trade policy is increasingly being influenced by political and security interests, as well as by how countries approach matters such as climate change and labor rights. These developments will affect not only whether globalization continues to advance but also its pattern. For example, there is growing concern about globalization becoming more fragmented and the cost to the world economy that might entail.[14]

US–China Rivalry

Since the mid-twentieth century, the United States has led the way in creating and maintaining a free-trade regime based on the GATT/WTO multilateral system. For the first time in history, nearly every country in the world agreed on the basic principles of free trade and sought to abide by them in good faith. By opening up its domestic market, the United States was able to spur other countries to liberalize trade and investment, and this in turn allowed the US economy to benefit from expanded markets abroad and lower costs at home. In the process, the United States revitalized the international division of labor by inducing China to open up its economy to international trade.

Under a more open trade regime, China has emerged as the world's manufacturing factory, taking advantage of its abundant and cheap labor, to achieve three decades of nearly double-digit economic growth. But China's state-led capitalism has led to controversies over its trade practices, considered to give an unfair advantage to Chinese firms, and infringement of intellectual property rights. The United States has called for reforms in China's policies, including making its financial and services markets more open, strengthening intellectual property protection, and reducing state subsidies.

Economic tensions between the United States and China began to intensify in the 2010s. The influx of imports from China and outsourcing to China were blamed for job losses, wage stagnation, and a surge in inequality in the United States. China's rising clout in the world economy increasingly led to a rivalry with the United States for global economic power. Also, China's political system was viewed as a threat to US democratic values. Concerns about China's unfair trade practices, technology theft, and human rights abuses triggered trade restrictions and economic sanctions against the country.

The current US-China hegemonic competition is reminiscent of the situation in the nineteenth century when Britain tried to curb the technological development of emerging competitors, notably Germany and the United States, by imposing restrictions on the export of capital goods and the movement of technical personnel. Despite Britain's efforts, the international trade network underwent a rapid restructuring, with the United States at the center.[15]

From a historical perspective, the current state of the global economy looks somewhat like that around 1914, when the first wave of globalization ended. Similarities include the emergence of competing global powers, rising protectionism, shifts in major energy sources, anti-immigrant sentiment, and elevated security concerns. On the other hand, there are also differences, such as lower trade barriers, higher interdependence through GVCs and the ICT revolution, more developed global capital markets, and greater servicification of manufacturing and trade in today's global economy. The hyperconnectedness that now exists between countries suggests that a large-scale economic disconnection, as in the past, is unlikely. Instead, a coexistence of cooperation, competition, and conflict based on weaponized interdependence is more likely.

In any case, the race for technological supremacy between the United States and China will be an important factor affecting GVCs. Friendshoring or reshoring could lead to the fractionalization of GVCs to some extent. However, an across-the-board decoupling of GVCs is unlikely. What seems more likely is a selective decoupling of some strategic industries, such as semiconductors, vehicle batteries, and critical minerals (that is, "a small yard and high fence" strategy). In particular, the pressure to reorganize supply chains is likely to affect more those industries that involve dual-use technologies, where technologies are used not only for commercial purposes but also for military applications.

Digital Transformation

Digital transformation refers to the creation of new business models through the use of digital technologies based on mobile, cloud, and digital platforms and, more recently, artificial intelligence (AI), going a step further than the digitization of data or the digitalization of operations (figure 7.18). Digital transformation is expected to drive further production automation and customization, with potentially important implications for GVCs.

Previous advances in digital technologies have enabled firms to coordinate complex production management across borders through the digitization of data and operations, which in turn has encouraged them to unbundle their production processes and engage in GVCs. But digital transformation goes further and could affect supply chains in different ways. Inevitably, there is uncertainty about the full range of impacts of the latest innovations. Depending on the nature, scope, and intensity of digital transformation, it can spur the expansion of GVC networks, but it can also act as a disincentive to participate in GVCs.

First, the development of new digital technologies can boost GVC networks by further lowering the costs of communication and coordination among firms. Digital transformation is likely to promote customized, multivariant production, which could accelerate GVC reorganization and the servicification of manufacturing. It can make a wider range of services deliverable across borders.[16] It can also expand opportunities for small-scale exports, promoting the participation of small and medium-size enterprises in GVCs.

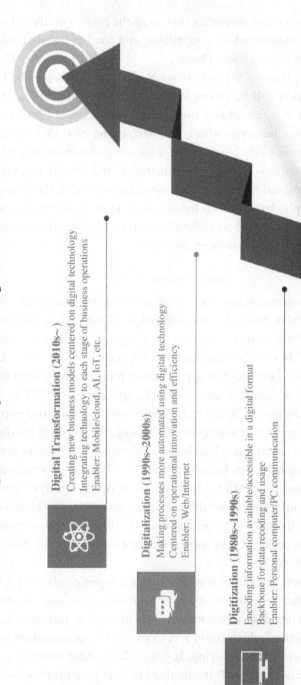

FIGURE 7.18. Digitization, Digitalization, and Digital Transformation

Digital Transformation (2010s~)
Creating new business models centered on digital technology
Integrating technology to each stage of business operations
Enabler: Mobile/cloud, AI, IoT, etc.

Digitalization (1990s~2000s)
Making processes more automated using digital technology
Centered on operational innovation and efficiency
Enabler: Web/Internet

Digitization (1980s~1990s)
Encoding information available/accessible in a digital format
Backbone for data recoding and usage
Enabler: Personal computer/PC communication

Source: Author's construction.

Second, given that one key motivation behind the GVC business model is to reduce labor costs, increased automation of production, by allowing further replacement of labor by machines, may reduce the incentive to engage in GVCs. At the same time, as automation helps a firm raise its productivity and increase its optimal scale, foreign outsourcing of intermediate goods may increase.[17]

Third, digital transformation could shorten the length of supply chains by encouraging the near-shoring or reshoring of production. Enhanced by the latest innovations such as AI, the Internet of Things, and 3D printing, it may facilitate mass customization. In this case, the location choice in the value chain becomes more about proximity to customers than labor cost levels. Also, in a platform economy where economies of scale from a larger network of customers are important, regional GVC networks may be formed around countries with large domestic markets and good digital infrastructure.

Digital transformation serves as a mechanism to create new types of trade and business models, but in the process of doing so, it can also increase trade frictions between countries, on issues such as the protection of privacy, cybersecurity, regulation of cross-border data flows, digital taxation, and competition policy. The expansion of digital trade transactions is accompanied by an increase in the flow of personal and confidential data that raises concerns about privacy and cybersecurity, which can prompt regulatory responses that, depending on their design, erect barriers to digital trade. With the expansion of non-face-to-face digital services, the market dominance of platform companies that generate profits without a fixed business location can grow, compounding the challenge of preventing tax erosion through income shifting. Unfair practices and cross-border competition policy issues in global digital markets and intellectual property protection also are matters that confront policymakers. Cross-border transfer of digital technologies could face increased barriers, as has recently been the case with some advanced digital technologies.

Climate Change

GVCs can affect climate change through several channels.[18] First, since GVCs are associated with longer distances between countries in the distribution network, they can entail greater emission of greenhouse gases from transportation. Second, participation in GVCs accelerates the growth of the global energy footprint, in which stronger backward linkages can increase

energy use. Third, international carbon leakage, which refers to the relocation of production to countries with less stringent climate policies, leads to
burden-shifting of emissions and can undermine climate-mitigation efforts.
Fourth, the cost-benefit of GVCs can lead to overproduction and excessive
waste, such as in electronics and plastics. Even so, GVCs can also help
reduce climate risks by improving productive efficiency through trade and
by diffusing environmentally friendly technologies and standards.

The current push for the green agenda by governments as well as by
private actors is driving a reorganization of the supply chains toward greater
sustainability. Companies are shifting from the traditional practice of passively complying with environmental regulations to actively engaging in
innovation to reduce environmental risks. One concern is that some of the
public policy responses to combat climate change, motivated by political and
protectionist reasons, could disrupt supply chains, such as domestic content
requirements for electric vehicles and renewable energy products.

As carbon neutrality becomes important, global demand for key minerals essential to the production of renewable energy is rising (figure 7.19).
For instance, electric vehicles require more than six times the use of key
minerals compared to vehicles with internal combustion engines. Renewable
energy such as solar and wind power requires more than three times the
use of key minerals compared to fossil fuel energy generation. If we are to
achieve net-zero carbon emissions in 2050, the total production value
of these minerals in 2040 would need to be more than four times that
in 2021.[19]

In contrast to the surge in demand for key minerals, the development of
new mines is likely to be limited, which can exacerbate the global supply-
demand imbalance. In developed countries, environmental regulations make
it more difficult to develop new mines. Developing countries could produce
more but, given the long time it takes to explore and develop mines and
the often-low probability of commercial success, the global market for core
minerals is likely to be tight in the period ahead.

The current production and processing of key minerals is heavily concentrated in a few countries, notably China, and a resurgence of resource
nationalism can increase risks to global supply chains for these minerals. The
United States and countries in Europe are stepping up efforts to strengthen
their domestic production capabilities and establish international cooperative
systems centered on allies. Nevertheless, ensuring reliable supply chains in
core minerals will be an important challenge in the coming years.

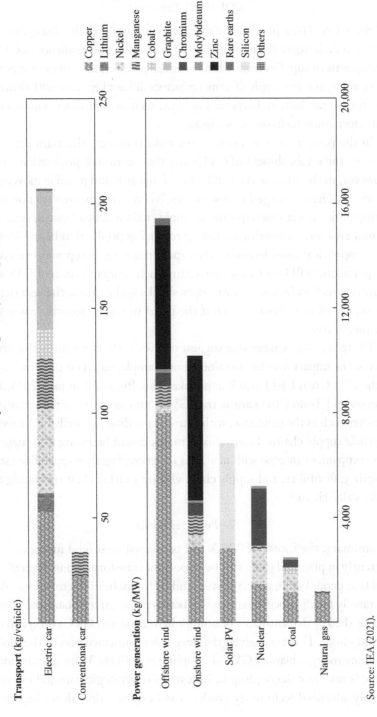

FIGURE 7.19. Key Mineral Inputs by Energy Source

Source: IEA (2021).

Note: kg = kilogram; MW = megawatt. Steel and aluminum are not included.

COVID-19 Pandemic

As the COVID-19 pandemic caused severe supply chain disruptions, it served to underscore the importance of the stability and resilience of GVCs. Disruptions in supplies from China affected production in many countries, for example, and the supply of semiconductors did not kept pace with demand, resulting in production delays for key items such as electronics, automobiles, and information technology products.

In the past, market access and cost reduction were the main determinants of the establishment of GVCs and the location of production bases. However, in the wake of the pandemic, biohazards and possible movement restrictions have emerged as new factors. Many governments are now preparing policy initiatives to promote supply chain independence in strategic sectors and core industries, including reshoring production bases. Alongside geopolitical considerations, the experience with disruptions caused by the pandemic will be a factor motivating such reorganization of GVCs as countries seek to insure against major shocks and increase the security of the supply of vital inputs—even if the gains in supply security come at a significant cost.[20]

There are some studies that suggest that while the pandemic will disrupt GVCs, the impact may be contained. For example, based on the experience of the 2011 Great East Japan Earthquake, Zhu, Ito, and Tomiura (2016) and Matous and Todo (2017) argue that GVCs may not contract after natural disasters such as the pandemic, with firms responding primarily by diversifying their supply chains. International management literature also suggests that companies can cope with new risks by leveraging their capabilities such as agility, flexibility, and supply chain visibility rather than realigning the entire value chain.[21]

The Future of GVCs

In summary, the future of GVCs will be shaped by several forces that are currently in play, and there will be important transformations. Overall, we find that geopolitical, geoeconomic, and technopolitical factors, especially the rapidly building hegemonic rivalry between the United States and China, will be the key determinants of how globalization and GVCs evolve in the period ahead. However, given the deep interconnectedness of the global economy today, a blanket GVC decoupling is unlikely. What appears more likely is selective decoupling in industries of strategic national interest, notably advanced technology products and critical minerals for high-tech industries and renewable energy. The full potential impact of digital transformation, particularly that of the latest wave of innovations, is still rather uncertain. But it will certainly change business models and practices, create new types of international transactions, and reshape the value chains.

GVCs are expected to be reorganized in different ways, depending upon industrial characteristics and geopolitical and geoeconomic considerations. These may range from reshoring to diversification and from regionalization to replication.[22] While the GVC network for traditional industries is likely to remain relatively stable, the pressure to reorganize supply chains will be much stronger in high-tech industries related to the quest of major countries for technological supremacy.

Conclusion

In this chapter, we have analyzed the changing patterns of GVCs and discussed factors that could have major implications for their future configuration. The slowdown in GVC-related trade to date has been driven largely by the recession and growth slowdown following the global financial crisis, falling relative prices of intermediate goods, and structural changes in the Chinese economy. Despite the shocks experienced, including the COVID-19 pandemic, the global economy and value chains remain quite resilient. More recently, however, the rise of geopolitical tensions, hegemonic rivalries for geoeconomic power and control of advanced technologies, and increased protectionism have created important new risks for the future of GVCs.

The risks in the current global conjuncture necessitate a renewed commitment to global cooperation. Today's challenges, from strengthening the resilience of GVCs to combating climate change to harnessing the powerful new technologies, are best met through multilateral engagement, not aggressive unilateralism. A key need in this context is a new form of multilateralism that maintains and augments an open, rules-based world trading order.

The WTO, established as the mainstay of trade multilateralism, has in recent years fallen short of playing its due role in the changing landscape of globalization. A critical shortcoming of the WTO system in the current trade climate is its practice of an all-or-nothing approach to multilateral negotiations,[23] that is, nothing is agreed to until everything is agreed to, and by every member country. While this consensus and single-undertaking approach has been instrumental in promoting the liberalization of the global trade system in the past, it has limitations in the current context of increased challenges to broad trade liberalization and divergent interests among countries.

An alternative approach is to enable a subset of WTO members who are willing to move forward on certain issues to enter into plurilateral agreements within the WTO framework, as well as encourage their extension over time to other members when they are ready to join, eventually achieving broader multilateral agreements.[24] Such a "club of clubs" approach within the WTO system could help maintain the centrality of the WTO in trade matters by discouraging the proliferation of conflicting arrangements and rules outside the WTO's legal framework.

Plurilateral agreements among WTO members could be instrumental in strengthening the resilience of GVCs. An example is the Supply Chain Agreement negotiated by members of the Indo-Pacific Economic Framework for Prosperity (IPEF) in May 2023. This was the first plurilateral GVC agreement between countries at different stages of economic development.[25] It provides for the establishment of several bodies to facilitate cooperation among the IPEF partners on supply chain issues, such as the Supply Chain Council and the Supply Chain Crisis Response Network. They aim to improve the efficiency, transparency, and resilience of supply chains through collaborative actions. The IPEF was designed to be open, inclusive, and flexible; its larger, global impact will depend on adherence to those principles.

As geopolitical tensions threaten international trade and GVCs, it is important to stress that a rules-based multilateral trade order is an essential prerequisite for geopolitical stability. The experience of the early twentieth century, when fragmentation into economic blocs contributed to a breakdown of global political and economic stability, is instructive in this context. The reason why a multilateral trading system was established after World War II was not only to increase economic growth and consumer welfare through freer trade but also to promote geopolitical stability by establishing a multilateral cooperative order in economic relations between countries. In recent years, rising economic nationalism and an emphasis on economic security have led to a tendency to view economic matters between countries as a zero-sum game. But rules-based international trade is a win-win game for all and is also an underpinning of geopolitical stability.

NOTES

1. Grossman and Rossi-Hansberg (2008).

2. World Inequality Lab (2022).

3. The WTO system allows for actions to address these issues under GATT Articles 21 (security exceptions) and 20 (general exceptions), but members have rarely used these provisions.

4. GVC-related trade refers to the value of traded goods that cross at least two national borders, while traditional trade refers to the value of goods and services that cross only one border (Borin and Mancini 2019).

5. Examples of international input-output tables used for this purpose are the OECD's TiVA database, the Groningen Growth and Development Centre's World Input-Output Database (WIOD), and the Asian Development Bank's Multiregional Input-Output (ADB-MRIO) database.

6. Asian Factory 6 countries include Indonesia, Japan, Korea, Malaysia, Philippines, and Taiwan.

7. Lodefalk (2013) and Miroudot and Cadestin (2017).

8. Auboin and Borino (2018).

9. Lessard (2013).

10. Moreover, there is a natural upper limit to the ratio of trade to GDP or the share of GVC-related trade in total trade, which makes hyper-globalization unsustainable. Antras (2020) argues that the current "slowbalization" is a kind of adjustment against the hyperglobalization seen in the period prior to the global financial crisis.

11. www.wearesocial.com. Users may not represent unique individuals.

12. Congressional Research Service (2019).

13. See (Rönnbäck 2009) for the pros and cons of these two measures.

14. IMF (2023).

15. Zinkina et al. (2019).

16. Baldwin (2019).

17. Antras (2020).

18. Solingen, Weng, and Xu (2021).

19. IEA (2021).

20. For example, Javorcik et al. (2022) estimate that friend-shoring may lead to real GDP losses of up to 4.6 percent of global GDP.

21. Miroudot (2020).

22. UNCTAD (2020).

23. Levy (2006, 2010); Lawrence (2006); Bacchus (2023).

24. Bacchus (2023).

25. The IPEF currently has fourteen members: Australia, Brunei Darussalam, Fiji India, Indonesia, Japan, Korea, Malaysia, New Zealand, Philippines, Singapore, Thailand, the United States, and Vietnam. The IPEF membership accounts for 40 percent of world GDP and 28 percent of world trade. Besides

supply chains, the IPEF includes three other pillars: trade, clean energy, and taxation. The IPEF members are not required to join all pillars.

REFERENCES

Antras, P. 2020. "De-globalisation? Global Value Chains in the Post-COVID-19 Age." NBER Working Paper 28115. National Bureau of Economic Research, Cambridge, MA.

Auboin, M., and F. Borino. 2018. "The Falling Elasticity of Global Trade to Economic Activity: Testing the Demand Channel." Working Paper 7228. Center for Economic Studies and ifo Institute (CESifo), Munich.

Bacchus, J. 2023. "The Future of the WTO: Multilateral or Plurilateral?" Cato Policy Analysis No. 947. Cato Institute, Washington, DC.

Baldwin, R. 2019. *The Globotics Upheaval: Globalization, Robotics, and the Future of Work.* Oxford: Oxford University Press.

Borin, A., and M. Mancini. 2019. "Measuring What Matters in Global Value Chains and Value-Added Trade." Policy Research Working Paper 8804. World Bank, Washington, DC.

Borin, A., M. Mancini, and D. Taglioni. 2021. "Measuring Exposure to Risk in Global Value Chains," Policy Research Working Paper 9785. World Bank, Washington, DC.

Congressional Research Service. 2019. "International Trade and E-commerce." May 1.

Grossman, G., and E. Rossi-Hansberg. 2008. "Trading Tasks: A Simple Theory of Offshoring." *American Economic Review* 98 (5): 1978–97.

International Energy Agency (IEA). 2021. "The Role of Critical Minerals in Clean Energy Transitions." World Energy Outlook Special Report. Paris.

International Monetary Fund (IMF). 2023. "Geoeconomic Fragmentation and the Future of Multilateralism." Staff Discussion Note 2023/001. International Monetary Fund, Washington, DC.

Javorcik, S., L. Kitzmueller, H. Schweiger, and A. Yildirim. 2022. "Economic Costs of Friend-Shoring." EBRD Working Paper 274. European Bank for Reconstruction and Development, London.

Kee, H. L., and H. Tang. 2016. "Domestic Value Added in Exports: Theory and Firm Evidence from China." *American Economic Review* 106 (6): 1402–36.

Lawrence, R. 2006. "Rulemaking Amidst Growing Diversity: A Club-of-Clubs Approach to WTO Reform and New Issue Selection." *Journal of International Economic Law* 9 (4): 823–35.

Lessard, D. 2013. "Uncertainty and Risk in Global Supply Chains." In *Global Value Chains in a Changing World*, edited by D. Elms and P. Low. New York: World Trade Organization.

Levy, P. 2006. "Do We Need an Undertaker for the Single Undertaking: Considering the Angles of Variable Geometry." In *Economic Development and Multilateral Trade Cooperation*, edited by Simon Evenett and Bernard Hoekman. New York: Palgrave-McMillan and World Bank.

———. 2010. "Alternatives to Consensus at the WTO." American Enterprise Institute, Washington, DC.

Lodefalk, M. 2013. "Servicification of Manufacturing—Evidence from Sweden." *International Journal of Economics and Business Research* 6 (1): 87–113.

Matous, P., and Y. Todo. 2017. "Analyzing the Coevolution of Inter-organizational Networks and Organizational Performance: Automakers' Production Networks in Japan." *Applied Network Science* 2 (1): 1–24.

Miroudot, S. 2020. "The Reorganization of Global Value Chains in East Asia before and after COVID-19." *East Asian Economic Review* 24 (4): 389–416.

Miroudot, S., and C. Cadestin. 2017. "Services in Global Value Chains: From Inputs to Value-Creating Activities." OECD Trade Policy Paper 197. Organization for Economic Cooperation and Development, Paris.

O'Rourke, K., and J. Williamson. 2002. "When Did Globalisation Begin?" *European Review of Economic History* 6 (1): 23–50.

Rönnbäck, K. 2009. "Integration of Global Commodity Markets in the Early Modern Era." *European Review of Economic History* 13 (1): 95–120.

Solingen, E., B. Meng, and A. Xu. 2021. "Rising Risks to Global Value Chains." *Global Value Chain Development Report 2021*: 134–78.

United Nations Conference on Trade and Development (UNCTAD). 2020. *World Investment Report 2020: International Production Beyond the Pandemic*. New York and Geneva: United Nations.

World Inequality Lab. 2021. *World Inequality Report 2022*. Paris.

Zhu, L., K. Ito, and E. Tomiura. 2016. "Global Sourcing in the Wake of Disaster: Evidence from the Great East Japan Earthquake." RIETI Discussion Paper Series 16-E-089. Research Institute of Economy, Trade, and Industry, Tokyo.

Zinkina, J., D. Christian, L. Grinin, I. Ilyin et al. 2019. *A Big History of Globalization: The Emergence of a Global World System*. New York: Springer.

PART IV

New Financial Dynamics

EIGHT

The Implications of Digital Technologies
for the International Monetary System

ESWAR PRASAD

New financial technologies have the potential to mitigate the substantial frictions that now cloud cross-border financial transactions. Some of the complications, especially the involvement of multiple currencies, cannot be eliminated by new technologies, but improvements in the speed, transparency, and costs of such transactions can help reduce the impact of these frictions. These changes will be a boon to exporters and importers, migrants sending remittances back to their home countries, investors looking for international diversification opportunities for their savings, and firms looking to raise capital.

Diminishing frictions in cross-border capital flows will help create a more global market for capital but could add to the volatility of those flows, further complicating the jobs of central bankers, especially in emerging-market economies (EMEs). The emergence of new conduits for cross-border flows will facilitate not just international commerce but also illicit financial flows, raising new challenges for regulators and governments.

New forms of money and new channels for moving funds within and between economies could have implications for international capital flows, exchange rates, and the structure of the international monetary system. The proliferation of channels for cross-border flows will make it increasingly difficult for national authorities to control these flows. Emerging-market economies, in particular, will face challenges in managing the volatility of capital flows and exchange rates because these economies are often subject to the whiplash effects of the whims of foreign investors. Surges in capital inflows can lead to higher inflation and rising exchange rates, which tend to hurt the competitiveness of their exports in foreign markets. When a country loses favor with investors, it can lose access to foreign funds and face a debilitating plunge in the value of its currency. Investor sentiments tend to be influenced not just by what is happening in EMEs themselves but also by interest rates in the United States and other major advanced economies. New channels for capital flows into and out of emerging markets will exacerbate such volatility and expose these economies to more significant spillovers from the monetary policy actions of the world's major central banks.

Neither the advent of central bank digital currencies (CBDCs) nor the lowering of barriers to international financial flows will do much by themselves to reorder the international monetary system or the balance of power among major currencies. Currencies such as the US dollar that are dominant stores of value will remain so because that dominance rests not just on the issuing country's economic size and financial market depth but also on a strong institutional foundation that is essential for maintaining investors' trust in a currency. For all its flaws, the US institutional framework—including a trusted and independent central bank, an independent judiciary that maintains the rule of law, and a system of checks and balances that restrains the unbridled power of any branch of government—has stood the test of time. While the dollar's dominance as a payment currency might erode, it will remain the dominant global safe haven currency for a long time to come.

International Payments

The transfer of funds across institutions globally is now intermediated through SWIFT, the Society for Worldwide Interbank Financial Telecommunication. SWIFT does not actually transfer funds; rather, it provides a financial messaging service that connects more than 11,000 financial institutions in virtually every country in the world through a common messaging protocol. Before SWIFT was founded in 1973, messages initiating international payments were sent as full sentences through Telex, posing security risks and creating room for human error at both ends of a transaction. The main components of the original SWIFT services included a messaging platform, a computer system to validate and route messages, and a set of message standards. The standards allowed for the automated transmission of messages, unfettered by differences in languages or computer systems across countries. These elements, in updated forms, remain the crux of SWIFT's operations.

SWIFT now faces competition from alternative international payment messaging systems that offer similar services at a lower cost.[1] Its major advantage over potential competitors is that it has become a widely accepted and trusted protocol, but this might not be a durable business model. Indeed, many countries such as China and Russia are setting up their own payment systems to reduce their reliance on foreign ones and in the process opening a gateway to a new international payment system. In other words, such countries could conceivably link their individual payment systems, routing bilateral international transactions through these rather than relying on SWIFT and the institutions that use it for messaging.

SWIFT is subject to political as well as technological risks, adding momentum to the search for alternatives. The United States has used the threat of punitive actions against SWIFT officials and banks represented on its board of directors to force the organization to stop providing service to central banks and financial institutions in countries that are subject to US financial sanctions.[2] In turn, the threat of losing access to SWIFT is a powerful one, as it would impose a huge economic cost on countries by cutting them off from the international financial system and hindering their trade.

The SWIFT system is also exposed to cybersecurity risks and faces technical challenges as well. The system passes payments through a number of nodes, slowing down the transaction process, but cryptocurrencies and other payment systems that use distributed ledger technologies (DLTs) might bypass the need for routing through multiple nodes. Moreover, vexed by the system's vulnerability to US pressure, many central banks, including the European Central Bank (ECB), have been studying the potential for expanding the interoperability of digital currencies for cross-border trade.

The central banks of Canada, Singapore, Hong Kong, and Thailand are also exploring new initiatives to process cross-border transactions independently of SWIFT.

The international payment messaging system is almost certainly an area ripe for disruptive evolution. For all its advantages, expansive reach, and attempts to innovate to stay ahead of the competition, SWIFT remains vulnerable to shifting political and technological winds. In fact, the very need for such common messaging protocols might be obviated by new financial technologies. As one example, the Interbank Information Network, a blockchain-based messaging and payment system being developed by a consortium of banks led by J. P. Morgan Chase, might altogether eliminate the need for SWIFT. This peer-to-peer network runs on Quorum, a permissioned variant of the Ethereum blockchain, and has attracted more than 400 participating banks across the world. More important, there are government-backed initiatives underway to create payment systems that could end up sidelining SWIFT.

A number of countries, even those not directly affected by US sanctions, have begun developing alternatives to SWIFT and international payment systems that rely on its messaging services. For instance, China's Cross-Border Interbank Payment System (CIPS), which commenced operations in 2015, offers clearing and settlement services for cross-border payments in renminbi. CIPS has the capacity to easily integrate with other national payment systems, which could help in promoting the international use of the renminbi by making it easier to use the currency for cross-border payments. CIPS currently uses SWIFT as its main messaging channel, but it could eventually serve as a more comprehensive system that includes messaging services using an alternative protocol. CIPS has adopted the latest internationally accepted message standard (ISO 20022) and also allows messages to be transmitted in either Chinese or English, with a standardization system that facilitates easy translations between the two.

In short, then, new financial technologies are likely to hasten the disruption of existing international messaging and payment systems.[3] The days of SWIFT's uncontested dominance of international payment messaging are numbered, which could have knock-on effects on the dollar's dominance of international payments. Admittedly, though, the ability of new payment messaging systems to ensure security and to be scaled up to handle large volumes while staying on the right side of domestic and international regulations is not yet assured and could take some years to come to fruition.

Vehicle Currencies and Exchange Rates

"Vehicle currencies" such as the US dollar play an important role in international trade as they serve as widely accepted units of account for denominating trade and financial transactions and as mediums of exchange for making payments to settle those transactions.[4] The US dollar is the dominant vehicle currency, with a few others such as the euro, the British pound sterling, and the Japanese yen also playing this role.

As EMEs grow larger and their financial markets develop, the cost of trading their currencies for other emerging-market currencies is likely to decline. New financial technologies that make international payments quicker and easier to track will also play a role. Risks arising from exchange rate volatility are mitigated if a payment for a trade transaction can be settled instantaneously rather than over a matter of days, which is typically the case now. A longer-term and perhaps less likely outcome is the emergence of cryptocurrencies, or at least decentralized payment systems, that function as mediums of exchange in international transactions. These forces, to varying extents, will diminish reliance on vehicle currencies.

As the role of vehicle currencies declines, many more bilateral exchange rates will become consequential for cross-border transactions, including exchange rates between EME currencies. Financial markets do provide instruments for hedging foreign exchange risk, but these are expensive. Changes in international payment systems that allow for faster payment and settlement will reduce the horizons over which it is necessary to hedge against exchange rate movements. For trade in many products, where contracts are negotiated weeks or months in advance, these changes will amount to only a modest change in the horizon of hedging needs. For financial transactions that have shorter horizons, there could be material decreases in hedging requirements and the associated costs. In some cases, instantaneous payment and settlement of transactions can remove the risks to revenues from short-term exchange rate volatility even without involving the costs of hedging.

What if one day it were possible to use a cryptocurrency such as Bitcoin or a private stablecoin for denominating and settling cross-border transactions? In that event, the only exchange rates that would matter would be those between domestic currencies and the relevant cryptocurrency. If the same cryptocurrency could be used both within and across countries, even that exchange rate might have less relevance. These are fanciful but unlikely outcomes, given the volatility of unbacked cryptocurrencies' values and the likelihood that CBDCs and official stablecoins will compete with each other only as mediums of exchange, with their values tightly linked.

For the foreseeable future, exchange rates for each country's currency relative to those of their trading partners, as well as major currencies that serve as units of account and mediums of exchange, will remain important in the functioning of the international monetary system. In short, while new financial technologies could over time influence the relative importance of various currencies in the denomination and settlement of cross-border transactions, the basic mechanics of foreign exchange markets are unlikely to be altered significantly.

A Global Market for Financial Capital

The promise of financial globalization was that it would allow capital to be allocated to its most productive uses worldwide. This would be good for firms looking to finance their investments and working capital requirements as they would no longer be constrained by domestic savings. It would also give savers the ability to invest in financial markets around the world.

These potential benefits should be greater for developing countries. Firms in these countries have a harder time obtaining financing because domestic savings levels tend to be lower, in part because people there are less wealthy. Moreover, savers have limited opportunities to make relatively safe investments that offer higher returns than bank deposits. Stock and bond markets tend to be small and volatile. Investing in foreign assets could help savers achieve better returns and also diversify their portfolios, but because their savings tend to be modest, it is cost-inefficient to look for investment opportunities abroad. When banks and investment managers in such countries offer opportunities for foreign investments, they tend to do so only for select wealthy clients who have more money to invest and can afford significant fees. For all these reasons, easier and cheaper access to international financial markets, reflected in larger cross-border flows of capital, would be good for both firms and households in poorer countries.

Two factors have constrained such flows of savings and investment across countries, especially for developing countries. First, it is costly for investors in one country to acquire information about firms in other countries, particularly if those firms happen to be small ones located in developing countries. This gives larger firms an advantage in scouring global markets for capital, further entrenching the advantages they already enjoy over smaller firms. Second, financial markets in developing countries are underdeveloped. The fact that domestic bond and equity markets are small and volatile affects not just savers looking for places to store their savings but also firms looking for capital. Small firms find it difficult to use these markets for raising capital, and they might also find it difficult to obtain bank financing if they do not have sufficient collateral.

Today, at least in principle, the first constraint is loosening, as it is now easier to obtain information about investment opportunities around the world. Fintech might soon provide a way around the second constraint—that financial markets in some countries are underdeveloped and unable to effectively channel capital to productive firms. Investing in a less-developed economy often carries much greater risk even if the potential for profit might be greater. Fintech firms could in principle help foreign investors assess risk better and also create channels for directly investing in productive firms, bypassing creaky domestic financial systems.

With rising integration of financial markets around the world and with more channels for taking money into and out of countries, there should logically be a global market for capital. If it were so, companies could tap into pools of savings from anywhere in the world, which is already the case for large corporations. For instance, Chinese companies such as Alibaba and Baidu have listed their shares on US stock exchanges, raising equity capital in the United States and giving US households and financial institutions the opportunity to invest in them through domestic rather than foreign equity exchanges. Yet issuing equity or corporate bonds abroad is a costly and complicated exercise. Foreign firms listed on US stock exchanges such as the New York Stock Exchange or NASDAQ have to meet a number of regulatory and reporting requirements, which might require changes in those firms' accounting and auditing procedures to meet US regulatory standards, in addition to having to pay accounting and legal fees to fulfill those requirements. The new financial technologies might make access to worldwide capital available to small and medium-size firms as well, through more direct and less expensive channels.

Fintech is unlikely to change the fundamental drivers of global capital flows, but by reducing explicit and covert barriers to such flows, it could influence the allocation of global capital. This could eventually set off a new wave of financial globalization and generate numerous benefits—even if it did not mean a return to the same scale of cross-border flows as in their recent heyday.

Significant changes are in store for retail investors as well. Fintech firms might eventually make it possible for retail investors to allocate part of their portfolios to stock markets around the world at a low cost. In many advanced countries, one can already do this simply by buying shares in a mutual fund that invests abroad. Such funds typically charge higher fees than funds that might invest in domestic stocks and bonds. New investment platforms are likely to reduce costs, forcing even existing investment management firms to charge lower fees.

Fintech firms are also reducing the costs of both obtaining information about foreign markets and investing in those markets. Moreover, new investment opportunities are also being opened up by technologies that allow for more efficient pooling of small individual savings accounts into larger pools that can be deployed more effectively and at lower cost.

One of the next frontiers in the Fintech evolution is likely to be the intermediation of capital flows at the retail level, enabling less-wealthy households and smaller firms in both rich and poor economies to more easily gain access to global financial markets. Diversifying one's portfolio should become easier as stock markets around the world open up to foreign investors and as the costs of transacting across national boundaries fall. Fintech firms that lower information barriers, reduce costs and other frictions in international capital movements, and create new saving and financial products are likely to experience significant demand for their services. Of course, as with any financial innovations, there will be risks and stumbles in this process, and financial regulators will face the usual tradeoffs between facilitating innovations and managing those risks. In fact, the capital flows themselves pose risks not just to individual investors but also at the country level.

Greater financial integration offers many benefits, but these potential benefits come at a price, especially for smaller and less-developed economies, which are particularly vulnerable to the whiplash effects of volatile capital flows, caused in part by monetary policy actions of the major advanced economies.[5] When the US Fed lowers rates, investors in the United States and elsewhere are willing to take on more risk to generate a better yield. When it hikes rates, money tends to flow out of emerging markets as investors opt for a decent return in a safe investment rather than a higher return in a riskier investment. Such "risk-on" and "risk-off" investor behavior leads to volatile swings in capital flows to emerging markets. To the exasperation of policymakers in these countries, they end up being subject to such volatility even when their policies are disciplined and their economies are doing well. In other words, they end up becoming collateral damage when the US Fed uses monetary policy levers to achieve its own (domestic) ends, with little regard for the effects of those policies on other economies.

New and relatively friction-free channels for cross-border financial flows could exacerbate these "spillover" effects across economies. These new channels could not only amplify financial market volatility but also transmit it more rapidly across countries. In other words, the availability of more efficient conduits for cross-border capital flows could intensify global financial cycles and all the domestic policy complications that result from them.

De jure capital account restrictions have become increasingly porous under greater pressures for capital to flow across national borders in search of yield or safety, or both, and also because financial institutions continue to expand their global footprint. This has led to rising de facto financial openness in all economies, including EMEs such as China and India, that maintain de jure capital controls. In the case of China, for instance, its large banks now have a global presence and provide channels for moving money into and out of the country more easily than when these banks' operations were primarily domestic.

Developments in financial markets and new technologies now threaten to undermine whatever capital controls remain in place. While governments around the world try to limit the use of cryptocurrencies to circumvent capital controls or for more nefarious purposes, it is unclear if and how long such measures will remain effective in the face of strong economic incentives for capital flows.[6]

Clearly, both official and private channels for cross-border capital flows are expanding. Official channels—such as the cross-border payment system on which the central banks of Canada, Singapore, and the United Kingdom have been collaborating—will make such flows easier while allowing governments to modulate these flows and reduce the risk of illegitimate financial activity.[7] Private channels, on the other hand, could become increasingly difficult to monitor and manage, especially if they are created and used by informal financial institutions that will be harder to regulate.

The existence of a privately issued stablecoin that is recognized and accepted worldwide would also affect governments' ability to control capital flows across their borders. If money can be moved electronically, without going through any financial institutions regulated by a nation's regulatory agencies, it becomes difficult for that government to control inflows and outflows of financial capital in any meaningful way.

Competing Fiat Currencies

The US dollar is by far the dominant international currency in all respects—as a unit of account, medium of exchange, and store of value.[8] A great deal of international trade, including virtually all international contracts for commodities such as oil, is denominated in dollars, far more than in any other currency. Thus, it is the main invoicing currency.[9] As noted earlier, the dollar is the leading payment currency as well—by some measures, about 40 percent of international payments are settled in dollars. The dollar is also the principal global reserve currency—roughly 60 percent of foreign exchange reserves held by the world's central banks are held in dollar-denominated assets. When firms or governments in developing countries borrow in foreign currencies, usually because foreign investors lack confidence in the value of those countries' domestic currencies, they tend to do so in dollars.

The dollar's overwhelming dominance, and the absence of any serious competition yet that might undermine this dominance, gives the United States outsize influence. In 1960, the United States accounted for about 40 percent of global GDP (at market exchange rates). By 2000, this share was down to 30 percent. In the two decades since then, as China, India, and other emerging markets have made enormous strides, this share has fallen further, to 24 percent.[10] The dollar's role in global finance and, with it, US influence on global financial markets, is far greater than its weight in the global economy.

The dollar's status as the principal global reserve currency means that the United States is able to borrow money at low interest rates from the rest of the world to finance its current account deficits. The dollar's dominance also gives the United States a powerful geopolitical tool that it does not hesitate to wield against its rivals. The dollar-centric global financial system gives US financial sanctions particular bite since they end up affecting any country or firm that has dealings of one sort or another with a US-based financial institution or that has even a secondary relationship with such institutions.

The demand for Bitcoin as a store of value rather than as a medium of exchange has stoked discussion about whether such cryptocurrencies could challenge that role of traditional reserve currencies. It is more likely that, as the underlying technologies become more stable and as better verification mechanisms are developed, such decentralized nonofficial cryptocurrencies will start playing a bigger role as mediums of exchange. Even that proposition is a tenuous one given the high levels of price volatility recently experienced by such currencies. Nevertheless, this shift could occur over time as the payment functions of cryptocurrencies take precedence over speculative interest in them, especially if private stablecoins gain more traction.

The decline in transaction costs and easier settlement of transactions across currency pairs could have a more direct and immediate impact—a decline in the role of the US dollar as a vehicle currency, as previous discussed. There are other possible changes as well. The dollar's role as a unit of account is also subject to erosion, so it is not a stretch to conceive of the denomination and settlement of contracts for oil and other commodities in other currencies, perhaps even emerging-market currencies such as the renminbi. Indeed, China's purchases of oil from Saudi Arabia are reportedly now being increasingly contracted for and settled in renminbi. China has begun issuing yuan-denominated oil futures as a way of shifting more of the financial transactions related to oil purchases and sales, including in derivatives markets, away from the dollar. Such developments are important but should be kept in proper perspective. While the very existence of yuan-denominated oil derivative contracts is a noteworthy development, this is a far cry from such contracts' playing a major role or in any significant way displacing dollar-denominated contracts.

Notwithstanding any such changes, the role of reserve currencies as stores of value is unlikely to be significantly affected. Safe financial assets—assets that are perceived as maintaining most of their principal value even in times of extreme national or global financial stress—have many attributes that cannot be matched by nonofficial cryptocurrencies.

One important characteristic of a store of value currency is *depth*. That is, there should be a large quantity of financial assets denominated in that currency, which means that both official investors such as central banks and private investors can easily acquire those assets. There is a vast amount of US Treasury securities, not to mention other dollar-denominated assets, that foreign investors can easily acquire. Another characteristic that is important for a store of value is its *liquidity*. That is, it should be possible to easily trade the asset even in large quantities. An investor should be able to count on there being sufficient numbers of buyers and sellers to facilitate such trading, even in difficult circumstances.

For an aspiring safe-haven currency, depth and liquidity in the relevant financial instruments denominated in that currency are indispensable. More important, both domestic and foreign investors tend to place their trust in such currencies during financial crises since they are backed by a powerful institutional framework, which includes such elements as an institutionalized system of checks and balances, the rule of law, and a trusted central bank.[11] These elements provide a security blanket to investors, assuring them that the value of those investments will be largely protected and that investors, both domestic and foreign, will be treated fairly. The US institutional framework has eroded somewhat in recent years, but there is no rival that can match the combination of US institutional, economic, and financial strength that underpins the dollar's dominance.

While reserve currencies might not be challenged as stores of value, digital versions of extant reserve currencies and improved cross-border transaction channels could intensify competition between reserve currencies themselves. In short, the finance-related technological developments that are underway or on the horizon portend some changes in domestic and international financial markets, but a revolution in the international monetary system is not quite in the cards for the foreseeable future.

New Safe Havens

The fervent desire of many government leaders and officials around the world to knock the US dollar off its pedestal has converged with the quest for alternative safe assets. These desires have been given new life by the emergence of cryptocurrencies and the technology underpinning them. In September 2019, Benoît Cœuré, then a member of the ECB's Governing

Council, gave a speech in which he speculated on whether a global stablecoin such as Libra "may be a contender for the Iron Throne of the dollar." He argued that "in specific circumstances, and if allowed to develop, private digital forms of money could challenge the supremacy of the US dollar more easily, and faster, than currencies issued by other sovereigns."[12]

Cœuré made two key points. First, it was no longer the case that the widespread usage of existing reserve currencies would confer on them a persistent advantage relative to new currencies. Such "network effects" usually make it hard to dislodge incumbents, but Cœuré noted that the costs of switching to new currencies are quite low in the case of retail consumer payments. Second, he argued that the factors driving international currency use are also changing and that new currencies have advantages. He noted that "it is probably easier to connect a new currency to an existing network—the case of Libra—than to build a new network on an existing currency—the case of the euro."

This line of argument suggests that international currencies could piggyback on other uses, turning on its head the conventional paradigm that a currency used for payments is then put to other uses over time. For instance, adding a payment function using a digital token or a global stablecoin to an existing messaging platform such as WhatsApp would enable direct transfers of money between users of the platform. The underlying business model, a messaging and communication service, would not be affected by these additional payment-related functions.

Stablecoin initiatives built on top of service platforms that have extensive international reach could indeed make domestic and cross-border payments, at least between individuals and small businesses, relatively seamless.[13] Thus, competition between international currencies, both new and old, could become more heated and dynamic in the future, with the advantages of incumbency no longer as powerful as they once were.[14]

Given the extensive frictions in international payments, it is certainly a plausible proposition that stablecoins could gain traction as mediums of exchange that supplement, but do not supplant, existing payment currencies. However, the dollar is least likely to be hurt by such competition. A more likely outcome is that alternative payment systems erode the shares of currencies such as the euro, the British pound sterling, and the Japanese yen, while leaving the dollar largely unscathed. After all, stablecoins pegged to the dollar would simply make it easier to gain access to the world's most dominant currency.

Moreover, it is unlikely that such stablecoins would represent alternative stores of value. Indeed, the allure of stablecoins is precisely that their value is tightly linked to existing reserve currencies in which savers and investors around the world are willing to place their trust. In short, the emergence of stablecoins linked to existing reserve currencies will reduce direct demand for those currencies for international payments but will not in any fundamental way transform the relative balance of power among the major reserve currencies.

At the August 2019 Jackson Hole conference, Mark Carney, then the governor of the Bank of England, gave a speech that spanned a broad expanse of policy issues.[15] He proposed the creation of a synthetic hegemonic currency (SHC) that would be "provided by the public sector, perhaps through a network of central bank digital currencies." He depicted the SHC as taking the form of an invoicing and payment currency whose widespread use could eventually lead central banks, investors, and financial market participants to perceive the currencies that comprised its basket as reliable reserve assets, thereby displacing the dollar's dominance in international trade and finance, including in credit markets. To achieve this objective, the basket would presumably tilt away from a large weight on the dollar.

Despite all the intentions to break free of the US dollar and the problems caused by a unipolar international monetary system, however, the viability of an SHC is likely to be limited. One reason is that setting up an SHC would require international cooperation, which is in rather short supply. Second, the economic and political stability of many of the major economies in the world seems fragile. For instance, an SHC that included the euro would be subject to persistent concerns about the centrifugal forces perpetually threatening the currency zone and the viability of its common currency. A third problem is the smaller size and lower liquidity of financial markets outside the United States and in international transactions that do not involve the dollar. Conducting transactions using an SHC would therefore be costlier, at least for the first few years, relative to transacting in dollars. It is not obvious who would bear the costs and what incentive transacting parties would have to use a costlier medium of exchange that would put them at a competitive disadvantage.

There is one potential SHC candidate in the wings—the Special Drawing Rights (SDRs) issued by the IMF. The IMF created the SDR, which it calls an international reserve asset, in 1969 to supplement the official reserves held by its member countries. One major difference between the

SDR and a national currency is that the SDR has no real backing. Unlike a central bank–issued fiat currency that has a national government's authority to levy taxes behind it, the IMF has no such power. The SDR is a unit of account for the IMF, which maintains its accounts in SDRs, and even a store of value for national central banks. It is not, however, a useful medium of exchange. Thus, the SDR is really just a composite currency, and the IMF takes pains to emphasize that "the SDR is neither a currency nor a claim on the IMF. Rather, it is a potential claim on the freely usable currencies of IMF members. SDRs can be exchanged for these currencies."[16]

Moreover, the IMF has a governance structure—determining how voting rights are distributed among countries—that remains heavily tilted toward advanced Western countries, which can collectively muster a majority of votes and therefore dominate the institution's policy decisions, a situation that does not engender a great deal of trust in the institution among the EMEs. In short, a viable new global currency issued by a multilateral organization requires a level of global cooperation that seems unrealistic for the foreseeable future. If countries could not agree on a relatively simple and costless measure to ramp up issuance of a common digital currency when the global economy faced an economic collapse, it is highly unlikely that in calmer times the major economic powers would put aside their competing interests to agree on a global currency, digital or otherwise.

Will China's CBDC Threaten the Dollar's Dominance?

The renminbi made a dramatic move onto the global financial stage after 2010, when the Chinese government started opening up China's capital account and promoting its currency through a variety of policy measures.[17] In 2016, the IMF gave the renminbi its official imprimatur as a reserve currency by including it in the SDR basket of currencies, potentially adding momentum to the progress the renminbi had already made as an international payment currency.

The renminbi has since come to be a modest player in international finance, accounting for about 2 to 3 percent of global payments intermediated through the SWIFT network in 2023.[18] Other indicators such as renminbi deposits in Hong Kong and the offshore issuance of renminbi-denominated bonds (dim sum bonds), all of which were on a rapidly rising trajectory in the first half of this decade, have fallen off sharply since 2015.

In mid-2023, the renminbi accounted for a little over 2 percent of global foreign exchange reserves, an important but still modest fraction.[19] Nevertheless, even these modest shares rank the renminbi fifth worldwide as an international payment currency and as a reserve currency.

In short, the renminbi's rise has been significant—especially for a currency issued by a country that does not have an open capital account or a market-determined exchange rate—but uneven. It has not proven to be the key challenger to the US dollar's dominance that some had expected it to be, particularly in its role as a store of value.[20]

Is China's CBDC—the eCNY—likely to be a game changer in the renminbi's putative rivalry with the US dollar or, more generally, in its status as a reserve currency? In some respects, especially regarding the technological sophistication of its retail payment systems, China has managed to leapfrog the United States. It therefore seems a plausible proposition that, with its CBDC likely to be in operation before those of other major economies, the eCNY will give the renminbi a boost in the tussle for global financial market dominance.[21]

The eCNY, in tandem with China's cross-border payment system, will eventually make it easier to use the currency for international transactions. Russia—or, for that matter, Iran and Venezuela—might now find it easier to be paid in renminbi for their oil exports to China, which means they can avoid US financial sanctions, a tempting prospect for many such governments. As the renminbi becomes more widely used, other smaller and developing countries that have strong trade and financial links with China might find it advantageous to invoice and settle their trade transactions directly in that currency.

The eCNY by itself will, however, make little or no difference to foreign investors' perception of the renminbi as a reserve currency. At a technical level, there are two major constraints on the renminbi's role as a reserve currency. The first is that capital flows into and out of the country remain subject to restrictions, even if these restrictions are being gradually dismantled. The second is that the renminbi's exchange rate is still managed by the People's Bank of China (PBC) rather than being determined by market forces. Neither of these conditions is likely to change significantly anytime soon. The Chinese government has indicated that it plans eventually to have an open capital account. Moreover, the PBC has committed to reducing its intervention in foreign exchange markets to prevent exchange rate appreciations or depreciations driven by market forces.[22]

Still, convincing foreign investors that these are durable commitments remains a challenge for the Chinese government.

Even if the government were to take these steps, however, the renminbi will not be seen as a safe-haven currency that foreign and domestic investors turn to in times of global financial turmoil. The Communist Party of China's control of the country's political system means that the country lacks a system of checks and balances. Some have argued that, while China has a one-party, nondemocratic system of government, there are sufficient self-correcting mechanisms built into the system that prevent the government from running amok. This is unlikely to be seen as a durable substitute for an institutionalized system of checks and balances such as that in the United States—where the executive branch, the legislative branch, and the judiciary have independence from, and serve as constraints on the unbridled exercise of powers by, the other branches.

In short, the eCNY is likely to help promote the role of the renminbi as an international payment currency. But it will not dent the US dollar's status as the dominant global reserve currency.

Conclusion

New and evolving financial technologies, including the advent of cryptocurrencies and CBDCs, will have implications for certain aspects of the international monetary system, but these are not likely to be revolutionary and will be realized only over a number of years. Some changes facilitated by Fintech could occur sooner, although their effects on global finance will be limited primarily to the operation and structure of financial markets themselves rather than any fundamental reordering of the international monetary system.

More efficient payment systems will bring a host of benefits, making it easier, for instance, for economic migrants to send remittances back to their home countries more easily than is currently possible. It will become easier even for investors with modest savings to diversify their portfolios and seek higher returns through better access to international investment opportunities. In principle, financial capital will be able to flow more easily within and across countries to the most productive investment opportunities, raising global economic welfare—at least as measured by GDP and consumption capacity. With easier capital flows across national borders, though, many countries will also face risks related to the volatility of those flows and the complications that it creates for managing their exchange rates and their economies. New channels for transmitting payments across borders more quickly and cheaply are likely to make it more difficult to regulate and control capital flows. The resulting challenges will be especially thorny for EMEs and other small open economies.

The landscape of global reserve currencies might seem to be at the threshold of disruption as cryptocurrencies gain traction as mediums of exchange and stores of value. In reality, despite all the hype, the proliferation of cryptocurrencies will not have a substantial disruptive effect on the major reserve currencies, especially the US dollar. Unbacked cryptocurrencies are much too volatile to be considered stable sources of value or reliable mediums of exchange. On the other hand, private stablecoins are likely to gain traction as means of payment. But insofar as their stable values depend on their being backed by fiat currencies, stablecoins are unlikely to become independent stores of value. Still, more effective global regulation and a strengthening of domestic payment systems in low-income countries is essential to ensure that their payment systems are not overrun by those managed by outside actors that are not under their regulatory purview.

The topography is likely to shift a great deal more for smaller and less developed economies. National currencies issued by their central banks could lose ground to private stablecoins and perhaps also to CBDCs issued by the major economies. These countries might also face some difficult choices in tying their economic destinies to specific currency blocs if rivalries between the major currencies (and the economies issuing them) result in a fragmentation of the international monetary system.

Such fragmentation could be particularly deleterious for some emerging-market and developing economies. For those not politically aligned with advanced economies, lower trade and financial flows could mean fewer technology and knowledge transfers, constraining their path to development. Access to export markets could also become more constrained over time. This might matter less for major emerging-market economies but could harm more those countries that are smaller and at earlier stages of economic development.

Even among the major reserve currencies, there are some shifts in store. The US dollar could lose some ground as a payment currency, although it will remain dominant both along this dimension and as a store of value. A digital renminbi will help the currency gain traction as a payment currency, but the digitization of the currency by itself will do little to boost its status as a reserve currency. The renminbi's further rise, even if gradual and modest, and the advent of additional stablecoins, could reduce the importance of the second-tier reserve currencies, including the euro, the British pound sterling, the Japanese yen, and the Swiss franc.

At most, the US dollar will lose a bit of ground as an international payment currency as alternative cross-border payment channels proliferate and as transactions between currency pairs that do not involve the dollar become cheaper and easier to execute. The dollar's dominance among global fiat currencies, however, will remain unchallenged in the foreseeable future, especially because other major currencies could see even greater erosions in their prominence as mediums of exchange and as safe havens.

NOTES

This article draws extensively on the author's book *The Future of Money: How the Digital Revolution Is Transforming Currencies and Finance*. An earlier version of this chapter appeared in the *Oxford Review of Economic Policy*.

1. Qiu, Zhang, and Gao (2019).
2. Katzenstein (2015) and Zoffer (2019).
3. Bech, Faruqui, and Shirakami (2020).
4. Goldberg and Tille (2008).
5. Clark et al. (2019) and Rey (2018).
6. Ju, Lu, and Tu (2016) and Pieters (2017).
7. See https://www.mas.gov.sg/news/media-releases/2018/assessment-on-emerging-opportunities-for-digital-transformation-in-cross-border-payments.
8. See Arslanalp, Eichengreen, and Simpson-Bell (2022); Chitu, Eichengreen, and Mehl (2017); Eichengreen (2011); Goldberg (2010); Gopinath and Stein (2018); Prasad (2014); Prasad (2019).
9. Gopinath (2016).
10. World Bank database.
11. Prasad (2014).
12. Cœuré (2019).
13. Cœuré (2019).
14. Brunnermeier, James, and Landau (2019).
15. Carney (2019).
16. IMF (2021, p. 59).
17. Prasad (2016) and Subacchi (2016).
18. See the SWIFT Renminbi Tracker, November 2023.
19. https://data.imf.org/?sk=e6a5f467-c14b-4aa8-9f6d-5a09ec4e62a4.

20. Prasad (2020).
21. Yao (2017) and Yao (2018).
22. Miao and Deng (2019).

REFERENCES

Arslanalp, Serkan, Barry Eichengreen, and Chima Simpson-Bell. 2022. "The Stealth Erosion of Dollar Dominance: Active Diversifiers and the Rise of Nontraditional Currencies." IMF Working Paper 2022/058. International Monetary Fund, Washington, DC.

Bech, Morten, Umar Faruqui, and Takeshi Shirakami. 2020. "Payments Without Borders." *BIS Quarterly Review* (March): 53–65.

Brunnermeier, Markus, Harold James, and Jean-Pierre Landau. 2019. "The Digitalization of Money." NBER Working Paper 26300. National Bureau of Economic Research, Cambridge, MA.

Carney, Mark. 2019. "The Growing Challenges for Monetary Policy in the Current International Monetary and Financial System." Speech at the Jackson Hole Symposium, Federal Reserve Bank of Kansas City, August 23.

Chitu, Livia, Barry Eichengreen, and Arnaud Mehl. 2017. *How Global Currencies Work: Past, Present, and Future.* Princeton, NJ: Princeton University Press.

Clark, John, Nathan Converse, Brahima Coulibaly, and Steven Kamin. 2019. "Emerging Market Capital Flows and U.S. Monetary Policy." *International Finance* 23 (1): 2–17.

Cœuré, Benoît. 2019. "Digital Challenges to the International Monetary and Financial System." Remarks at the Banque Centrale du Luxembourg-Toulouse School of Economics conference on "The Future of the International Monetary System," September 17.

Eichengreen, Barry. 2011. *Exorbitant Privilege: The Rise and Fall of the Dollar and the Future of the International Monetary System.* New York: Oxford University Press.

Goldberg, Linda. 2010. "Is the International Role of the Dollar Changing?" *Current Issues in Economics and Finance* 16 (1). Federal Reserve Bank of New York.

Goldberg, Linda, and Cédric Tille. 2008. "Vehicle Currency Use in International Trade." *Journal of International Economics* 76 (2): 177–92.

Gopinath, Gita. 2016. "The International Price System." Proceedings of the Jackson Hole Symposium, Federal Reserve Bank of Kansas City.

Gopinath, Gita, and Jeremy Stein. 2018. "Banking, Trade, and the Making of a Dominant Currency." NBER Working Paper 24485. National Bureau of Economic Research, Cambridge, MA, March 28.

International Monetary Fund. 2021. *Build Forward Better: IMF Annual Report 2021.* Washington, DC: IMF.

Ju, Lan, Timothy (Jun) Lu, and Zhiyong Tu. 2016. "Capital Flight and Bitcoin Regulation." *International Review of Finance* 16 (3): 445–55.

Katzenstein, Suzanne. 2015. "Dollar Unilateralism: The New Frontline of National Security." *Indiana Law Journal* 90 (1/8): 293–351.

Miao, Yanliang, and Tuo Deng. 2019. "China's Capital Account Liberalization: A Ruby Jubilee and Beyond." *China Economic Journal* 12 (3): 245–71.

Pieters, Gina. 2017. "Bitcoin Reveals Exchange Rate Manipulation and Detects Capital Controls." Available at SSRN: https://ssrn.com/abstract=2714921 or http://dx.doi.org/10.2139/ssrn.2714921.

Prasad, Eswar. 2014. *The Dollar Trap: How the U.S. Dollar Tightened Its Grip on Global Finance.* Princeton, NJ: Princeton University Press.

———. 2016. *Gaining Currency: The Rise of the Renminbi.* New York: Oxford University Press.

———. 2019. "Has the Dollar Lost Ground as the Dominant International Currency?" Working Paper. Brookings Institution, Washington, DC, September.

———. 2020. "China's Role in the Global Financial System." In *China 2049: Economic Challenges of a Rising Global Power,* edited by David Dollar, Yiping Huang, and Yao Yang, 355–72. Washington, DC: Brookings Institution.

Qiu, Tanh, Ruidong Zhang, and Yuan Gao. 2019. "Ripple vs. SWIFT: Transforming Cross Border Remittance Using Block Chain Technology." *Procedia Computer Science* 147: 428–34.

Rey, Hélène. 2018. "Dilemma Not Trilemma: The Global Financial Cycle and Monetary Policy Independence." NBER Working Paper 21162. National Bureau of Economic Research, Cambridge, MA, February.

Subacchi, Paola. 2016. *The People's Money: How China Is Building a Global Currency.* New York: Columbia University Press.

Yao, Qian. 2017. "The Application of Digital Currency in Interbank Cash Transfer Scenario." *Finance Computerizing* 5: 16–19.

———. 2018. "A Systematic Framework to Understand Central Bank Digital Currency." *Science China Information Science* 61 (January).

Zoffer, Joshua P. 2019. "The Dollar and the United States' Exorbitant Power to Sanction." *American Journal of International Law* 113 (AJIL Unbound): 152–56.

NINE

Strengthening the Global Financial Architecture

JOON-HO HAHM AND WOO JIN CHOI

The postwar global financial architecture (GFA) has undergone profound changes over nearly a century. These changes have been particularly significant in recent decades as economic and financial globalization has advanced. In this chapter, we review the evolution of the GFA and discuss areas for further reform in light of the recent and ongoing changes in global economy and finance.

We begin with an overview of the GFA and its institutional arrangements and policy frameworks and then assess the new risks and challenges for the global financial system arising in the aftermath of the global financial crisis (GFC) of 2008–2009. Next, we discuss the main elements of the current agenda for GFA reform. The last section of the chapter provides some concluding observations. In assessing developments in the GFA and the reform agenda, we pay particular attention to the perspective of emerging-market economies (EMEs).

Overview of the Global Financial Architecture

Today's GFA has been shaped by several phases of change and reform. We review this evolution here from both historical and functional standpoints.

Conceptual and Historical Perspectives

The concept of the GFA is multifaceted and has been evolving, with various authors providing different definitions. For instance, Giovanoli (2009) sees the GFA as encompassing the institutions responsible for setting and implementing international financial standards, which are defined as a set of minimum financial requirements applied globally to mitigate systemic risk. International financial standards are typically formulated as recommendations that embody widely accepted principles and practices. Countries adopt these standards by incorporating them into national policies. Taking a broader perspective, Crockett (2009) defines the GFA as the fundamental economic model governing international financial relations. It includes the network of institutional arrangements established to manage these relations and determine how decision-making power is distributed among countries. Baker (2009) uses the term GFA as a concise way to refer to the collection of key decision-making processes and deliberative spaces that aim to organize the global financial system. Elson (2010) describes the GFA as the collective governance arrangements at the international level that safeguard the effective functioning of the global monetary and financial systems.

Despite its multifaceted nature, the common thread running through all these definitions of the GFA is that it refers to a system of institutions, agreements, and regulations governing the flow of capital and financial services across countries. Its primary objective is to promote economic growth and financial stability in the global economy.

The GFA has undergone multiple reforms over time, often in response to economic and financial crises.[1] The first reform, known as the Bretton Woods Agreement of 1944, aimed to foster an open and stable system of international trade by avoiding competitive devaluations and exchange controls that had contributed to the Great Depression. However, the Bretton Woods system collapsed in the early 1970s due to an unsustainable increase in US foreign liabilities and rising capital flows among advanced countries, despite the presence of capital controls.

The second reform of the GFA took place in the late 1970s, replacing the Bretton Woods system with a mixed system of fixed and flexible exchange rates, based on the preferences of individual countries. The role of the International Monetary Fund (IMF) shifted to conducting surveillance over a country's macroeconomic policies, while the GFA also focused on addressing the needs of developing countries through closer coordination between the IMF and the World Bank. Additionally, the Bank for International Settlement (BIS) assumed the responsibility of overseeing and monitoring payment and settlement systems, as well as capital flows, under the leadership of the Group of Ten (G10).

The third reform of the GFA, implemented in 1999, was a response to the financial crises experienced by EMEs in the 1990s.[2] These crises were caused by extreme volatility in private financial flows to EMEs. The Financial Stability Forum (FSF) was established to address this issue, and it aimed to coordinate the efforts of various standard-setting bodies such as the International Organization of Securities Commissions (IOSCO) and the International Association of Insurance Supervisors (IAIS). Its objective was to oversee global capital flows and strengthen the regulatory systems of EMEs.

Extending Elson's framework, we can characterize the fourth reform of the GFA, pursued after the GFC, as being driven by the underlying causes of that crisis. It is important to note that the GFC originated in advanced economies (AEs), with factors such as the US subprime mortgage bubble, wholesale funding, and off-balance sheet activities of major financial institutions playing significant roles. Some argued that the accumulation of large amounts of foreign reserves in EMEs and their "savings glut" were important causes of the widening US external imbalances at the onset of the crisis.[3] However, more recent evidence suggests that the US external imbalances were primarily financed by capital flows from European sources rather than EMEs.[4]

Despite having improved external accounts and bank balance sheets, many EMEs experienced contagion and negative spillover effects from the GFC, including sudden reversals of capital flows. This led to a reassessment of financial globalization, prompting international financial institutions to reconsider the role of capital flow management in protecting the financial stability of EMEs. The FSF was transformed into the Financial Stability Board (FSB) to strengthen the regulatory framework and address newly exposed financial vulnerabilities. Previous prudential standards, such as the *Basel Accord*, were revised, and a new policy framework of macro-prudential regulation was introduced to tackle systemic risks arising from the procyclicality of financial credits and the interconnectedness of financial institutions. Parallel to the Group of Seven (G7), the Group of Twenty (G20), established in 1999 to include major EMEs whose role in the global economy was rising, was elevated to the level of heads of government.

However, despite reform efforts, criticisms of the GFA persist, particularly regarding its functionality and governance mechanism. First, the current system still disproportionately represents the interests of developed countries and inadequately addresses the concerns of emerging markets and developing economies. Second, it relies heavily on the US dollar as the dominant currency, which can create instability and expose the global financial system to changes in US monetary policy. Third, it lacks effective global governance, resulting in suboptimal coordination and cooperation among participating countries in addressing global financial challenges. Critics argue that the decision-making processes of major institutions and actors within the GFA lack transparency and accountability. Additionally, the existing architecture lacks adequate regulations for big financial institutions with systemic implications (though the related regulatory framework has improved) and is ill-equipped to effectively respond to financial crises, particularly in emerging markets and developing economies. Finally, it does not sufficiently address emerging challenges such as climate financing and climate-related financial risks.

Functional Scope and Current State of the Architecture

If one envisions a domestic version of the financial architecture, it would comprise the structure and organization of a country's financial system, including institutions, markets, and regulations that enable the smooth flow of funds within the country. In modern days, there seems to be a broad consensus about how to organize a financial system that supports economic growth while maintaining financial stability. Key elements include a credible central bank, competitive financial institutions, well-functioning money and capital markets, a robust financial infrastructure such as payment and settlements systems, and an effective financial supervision and regulation framework.

Like the domestic version, one can envision an ideal global financial architecture that facilitates financial intermediation and governance at the international level. This entails efficient allocation of financial resources, accurate pricing and risk determination, risk diversification and monitoring, and effective resolution of defaults and insolvencies on a global scale.

However, there are notable differences between the international and domestic financial systems. One key difference is in the degree of integration. Domestic financial systems tend to be more integrated, with a centralized banking system, a unified currency, and relatively homogenous regulations. In contrast, the GFA is more decentralized, involving a larger number of actors with different currencies. Another important difference arises from the absence of centralized sovereignty at the international level. Unlike domestic financial systems, the role of government is much more limited in the international context. There is no central bank, government, or judicial system that supports regulation, supervision, or legal measures to address financial failures. Consequently, the GFA must rely on international institutions and frameworks resulting from negotiations and cooperation among national authorities.

Nonetheless, it is instructive to compare the current state of the GFA with an ideal financial structure from a functional perspective. We specifically focus on the role of the GFA in promoting financial stability. We define the GFA as a system of institutional arrangements, policies, and governance mechanisms aimed at achieving an efficient allocation of financial resources across countries while safeguarding the global financial system's stability. We examine the functional aspects of a financial stability policy framework. In a domestic setting, a financial stability framework typically comprises three dimensions: monetary stability, encompassing monetary policy and the central bank's role as lender of last resort; ex-ante financial stability, involving macroprudential and microprudential measures and supervision; and ex-post financial stability, focusing on crisis management and resolution of insolvencies. By comparing domestic and global counterparts within this functional framework (as shown in table 9.1), we can better identify relative deficiencies in the current GFA structure and areas for reform.

Considering the functional structure outlined above, it becomes apparent that the current GFA exhibits several deficiencies compared to its domestic counterpart. First, the absence of a central bank, a unified monetary policy, and a credible international lender of last resort amplify the vulnerability of the global financial system to adverse shocks. The GFC highlighted the need for a global lender of last resort facility that can provide quick and adequate liquidity support during crises and mitigate negative spillovers, but the absence of an effective liquidity provision mechanism, especially in the early stages of financial crises, hampers the GFA's ability to respond promptly and effectively to financial disruptions.

Second, the lack of an effective surveillance scheme to identify financial imbalances and cross-country spillovers, along with the absence of coordination in macroprudential policies, represents another weakness of the current GFA. As Elson (2010) emphasizes, the GFA's governance structure

Table 9.1. Functional Framework of Domestic and Global Financial Architecture

	Monetary stability (Monetary policy / Payment & settlement / Lender of last resort)	Financial stability policy framework						
		Ex-ante financial stability (surveillance and regulation)					Ex-post financial stability	
		Macroprudential policy		Microprudential policy				
		Macroprudential oversight	Macroprudential regulation	Microprudential supervision	Capital market regulation	Consumer protection	Deposit insurance Bank resolution	Crisis management Public funds
[US]	FRB	FSOC		FRB/OCC/NCUA	SEC/CFTC	CFPB	FDIC	Treasury
[EU]	ECB	ESRB		EBA	ESMA	EIOPA	EDIS	ESM
[GFA]	IMF/Fed Swap/CPMI	IMF/FSB/BIS		BCBS	IOSCO	IAIS/IOPS	IADI	(IMF/WB)
[RFA]	CMIM/NAFA/FLAR	AMRO						

Source: Authors' compilation.

Note: Acronyms: ASEAN+3 Macroeconomic Research Office (AMRO); Basel Committee on Banking Supervision (BCBS), Bank for International Settlements (BIS), Consumer Financial Protection Bureau (CFPB), Commodity Futures Trading Commission (CFTC), Chiang Mai Initiative Multilateralization (CMIM), Committee on Payments and Market Infrastructures (CPMI), European Banking Authority (EBA), European Central Bank (ECB), European Deposit Insurance Scheme (EDIS), European Insurance and Occupational Pensions Authority (EIOPA), European Stability Mechanism (ESM), European Securities and Markets Authority (ESMA), European Systemic Risk Board (ESRB), Federal Deposit Insurance Corporation (FDIC), Latin American Reserve Fund (FLAR), Federal Reserve Board (FRB), Financial Stability Board (FSB), Financial Stability Oversight Council (FSOC), Global Financial Architecture (GFA), International Association of Deposit Insurers (IADI), International Association of Insurance Supervisors (IAIS), International Organization of Pension Supervisors (IOPS), International Organization of Securities Commissions (IOSCO), North American Framework Agreement (NAFA), National Credit Union Administration (NCUA), Office of the Comptroller of the Currency (OCC), Regional Financing Arrangement (RFA), Securities and Exchange Commission (SEC).

faces challenges in terms of clear lines of authority and coordination among its components. Despite the regulatory responsibilities of the FSB and the macrofinancial stability role of the IMF, coordination between these entities appears rather limited. Insufficient coordination among international institutions makes it difficult for the GFA to proactively identify and address potential financial stability risks.

Third, the absence of an explicit deposit insurance scheme and a well-functioning insolvency resolution mechanism represents a major weakness of the GFA. There is a lack of coordination in the implementation of deposit and investor protection measures across major countries, and there is no coordinated framework for resolving the insolvency of multinational financial institutions in an orderly manner or effectively restructuring the debt of crisis-affected countries.

A fourth deficiency of the GFA stems from the absence of a crisis management mechanism backed by fiscal resources. This hinders the GFA's ability to respond promptly and effectively to financial crises, as it relies on ad-hoc bilateral arrangements rather than a well-coordinated multilateral response. These weaknesses suggest a broad agenda of reform to address the challenges faced by the global financial system and ensure its stability and resilience in the face of future disruptions. They also point to major areas where the GFA needs bolstering.

From a complementary perspective, Gallagher et al. (2020) describe the current gaps in the global financial safety net, as shown in table 9.2. They note that foreign reserves and prudential and capital flow management measures exhibit inadequacies, bilateral arrangements are asymmetric and uncertain in availability, regional financing arrangements have limited coverage and insufficient funding, and multilateral facilities such as IMF lending programs reveal various deficiencies, including inadequate resource levels and the stigma effect.

Post-GFC Trends in Global Imbalances and New Challenges to the Global Financial System

As we have reviewed, the GFA has evolved over time, enduring significant shocks and crises in the global economy. In this section, we analyze the current state of global financial imbalances and newly emerging vulnerabilities. These factors must play a key role in shaping future reforms for the GFA.

Table 9.2. Gaps in the Global Financial Safety Nets

	Surveillance	Precautionary platforms	Liquidity provision
National governments	Limited attention to national-global links Lack of reliable information	Inadequate currency reserves Weak efficacy of prudential measures Limited efficacy of CFMs	Limited efficacy and availability of fiscal/monetary policy Lack of adequacy and efficacy of currency reserves
Bilateral arrangements	Largely without formal surveillance activity	Asymmetric and uncertain availability Ex-ante conditionality concerns	Asymmetric and uncertain availability Ex-ante conditionality concerns
Regional financing arrangements	Incomplete geographic coverage Narrow thematic coverage	Limited level and coverage of swaps Linkages to the IMF	Limited level and coverage of swaps Linkages to the IMF
Multilateral facilities	Uneven quality of IMF surveillance Narrow thematic coverage (IMF surveillance) Limited attention to global-country specific links (FSB/BIS)	Absence of multilateral swap facility Inadequate level of IMF resources available Stigma attached to IMF credit lines Ex-ante conditionality of IMF facilities	Inadequate level of IMF resources available Lack of IMF voice and representation of EMDEs Procyclical conditionality of IMF programs Stigma and mixed outcomes of IMF programs

Source: Gallagher et al. (2020).
Note: Acronyms: Capital flow management measures (CFMs); emerging-market and developing economies (EMDEs).

Current account imbalances between AEs, particularly the United States, and EMEs such as China and oil-exporting nations had been steadily widening from the 1990s until the GFC and were considered an important factor setting the stage for the crisis. After the crisis, we witnessed a stabilization of these imbalances, which were on a declining trend until the outbreak of the COVID-19 pandemic. External imbalances seem to be widening again after the pandemic. As shown in figure 9.1, not only did current account imbalances increase but the cumulative stock of net international investment positions also began to expand in 2020. This resurgence of imbalances is most pronounced in the United States. As a result of highly expansionary monetary and fiscal policies after the pandemic, coupled with commodity price shocks, the US current account deficit has started to rise again, affecting the overall global imbalances. Other advanced economies with highly developed information and communication industries have moved into surplus positions. China, a typical counterparty to US imbalances, is again experiencing an increase in capital outflows.

The United States possesses the capacity to manage external imbalances, although further increases in external debt seem inevitable as its external deficits are expected to remain sizable, at least for the time being. Given the status of the US dollar as a global reserve currency, the United States will continue to enjoy the "exorbitant privilege"—the ability to issue external bonds in its own currency, invest without limitations imposed by its own savings, and finance fiscal deficits at a low cost.

In general, history has shown that the adjustment process at the international level, to resolve persistent imbalances in countries' external positions through exchange-rate adjustments or underlying macroeconomic measures, has not been fully effective. The resurgence of US external imbalances could pose potential threats to global financial stability that may arise from the rebalancing of the US current account, the value of the US dollar, and interest rates.

We also observe noticeable shifts in the composition of capital flows after the GFC. These shifts include a decline in bank lending relative to bond flows, a rise in nonbank financial intermediary (NBFI) flows, and a growing role of EMEs in shaping global capital flows. EMEs have emerged at the forefront of global financial flows and have significantly influenced overall capital allocation since the GFC. Figure 9.2 provides a breakdown of global debt flows in advanced, emerging, and developing economies. Before the GFC, the US external imbalances were financed primarily by

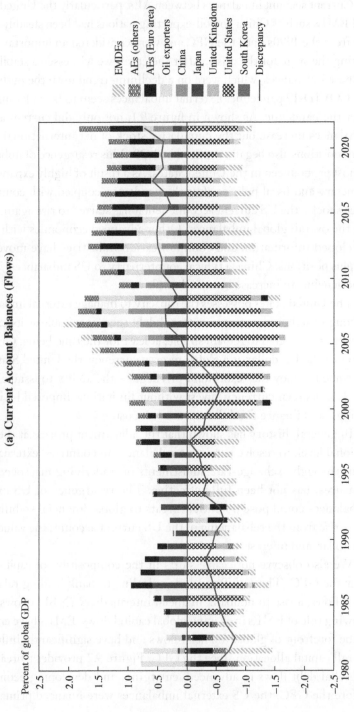

FIGURE 9.1. Global External Imbalances
(a) Current Account Balances (Flows)

(b) Net International Investment Positions (Stocks)

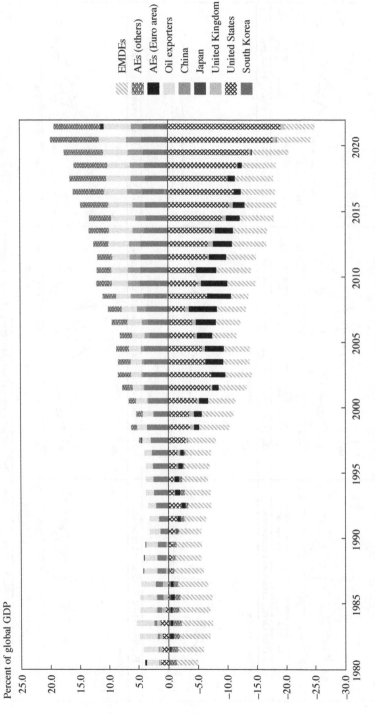

Percent of global GDP

Legend:
- EMDEs
- AEs (others)
- AEs (Euro area)
- Oil exporters
- China
- Japan
- United Kingdom
- United States
- South Korea

Source: Authors' calculations based on IMF World Economic Outlook database, Milesi-Ferretti (2022), and Lane and Milesi-Ferretti (2018).

Note: AEs = advanced economies; EMDEs = emerging-market and developing economies.

FIGURE 9.2. Aggregate External Debt Inflows

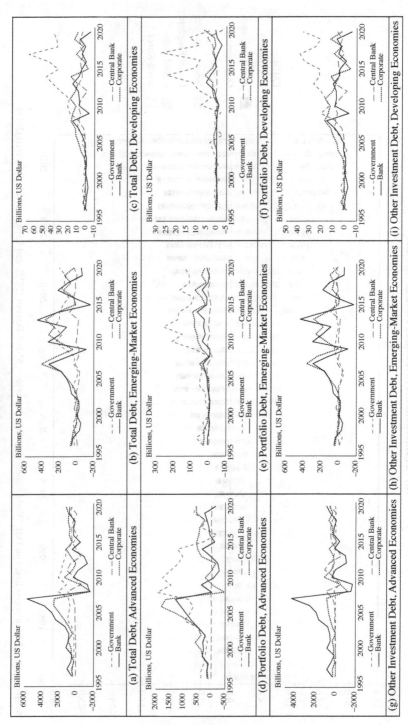

(a) Total Debt, Advanced Economies

(b) Total Debt, Emerging-Market Economies

(c) Total Debt, Developing Economies

(d) Portfolio Debt, Advanced Economies

(e) Portfolio Debt, Emerging-Market Economies

(f) Portfolio Debt, Developing Economies

(g) Other Investment Debt, Advanced Economies

(h) Other Investment Debt, Emerging-Market Economies

(i) Other Investment Debt, Developing Economies

Source: Authors' calculations based on data from BIS, IMF, and World Bank, following the approach in Avdjiev et al. (2022).

Note: Total debt is portfolio debt plus other investment debt.

banking flows from European sources. As the figure shows, the increasing level of total debt among AEs until the GFC largely took the form of other investment debt, primarily bank lending. However, after the GFC, bank debt flows declined significantly in AEs, while they continued in emerging and developing economies. A notable change after the GFC is the increase in bond flows (portfolio debt) across all country categories, particularly in the government sector.

Another notable aspect of post-GFC capital flows to EMEs is the expansion of US dollar-denominated flows and funding by NBFIs. External debt of EMEs increased from 25 percent of GDP (or $3.3 trillion) at the end of 2010 to 30 percent of GDP (or $5.6 trillion) at the end of 2019 (figure 9.3). Eighty percent of this debt was denominated in foreign currency, primarily the US dollar, leading to currency mismatches, particularly in the nonfinancial corporate sector. The growing reliance on debt markets and NBFIs for funding has made liquidity, especially in the US dollar, increasingly crucial for the stability of the global financial system. Figure 9.4 indicates a rising trend in US dollar-denominated bonds issued by nonbanks. The share of debt securities in overall US dollar-denominated credit to nonbanks is at an unprecedentedly high level.

Currency mismatches, combined with an increased dependence on NBFIs for financing external debt, create significant vulnerabilities for EMEs. For instance, in response to sudden deteriorations in global financial conditions, investment funds facing redemptions from investors seeking liquidity could initiate large selling of EME assets. This, in turn, could result in sharp declines in EME asset prices, substantial currency depreciation against the US dollar, and significant capital outflows.

Besides external imbalances, internal financial imbalances have tended to increase due to monetary spillovers and the expansionary global financial cycle. The interconnected nature of the global financial system has intensified the spillover effects of financial conditions across borders. As argued by Rey (2015), monetary policy autonomy is undermined, even with exchange-rate flexibility. The global financial cycle is often not aligned with countries' specific macroeconomic conditions. The channels through which cross-border spillovers occur have been diverse, including exchange rates and bank credits,[5] corporate risk spreads,[6] and bond market flows and long-term interest rates.[7]

The prolonged unconventional monetary policies of AEs, such as the policy of quantitative easing by the US Federal Reserve, have resulted in

FIGURE 9.3. External Debt of Emerging-Market Economies

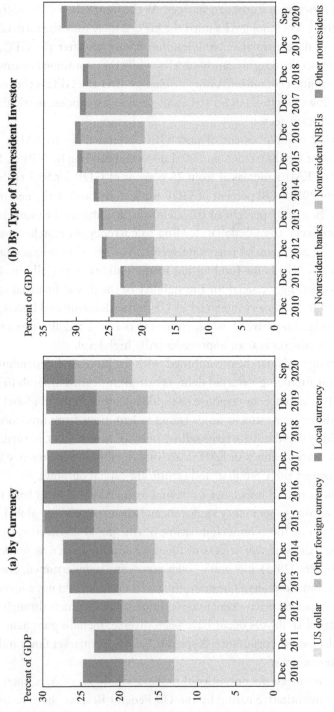

(a) By Currency

(b) By Type of Nonresident Investor

Source: Authors' calculations based on data from BIS and IMF.

Note: The figures do not include China. See FSB (2022a) for details.

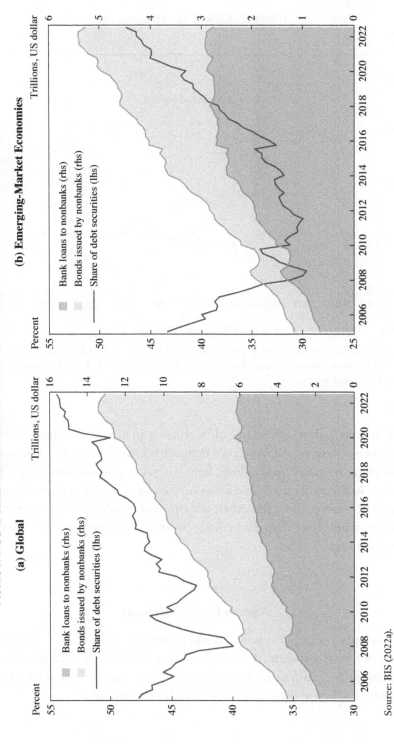

FIGURE 9.4. US Dollar–Denominated Credit to Nonbanks Outside the United States

(a) Global

(b) Emerging-Market Economies

Bank loans to nonbanks (rhs)
Bonds issued by nonbanks (rhs)
Share of debt securities (lhs)

Source: BIS (2022a).

FIGURE 9.5. Global Macro Leverage

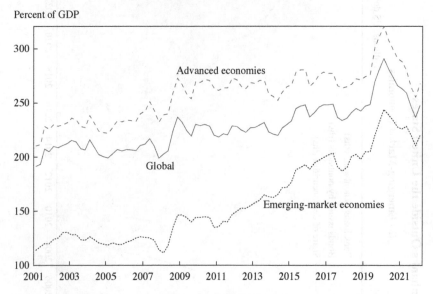

Source: Authors' calculations based on the data from BIS Statistics.

Note: The figure shows total credit to the nonfinancial sector (core debt). It includes forty-three countries covered by the BIS data. "Global" in this figure is the sum of advanced economies and emerging-market economies.

significant spillover effects in EMEs, creating an unusually accommodative financial environment. As shown in figure 9.5, the low-interest-rate environment, surging capital inflows, improving risk appetites, and rising asset prices have contributed to an expansionary credit cycle and an unprecedented level of leverage in EMEs. Alongside external imbalances, rising internal financial imbalances also pose a threat to various countries' and global financial stability.

Agenda for GFA Reforms

Developments in global economy and finance raise new challenges for the global financial system. While the institutional and policy framework for global finance has changed a great deal, there is a need to build on earlier reforms to better align the GFA with today's imperatives.

Reinforcing the Lender of Last Resort Capacity

The GFC exposed a key flaw in the GFA: the lack of a credible international lender of last resort. When confronted with the contagion resulting from the financial crisis in AEs, many EMEs were unable to withstand the severe downward pressure on their currencies caused by the sudden reversal of capital flows. The availability of official financing for EMEs facing adverse spillover effects was quite limited, except for swap arrangements established by the US Federal Reserve, which surpassed the resources provided by the IMF.[8]

In response to the GFC, two strands of reform proposals have emerged to strengthen the capacity of the international lender of last resort. The first focuses on enhancing the role and resources of the IMF as the primary monitor and lender of last resort. The second involves institutionalizing multilateral swap lines and exploring the intermediary role of the IMF.

Gallagher et al. (2020) observe that it is crucial to expand the available resources of the global financial safety net (GFSN), which is not keeping pace with the size of the global financial system. Excluding swap arrangements, the GFSN's core capital is approximately $13 trillion (including global currency reserves), amounting to just 4 percent of the total global financial assets as measured by the FSB.[9] They argue that the G20 should urge member states to provide significant new resources to the IMF, the regional financing arrangements (RFAs), and the new swap facilities. Along with increasing IMF resources, creative alternatives should be considered, such as broadening the role and use of the Special Drawing Rights (SDRs) as an instrument of international policy cooperation. They also argue that the G20 should support the development of RFAs to extend the geographic coverage of the GFSN, as many countries lack access to current regional and multilateral swap and credit lines.

Not only is the size of financial resources a concern, but the role of the IMF as a core monetary institution also needs strengthening. Elson (2010) argues that the proliferation of other formal and informal institutional arrangements within the GFA has led to a fragmentation of decision-making and a weakening of the authority of the IMF, which was initially created as the central monetary institution of the global financial system. In addition to the fragmentation of decision-making within the GFA, the legitimacy of the IMF has been undermined by the lack of involvement of EMEs, reflecting their relatively small weight in the IMF's decision-making and their lack of confidence in the financial arrangements offered by the institution. Furthermore, the constrained role of the IMF reflects the unwillingness of AEs to use the institution as a coordinating mechanism and allow it to play an independent role in resolving global financial problems.

On a slightly different note, Ocampo (2019) points to the limitation of using SDRs only for payments among central banks, due to the division between the IMF's general resources and SDR accounts. To enable global monetary creation similar to domestic money creation by central banks, Ocampo suggests consolidating the two accounts. This would allow the financing of IMF programs with allocated SDRs, treating the SDRs held by countries as deposits in the IMF that can be lent to them in need. Implementing such use of SDRs, however, would require a change in the IMF's Articles of Agreement.

In a similar vein, Gourinchas (2023) proposes a "Safe Reserve Deposit" (SRD) offered by the IMF. The SRD would be a reserve account held at the IMF that countries can redeem at their discretion. Member countries would fund their SRD balances by transferring a portion of their official reserve holdings. The liquidity and safety of the SRD would be indistinguishable from official reserves from the perspective of member countries. Meanwhile, the IMF would pool these deposits globally, up to a liquidity buffer, and passively invest in global investable assets based on their market capitalization. This approach would allow the IMF to offer higher returns to countries compared to official reserves, thus reducing the quasi-fiscal cost of purchasing insurance.

In an effort to strengthen the IMF's role as an international lender of last resort, various facilities have been introduced, such as the Flexible Credit Line and the Precautionary and Liquidity Line. These facilities aim to provide financial assistance to countries facing liquidity crises and can help reduce the need for them to accumulate large foreign reserve. However, as noted by Eichengreen (2020), the overall lending capacity of the IMF is limited to $1 trillion, which is insufficient to fully address the potential impact of future challenges. Efforts to increase IMF quotas and reform its governance through the General Review of Quotas, as well as enhance the international role of the SDR, have been longstanding issues.

The swap facilities provided by the US Federal Reserve have proven to be effective and preferable to recipient countries as an alternative to new IMF borrowing facilities. During the pandemic crisis, however, the Fed offered swaps only to a select group of countries, and the criteria for selection were not transparent. This has led to suggestions that the decision to extend swaps, when systemic risk emerges on a global scale, should be delegated to an impartial arbiter such as the IMF rather than relying solely on the discretion of the US Federal Reserve or other AE central banks.

Indeed, the multilateral expansion of central bank swap lines is not a new concept. As a component of the GFSN, a central bank swap facility offers several advantages over other instruments such as foreign exchange reserves and IMF loans. Unlike IMF loans, it can provide liquidity quickly and without the stigma associated with borrowing from the Fund. Maintaining a swap line is also much less costly than holding foreign reserves during normal times.

Truman (2008) suggests that the US administration could authorize the Federal Reserve to engage in unlimited currency swaps, exchanging US dollars for SDRs issued by the IMF during crisis times. This would require the IMF's Articles of Agreement to be amended, allowing the Fund to swap SDRs for the national currencies of the US (and other countries that issue key currencies).

Yeyati (2020) argues that a genuine global lender of last resort differs significantly from a network of central bank swaps, as it should be available broadly and on-demand rather than selectively at the discretion of the lender. He suggests that the IMF should assume the role of a true lender of last resort by acting as a bridge between the Federal Reserve and other central banks. Specifically, the IMF could function as a broker, credit risk assessor, and risk retainer in a more functional manner for addressing liquidity crises. It could serve as an independent broker that consolidates central bank swaps into a comprehensive liquidity network, encompassing a larger group of eligible countries. The IMF would be prepared to intervene with its traditional toolkit, such as loan programs, if necessary. Under this arrangement, the IMF would act as an intermediary between the funding central bank and the borrowing country, similar to its current management of contingent funds in borrowing agreements. Functioning as a "central bank swap clearing house," the IMF could better fulfill the international lender of last resort role.

Coulibaly and Prasad (2021) propose the establishment of a swap framework aimed at systematically expanding access to temporary foreign exchange liquidity for a wide range of countries. Institutionalized mechanisms for emergency liquidity assistance would be more effective and reduce the incentive for countries to rely on self-insurance through reserve accumulation, which is inefficient at both the national and global levels. Strong support from the IMF's shareholders is crucial for formalizing swap lines offered by the G3 central banks (Federal Reserve, European Central Bank, and Bank of Japan) and expanding their access to more countries. The IMF could assist in unlocking such swap lines for a broad group of countries by providing guarantees that mitigate counterparty risks.

Gislen et al. (2021) concur with Truman (2008) in suggesting that the IMF's role should involve analyzing the need for increased global liquidity in the international financial system and, if necessary, recommending the activation of swap agreements between central banks. However, there has been little support for expanding the IMF's role, as the leading central banks have desired to retain control over swap arrangements.

Bahaj and Reis (2022) argue that the lender of last resort function can be performed through swap lines established between central banks. These swap lines enable a source central bank to provide liquidity in its currency to a counterparty central bank in exchange for collateral. This arrangement ensures that the counterparty central bank can supply liquidity to its domestic banks and contributes to stabilizing the global financial system during times of crisis. The authors find supporting evidence that swap lines establish a limit on deviations from covered interest parity and reduce the average borrowing costs for banks in recipient countries.

The People's Bank of China (PBOC) has been active in expanding its swap lines in recent years. As of 2022, the PBOC had established swap agreements with thirty-eight central banks, with a total value of around $4 trillion. It has entered into agreements with other major central banks, such as the European Central Bank, but notably not with the US Federal Reserve. Along with regional agreements like the Chiang Mai Initiative, these swap lines from the PBOC have helped to build a buffer against external vulnerabilities for the participating countries. It is important to note, however, that in the case of China, central bank swap lines serve multiple purposes. They are strongly linked to the promotion of payments in RMB and the currency's internationalization.[10] The primary aim of the PBOC swap lines appears to be the attainment of a reserve currency status for the RMB rather than simply providing credit lines in times of financial distress.

In our view, along with continued efforts to substantially increase IMF quotas, it is necessary to establish a standing and nondiscretionary, multilateral central bank swap facility, with the US Federal Reserve at its center and a strengthened intermediary role for the IMF. As emphasized by Rey (2015), the global financial cycle is influenced by several factors, including the global supply and demand for credit, changes in asset prices, and the risk attitude of global investors, all of which are impacted by US monetary policy. These factors can lead to the creation of financial imbalances and vulnerabilities that can ultimately result in financial crises in EMEs. While it is natural for the US Federal Reserve to conduct monetary policy to achieve domestic policy goals, it should also recognize the potential spillover effects on EMEs and adopt a more coordinated and cooperative approach with other central banks to mitigate the risks of global financial instability.[11] For instance, in the process of its monetary policy normalization, the US Federal Reserve could help mitigate negative externalities in international financial markets by leveraging the swap facility.

The US Federal Reserve recognizes this problem and maintains a standing swap facility with major reserve currency central banks—European Central Bank, Bank of England, Bank of Japan, Bank of Canada, and Swiss National Bank. It also maintains the Foreign and International Monetary Authorities (FIMA) repurchase facility, which allows foreign central banks and other foreign monetary authorities to temporarily raise US dollars by selling US treasuries to the Fed and agreeing to buy them back at maturity. However, note that the key difference between the central bank swap and the FIMA repo facility is the collateral. In the case of swaps, it is foreign currencies, but in the case of the repo, it is US treasury bonds. Hence, access is limited to central banks that have enough US treasuries.

We support a standing multilateral central bank swap mechanism intermediated by the IMF. Under this mechanism, the IMF would hold swap lines with the central banks of major currencies such as the US dollar, euro, and the Japanese yen, and become the counterparty of a swap. Because the counterparty is the IMF, default risk can be significantly mitigated for major central banks. The IMF would act as the intermediary between participating central banks, which would be able to request a currency swap from the IMF in times of a foreign currency liquidity crisis. The central bank requesting the swap would need to provide collateral in the form of its own currency or IMF-approved securities. The IMF would determine the terms of the swap, including the exchange rate and duration of the swap, based on the specific circumstances of the requesting central bank. Finally, the IMF would monitor the usage of the swap facility and ensure that the borrowing central bank is making progress toward resolving its liquidity crisis.

An alternative approach would be to create a multilayered network of central bank swap lines. For instance, as a guard against potential liquidity problems due to the US Federal Reserve policy normalization in 2017–2018, the Bank of Korea was able to obtain an indirect liquidity line by entering into swap agreements with the Bank of Canada and the Swiss National Bank, which already have standing swap lines with the Fed. Although those swap agreements were bilateral and non-US-dollar-based, they contributed to the stabilization of the exchange rate and the credit default swap premium on Korean bonds. We could envision a similar swap network based on the US dollar in which the US Federal Reserve would establish swap lines with a set of major regional hub central banks, and then those regional hub central banks would maintain swap lines with local central banks in their respective regions. In case a US dollar-based, multilayered swap network is not feasible, a bilateral currency-based swap network could also help if the US Federal Reserve could expand the counterparties of its swap facility beyond the five major central banks to include more regional hub central banks.

Strengthening Surveillance and Coordination of Macroprudential Policies

Global financial cycles and their implications for global financial stability, particularly for open EMEs, underscore the need for an effective global surveillance system to identify and address potential risks in advance. They also call for more coordinated macroprudential policies among both providers and recipients of capital flows. However, the current global financial surveillance and regulatory framework, which consists of national regulators coordinated by multiple international institutions such as the IMF, FSB, and BIS, has several deficiencies.

First, as emphasized by Elson (2010), the policy governance scheme for macroprudential risk and financial stability has not been effectively established at either the national or global level. At the national level, there is an ongoing debate about whether the central bank or a regulatory authority should take responsibility. At the global level, even though the FSB was intended to focus on the regulatory aspects of global financial stability, and the IMF was to focus on macrofinancial aspects, coordination between these two bodies has been relatively limited, in part reflecting different channels of vertical accountability. Also, EMEs are underrepresented in both the FSB and the IMF despite their growing share of the global economy, and there is a lack of effective channels to reflect their views in formulating a macroprudential regulatory framework.

Second, the surveillance framework remains largely focused on individual countries, especially capital recipient countries, with less than adequate capacity to identify and monitor financial vulnerabilities from a global perspective. The limited availability of comprehensive and standardized data on cross-border financial flows and interlinkages between global financial centers and institutions makes it difficult to accurately monitor and assess risks. The framework also primarily focuses on traditional banking sectors, neglecting the fast-growing NBFIs such as investment funds, insurance companies, and other shadow banking entities. The limited scope and timeliness of data availability constrain the effectiveness of macroprudential measures to address rapidly evolving financial risks.

Third, there is inadequate coordination and collaboration between different national and international regulatory agencies, leading to regulatory arbitrage and an excessive regulatory burden on capital-recipient countries. There is resistance from financial industries in capital-exporting countries to regulatory changes proposed in a multilateral framework, as they tend to view them as limiting their scope for business, ignoring cross-border externalities of their actions. In many cases, however, negative externalities could be better addressed in the source countries than by recipient countries.

One positive change after the GFC has been the increased adoption of macroprudential policies. For example, both AEs and EMEs have implemented an array of measures regarding household credit or housing sector risks.[12] Typical instruments include maximum loan-to-value, debt service-to-income, and debt-to-income ratios, as well as sectoral risk weights in minimum capital requirements. More recently, in compliance with Basel III, many AEs and EMEs have introduced countercyclical bank capital buffers. Some EMEs have also used macroprudential measures in foreign exchange markets designed to operate in a preemptive manner during capital inflow periods.

It is encouraging to see that international financial institutions are changing their views on the use of capital management and macroprudential measures in EMEs because they have recognized the challenges faced by many open EMEs. The IMF began developing an institutional view on capital controls, allowing for their use in certain circumstances, such as when financial flows threaten economic or financial stability and capital flow management measures (CFMs) do not substitute for necessary adjustments in macroprudential, monetary, or fiscal policies. Some concerns were raised that the view was too restrictive, however, and countries still feared that markets might stigmatize them for using CFMs. Subsequently, the IMF proposed an Integrated Policy Framework (IPF) that conceptualizes the use of CFMs, foreign exchange intervention, monetary policy, fiscal policy, and macroprudential policy as distinct instruments—all of which may be necessary to achieve multiple policy goals in an open economy.[13]

The IMF has recently reexamined its institutional view on capital controls, concluding that CFMs with a macroprudential rationale (CFMs/ macroprudential measures) could be justified as preemptive measures if they aim to prevent a build-up of financial vulnerabilities such as an overhang of foreign currency debt.[14] While this is a step forward, Obstfeld (2022) argues that it does not yet fully realize the potential of the IPF to place capital control and foreign exchange intervention policies on an equal footing with monetary, fiscal, and macroprudential policies, and he suggests that the IMF should take its reconsideration further.

Similarly, the BIS has suggested the development of Macro-Financial Stability Frameworks (MFSFs) to guide the formulation of policies to foster macrofinancial stability and avoid the buildup of systemic risk. The BIS MFSF is a comprehensive policy framework that seeks to achieve macroeconomic and financial stability through a combination of monetary policy, foreign exchange market intervention (FXI), micro- and macroprudential measures (MPMs), fiscal policy, and CFMs. AEs have primarily relied on monetary policy and MPMs, while EMEs have also used CFMs and FXI. In evaluating the MFSF, Borio et al. (2022) find that MPMs, CFMs, and FXI have generally been effective in stabilizing domestic credit. They also highlight the importance of effective communication and coordination among the various authorities responsible for implementing the MFSF, including central banks, regulatory agencies, and other government bodies.

Overall, recent efforts of international financial institutions to allow more flexible approaches based on the realities of EMEs are encouraging. More concerted efforts are needed, however, to improve consistency among the views and guidelines of the various institutions—IMF, BIS, FSB, and the OECD.

Despite the advances in the reform of global surveillance and regulatory framework since the GFC, there remain some weaknesses that need to be addressed. One important weakness is that the current framework is not fully equipped with policy tools to mitigate potential risks emanating from shifts in global capital flows, particularly from previous bank-centered flows to more bond- and NBFI-centered flows. The various macro- and microprudential policies introduced after the GFC have helped increase the resilience of the global banking system. Indeed, progress made in strengthening the capital and liquidity of the banking system prevented banks from amplifying the recent pandemic shock. However, while the banking system is better protected, new sources of risks are emerging in NBFIs.

As noted above, since the GFC, cross-border bond liabilities of EMEs have increased substantially, driven by a shift from bank borrowing to bond markets, also known as the "second phase of global liquidity."[15] While EMEs have made efforts to develop local currency bond markets to overcome the "original sin" of not being able to borrow externally in domestic currency, foreign investors have played a crucial role in these local currency markets, leading to the emergence of the "original sin redux," where EMEs continue to face currency risks.[16] A weaker exchange rate now hampers the balance sheets of lenders as they are now faced with a currency mismatch risk, making them more sensitive to signs of potential problems.

Borio et al. (2022) highlight the role of collective investment vehicles domiciled in Europe or the United States as important investors in EME local and foreign currency bond markets. National authorities should engage in international discussions about prudential regulations or risk management guidelines for NBFIs involved in cross-border portfolio investments. For instance, national authorities in AEs could encourage improved liquidity risk management practices in collective investment vehicles, especially those investing in less liquid EME assets, by guiding them to maintain adequate cash buffers during favorable times, as suggested by Schrimpf et al. (2021).

The FSB identifies NBFI vulnerabilities as a priority area for attention. A recent FSB report on NBFIs focuses on reducing excessive spikes in demand for liquidity by addressing the underlying vulnerabilities, such as liquidity mismatches or the build-up of leverage, and mitigating their financial stability impact.[17] The policy proposals involve repurposing existing NBFI policy tools and focusing on reducing liquidity mismatch risks in open-ended funds. The FSB's work program includes analytical and policy work to enhance the resilience of NBFIs and assess the interactions between US dollar funding, external vulnerabilities, and NBFI financing in emerging markets.

The FSB (2022b) also notes that closing data gaps is crucial for risk monitoring and timely adoption of policies to mitigate vulnerabilities. There is no comprehensive dataset on cross-border investment by NBFIs in EMEs, even though their role in financing EMEs has grown significantly. International organizations and national statistical agencies should develop more comprehensive information on the sources and currency denomination of capital flows and external debt. Greater information on investment funds would support assessing vulnerabilities in the sector.

Finally, it is important to better coordinate macrofinancial policies between AEs and EMEs. As Claessens (2014) notes, the need for international coordination of macroprudential policies stems from the presence of externalities. Policy spillover problems can arise when countries vary in policies or calibrations to deal with similar risks. Better coordination of the macroprudential policies of capital-source countries with those of recipient countries, taking into account the potential negative externalities that may arise during fluctuations in the global financial cycle, can help. For instance, in periods of upturns in the global financial cycle, AEs can tighten countercyclical macroprudential measures to alleviate the prudential policy burdens faced by capital-recipient countries.

Promoting Market-Based Resilience against Global Financial Cycle

Along with efforts to enhance the institutional capacity and functionalities of existing international financial institutions, there have been suggestions to strengthen the market-based resilience of the global financial system. For instance, Brunnermeier and Huang (2019) propose using sovereign bond-backed securities (SBBS) to redirect potentially destabilizing capital flows caused by flight-to-safety during contractions in the global financial cycle. By redirecting these flows, capital can move across different asset classes of EMEs instead of flowing only from these economies to AEs. An international special-purpose vehicle could be established to purchase a fraction of the bonds from EMEs, pool them, and divide them into senior and junior bond tranches. The senior bonds would then serve as a global safe asset for EMEs.

Although this proposal can have benefits, potential problems also need to be considered. It would involve setting up special-purpose vehicles and pooling and tranching bonds from multiple EMEs, which can be difficult to implement due to heterogeneous bond standards across countries and challenges in achieving a sufficiently diversified pool of bonds to reduce credit risk given that most EMEs tend to be exposed to risks in the same direction during fluctuations in the global financial cycle. The proposal also relies on market participants accepting the SBBS as safe assets, which may take time to develop. In addition, currency risk issues still remain. If the bonds are issued in local currencies, global investors are exposed to currency mismatches ("original sin redux"). If the bonds are denominated in US dollars, it would be questionable whether these bonds could genuinely be considered a global safe asset.

In a similar vein, there has been an initiative to recycle capital flows within regional capital markets in Asia. In 2003, the ASEAN+3 Asian Bond Markets Initiative (ABMI) was launched to promote the development of a regional bond market in Asia.[18] The participating countries aimed to foster liquid and efficient bond markets by facilitating the harmonization of bond standards and regulations. The absence of robust and vibrant capital markets in Asia was identified as one of the primary structural weaknesses that caused and exacerbated the 1997 Asian crisis. A more balanced financial system and well-developed bond markets would reduce the likelihood of a recurrence of financial crises in Asia by mitigating the problems of "double mismatches," namely, the mismatches in maturities and currencies in external financing. The development of regional bond markets would also contribute to greater mobilization and recycling of abundant savings within the region. As a result of such regional and individual country efforts, local currency-denominated bond markets in Asia have grown remarkably in terms of the size and diversity of issuers.

Despite their growth in volume and liquidity, local currency sovereign bonds in Asia have not yet attained the status of safe assets, even within the region. We propose a solution that combines the suggestion of Brunnermeier and Huang with the efforts of the ABMI. The ABMI has consistently worked toward harmonizing bond standards and regulations, positioning it well to consider establishing a special-purpose vehicle that can issue sovereign bond-backed securities by pooling and securitizing local sovereign bonds of member countries. Credit enhancement from regional institutions such as the Asian Development Bank could strengthen the creditworthiness of these securities and help them attain safe asset status in regional capital markets. This approach would also contribute to multipolarization of global capital markets, mitigating excessive swings in capital flows driven by shifts in US monetary policy.

Improving Restructuring Schemes for Sovereign Debt

The debt burden of EMEs has increased rapidly, compounded by the COVID-19 crisis. Total nominal debt in thirty large low- and middle-income countries rose to $98 trillion in 2022 from $75 trillion at the end of 2019.[19] The recent tightening of monetary policies by the United States and other AE central banks, along with the rising value of the US dollar, have placed increased pressure on the debt service capacity of emerging-market and developing economies, which implies that the demand for debt suspension and restructuring could increase in the future.

Borrowers in EMEs are facing an increasingly complex landscape with a diverse group of lenders, both official and private, utilizing different instruments with varying contractual terms and restrictions that may not always be transparent or made public. Official figures from international institutions likely understate the size of actual debts, as some creditors are not reporting all their lending to multilateral bodies. Additionally, there exist sizable contingent liabilities, such as those related to public-private partnership projects. Such factors add to the challenge and complexity of ensuring efficient debt restructuring, when needed, that also provides for an equitable burden-sharing among creditors.

Efforts to improve the multilateral framework for sovereign debt restructuring have been ongoing, but various hurdles have hindered progress, including a lack of creditor coordination, difficulties in reaching collective action, uneven involvement of all creditors in the restructuring process, and, more fundamentally, a lack of an adequate legal framework.

While recent sovereign debt restructuring has improved, with faster action and higher creditor participation due to the use of collective action clauses (CACs), there are still significant issues to address.[20] These include, for example, a lack of CACs in a large stock of international bonds, the absence of majority restructuring provisions in other forms of debt such as syndicated loans or subsovereign debt, increased use of collateral and collateral-like instruments, and information asymmetry problems leading to complications in the restructuring process and tensions among creditors.

A Debt Service Suspension Initiative (DSSI) was launched in May 2020 as a global effort to respond to the COVID-19 pandemic. It enabled low-income countries to temporarily suspend their debt payments to official bilateral creditors to free up resources for spending on health care, social protection, and other priority areas during the pandemic. The DSSI expired at the end of 2021. While a useful and timely initiative, the DSSI has also faced criticism for several reasons. It did not cover all countries that needed debt relief, including many middle-income countries struggling to repay debts. Because of its temporary nature, many countries still faced debt repayment challenges at the end of the suspension period. The DSSI only deferred debt repayments instead of providing an enduring solution to the problem of unsustainable debt levels. Most critically, it only covered debt owed to official creditors, excluding private creditors. Overall, the DSSI is viewed as a stopgap measure that provided some short-term relief for low-income countries in a crisis situation, but it failed to address the underlying issues of unsustainable debt and debt restructuring. As such, further action is needed to confront the debt challenges faced by low and middle-income countries.

A major gap in sovereign debt restructuring is the lack of an adequate sovereign debt workout arrangement that involves private creditors.[21] In the case of the DSSI, the G20 asked private creditors to participate on comparable terms, but only one private creditor participated.

Eichengreen (2020) suggests that the Paris Club, an organization of official creditors, should be expanded, and official institutions should play a bigger role in negotiating the restructuring of private debt and setting standards for these negotiations. To support this, governments and regulators could mandate the inclusion of clauses in loan contracts that facilitate rapid restructuring during global crises and prohibit the trading of bonds without these clauses.

In November 2020, the G20 launched the Common Framework for Debt Treatments beyond the DSSI to facilitate restructuring of the debts of the DSSI eligible low-income countries in cases of persistent liquidity problems or insolvency. Importantly, it includes non-Paris Club members such as China, the biggest official creditor to developing countries, in a framework that effectively extends Paris Club procedures to all official bilateral creditors. While it is clearly a step forward, there are several concerns about the effectiveness of the Common Framework due to its lack of binding commitments. There are no enforcement mechanisms in place to ensure that countries adhere to the framework's guidelines, which can lead to inconsistent implementation and unequal treatment. In addition, the framework's focus is still on debt standstills, rather than debt relief, which may be inadequate for addressing the scale of the debt sustainability challenges facing developing countries.

Obstfeld (2022) suggests that the Common Framework should include more debtor countries and engage the entire range of private sector creditors early in the restructuring process. He argues that the G20 should regularize the formation of creditor committees within the framework to reduce coordination problems and information asymmetries. The G20 should also encourage reforms in debt contracts and transparency and establish a standing consultative mechanism to coordinate the framework.[22]

According to Bulow et al. (2020), the involvement of private creditors in sovereign debt restructuring is critical. They emphasize the need to ensure that the burden of debt restructuring is shared fairly between official and private creditors. Even though official creditors should have priority in repayments, private creditors typically have pushed hard to secure repayments due to them. This means that, in situations like that faced by Greece, official creditors may end up shouldering most of the losses, even though they held much less of the debt originally. Moreover, private investors are using new tactics to resist debt write-downs and restructuring, compounding the challenge of maintaining fairness and equity among all creditors.

To encourage more active participation from non-Paris Club official lenders such as China and from private creditors, multilateral institutions may need to participate in loss-sharing to some extent while not undermining the principle according these institutions a preferred creditor status. In doing so, it is important to establish a fair loss-sharing rule that can be applied to all participating creditors. One potential approach would be to establish a loss-sharing rule based on the price mechanism, utilizing differential lending spreads across creditors. Although standardizing and comparing lending spreads across highly heterogeneous loan contracts presents challenges, it may be possible to establish a principle that loss-sharing be commensurate with lending spreads. These spreads indicate relative returns to creditors when the loans were being serviced.

Private creditors that seek high profits and charge interest rates to cover the full risk premium should bear higher losses in debt relief. In contrast, development institutions that provide concessional loans with submarket lending rates should bear lower losses. The establishment of such a fair loss-sharing rule can help create a more level playing field among creditors, promoting greater cooperation and coordination among them. Ultimately, increasing the burden-sharing of private creditors in debt restructuring will require a combination of regulatory changes, market incentives, and international cooperation.

Conclusion

The GFA has undergone considerable change over time. Much of the reform action occurred in response to financial crises. As global finance continues to evolve and new challenges emerge, the world would benefit from a more proactive approach to GFA reform, one that is more agile in aligning the GFA to the changing dynamics and emerging vulnerabilities.

Since the GFC and the reform actions taken in its aftermath, there have been important developments in global financial flows. The global financial system has seen the emergence of new risks. The composition of capital flows has been shifting, including a declining role of bank lending relative to bond flows and a rise in flows intermediated by NBFIs. The increased reliance on debt markets and NBFIs, together with currency mismatches, create significant vulnerabilities for emerging-market and developing economies. Many of them face an increased debt burden, with a growing number experiencing heightened debt service pressures. Moreover, global imbalances have widened again, especially after the pandemic. The resurgence of imbalances has been particularly pronounced in the United States, implying potential threats to global financial stability from a US rebalancing. Emerging-market and developing economies have faced important spillover effects from shifts in the global financial cycle and in the monetary policy stance of AEs.

This chapter has outlined a few key areas for strengthening the GFA. First, the international lender of last resort capacity should be bolstered, including by augmenting IMF resources, enhancing the role of the SDR, and improving the functioning and coverage of central bank swap facilities. Second, the global macroeconomic surveillance framework, which remains predominantly focused on individual countries, especially those receiving capital, should be strengthened to better address global linkages, spillovers, and policy coordination challenges. And the financial system regulatory and monitoring framework, which has been substantially strengthened for banks, needs to pay more attention to NBFIs in view of their expanded role and associated risks. Third, market-based resilience of the global financial system can be enhanced. In EMEs, for example, the development of local capital markets, harmonization of bond standards, and innovations such as sovereign bond-back securities can help better insulate their financial systems and curb contagion from shifts in the global financial cycle. Fourth, the process for sovereign debt restructuring should be improved. There is a need to establish a multilateral sovereign debt restructuring framework that can be put into action in a timely fashion when needed and that provides for fair burden sharing and full participation of both official and private creditors.

While beyond the scope of this chapter, there are also other important new challenges for the GFA. One is climate change. The global financial system will be called upon to help mobilize large amounts of financing in support of countries' efforts to address climate transition, including by augmenting public funding, bolstering the role of multilateral development banks, and incentivizing private investment. Its resilience to climate-related risks will need to be boosted. Another is technological change. The digital transformation of finance can facilitate financial flows, improving access and lowering cost, but it can also create new risks to financial stability that will need to be managed.[23]

NOTES

1. Elson (2020).
2. In this chapter, we mainly follow the classification of advanced, emerging-market, and developing economies used by the IMF in its World Economic Outlook reports. However, in the case of citations of data from other institutions such as the BIS and FSB, we use the country classification of the respective institution.
3. Bernanke (2005).
4. Borio and Disyatat (2011).
5. Bruno and Shin (2015).
6. Chen et al. (2016).
7. Miyajima et al. (2014).
8. Elson (2010).
9. FSB (2019).
10. Bahaj and Reis (2020) and Perez-Saiz and Zhang (2023).
11. In this regard, it is noteworthy to mention that the European Central Bank has recently introduced a tool to alleviate the negative externalities that peripheral countries may experience due to the normalization of its monetary policy. This tool, known as the Transmission Protection Instrument (TPI), can be utilized to counteract unwarranted and disorderly market developments that may seriously impede the smooth transmission of monetary policy across the euro area. In such cases, the Eurosystem could purchase securities from individual countries to address any deterioration in financing conditions that is not warranted by country-specific fundamentals. These purchases would be conducted in the secondary market and would focus on public sector bonds.
12. BIS (2022b).
13. IMF (2020b).
14. IMF (2022).
15. Shin (2013).
16. Carstens and Shin (2019).
17. FSB (2022b).

18. ASEAN+3 include ten members of the Association of Southeast Asian Nations plus China, Japan, and Korea.

19. Institute of International Finance (2023).

20. IMF (2020a).

21. Gallagher et al. (2020).

22. Chorzempa and Mazarei (2021) argue that the success of the Common Framework also depends on the implementation of IMF policies for lending into private and official arrears, which would facilitate the participation of non-Paris Club and private/hybrid creditors in debt restructuring. They recommend creating a flexible framework of creditor committees, including China, as part of the Common Framework or a broader initiative. The IMF could play the role of the secretariat and provide debt sustainability analyses. Georgieva and Pazarbasioglu (2021) suggest that the Common Framework needs to deliver more quickly and provide greater clarity on the steps and timelines in the process, as well as a comprehensive and sustained debt service payment standstill. The framework should also clarify the enforcement of comparability of treatment, including through the IMF arrears policies, and be expanded to cover a wider range of highly indebted countries.

23. Chapter 8 of this book examines the implications of digital technologies for the international monetary system.

REFERENCES

Avdjiev, Stefan, Bryan Hardy, Sebnem Kalemli-Ozcan, and Luis Serven. 2022. "Gross Capital Flows by Banks, Corporates, and Sovereigns." *Journal of the European Economic Association* 20 (5): 2098–135.

Bahaj, Saleem, and Ricardo Reis. 2020. "Jumpstarting an International Currency." Bank of England Staff Working Paper 874. Bank of England, London.

———. 2022. "Central Bank Swap Lines: Evidence on the Effects of the Lender of Last Resort." *Review of Economic Studies* 89 (4): 1654–93.

Baker, Andrew. 2009. "Deliberative Equality and the Trans-governmental Politics of the Global Financial Architecture." *Global Governance* 15 (2): 195–218.

Bank for International Settlements (BIS). 2022a. "BIS International Banking Statistics and Global Liquidity Indicators at End-June 2022." Basel. October.

———. 2022b. "Macro-Financial Stability Frameworks and External Financial Conditions." Basel. July.

Bernanke, Benjamin. 2005. "The Global Savings Glut and the U.S. Current Account Deficit." Remarks at the Sandridge Lecture, Virginia Association of Economists, Richmond, Virginia, March 10.

Borio, Claudio, Ilhyock Shim, and Hyun Song Shin. 2022. "Macro-Financial Stability Frameworks (MFSF): Experience and Challenges." BIS Working Paper 1057. Bank for International Settlements, Basel.

Borio, Claudio, and Piti Disyatat. 2011. "Global Imbalances and the Financial Crisis: Link or No Link?" BIS Working Paper 346. Bank for International Settlements, Basel.

Brunnermeier, Markus, and Lunyang Huang. 2019. *A Global Safe Asset from and for Emerging Economies.* Santiago de Chile: Central Bank of Chile.

Bruno, Valentina, and Hyun Song Shin. 2015. "Capital Flows and the Risk-Taking Channel of Monetary Policy." *Journal of Monetary Economics* 71 (C): 119–32.

Bulow, Jeremy, Carmen Reinhart, Kenneth Rogoff, and Christoph Trebesch. 2020. "The COVID-19 Debt Pandemic." *IMF Finance and Development* (September): 12–16.

Carstens, Agustin, and Hyun Song Shin. 2019. "Emerging Markets Aren't Out of the Woods Yet." *Foreign Affairs*, March 15.

Chen, Qianying, Andrew Filardon, Dong He, and Feng Zhu. 2016. "Financial Crisis, U.S. Unconventional Monetary Policy, and International Spillovers." *Journal of International Money and Finance* 67 (C): 62–81.

Chorzempa, Martin, and Adnan Mazarei. 2021. "Improving China's Participation in Resolving Developing-Country Debt Problems," Policy Brief 21-10. Peterson Institute for International Economics, Washington, DC.

Claessens, Stijn. 2014. "An Overview of Macroprudential Policy Tools," IMF Working Paper 14/214. International Monetary Fund, Washington, DC.

Coulibaly, Brahima, and Eswar Prasad. 2021. "Strengthening the Global Financial Safety Net by Broadening Systematic Access to Temporary Foreign Liquidity." Policy Brief, G20 Think20, September.

Crockett, Andrew. 2009. "Reforming the Global Financial Architecture." Remarks at the Federal Reserve Bank of San Francisco Conference on Asia and the Global Financial Crisis, October.

Eichengreen, Barry. 2020. "Cultivating Global Financial Cooperation." *IMF Finance and Development* (September): 21–23.

Elson, Anthony. 2010. "The Current Financial Crisis and Reform of the Global Financial Architecture." *The International Spectator* 45 (1): 17–36.

Financial Stability Board (FSB). 2019. "Global Monitoring Report on Non-Bank Financial Intermediation 2018." Basel. February.

———. 2022a. "US Dollar Funding and Emerging Market Economy Vulnerabilities." Basel. April.

———. 2022b. "Enhancing the Resilience of Non-Bank Financial Intermediation." Basel. November.

Gallagher, Kevin, Haihong Gao, Ulrich Volz, Jose Antonio Ocampo et al. 2020. "Expanding the Global Financial Safety." G20 Insights.

Georgieva, Kristalina, and Ceyla Pazarbasioglu. 2021. "The G20 Common Framework for Debt Treatments Must be Stepped Up." *IMF Blog*, December 2.

Giovanoli, Mario. 2009. "The Reform of the International Financial Architecture after the Global Crisis." *NYU Journal of International Law and Politics* 42 (1): 81–122.

Gislen, Marushia, Ida Hansson, and Ola Melander. 2021. "Dollar Liquidity from the Federal Reserve to Other Central Banks." *Sveriges Riksbank Economic Review* 2021:1: 27–51.

Gourinchas, Pierre-Olivier. 2023. "International Macroeconomics: From the Great Financial Crisis to COVID-19 and Beyond." *IMF Economic Review* 71 (1): 1–34.

Institute of International Finance (IIF). 2023. "Global Debt Monitor: A Many-Faceted Crisis." Washington, DC. February.

International Monetary Fund (IMF). 2020a. "The International Architecture for Resolving Sovereign Debt Involving Private Sector Creditors: Recent Developments, Challenges, and Reform Options." Washington, DC. September.

———. 2020b. "Toward an Integrated Policy Framework." IMF Policy Paper. Washington, DC. October.

———. 2022. "Review of the Institutional View on the Liberalization and Management of Capital Flows." IMF Policy Paper. Washington, DC. March.

Lane, Philip, and Gian Maria Milesi-Ferretti. 2018. "The External Wealth of Nations Revisited: International Financial Integration in the Aftermath of the Global Financial Crisis." *IMF Economic Review* 66 (1): 189–222.

Milesi-Ferretti, Gian Maria. 2022. "The External Wealth of Nations Database." Brookings Institution, Washington, DC.

Miyajima, Ken, Madhusudan Mohanty, and James Yetman. 2014. "Spillovers of U.S. Unconventional Monetary Policy to Asia: The Role of Long-Term Interest Rates" BIS Working Paper 478. Bank for International Settlements, Basel, December.

Obstfeld, Maurice. 2022. "Global Economic Recovery in the Face of COVID-19." In *G20 Indonesia 2022: New Normal, New Technologies, New Financing*, edited by Lili Yan Ing and Dani Rodrik. Economic Research Institute for ASEAN and East Asia (ERIA), Jakarta.

Ocampo, Jose Antonio. 2019. "The SDR's Time Has Come." *IMF Finance and Development*, December.

Perez-Saiz, Hector, and Longmei Zhang. 2023. "Renminbi Usage in Cross-Border Payments: Regional Patterns and the Role of Swap Lines and Offshore Clearing Banks." IMF Working Paper 23/77. International Monetary Fund, Washington, DC.

Rey, Helen. 2015. "Dilemma Not Trilemma: The Global Financial Cycle and Monetary Policy Independence." NBER Working Paper 21162. National Bureau of Economic Research, Cambridge, MA.

Schrimpf, Andreas, Ilhyock Shim, and Hyun Song Shin. 2021. "Liquidity Management and Asset Sales by Bond Funds in the Face of Investor Redemptions in March 2020." *BIS Bulletin* 39, March.

Shin, Hyun Song. 2013. "The Second Phase of Global Liquidity and Its Impact on Emerging Economies." Keynote Address at the Federal Reserve Bank of San Francisco Asia Economic Policy Conference, November 3–5.

Truman, Edwin. 2008. "On What Terms Is the IMF Worth Funding?" Working Paper 08-11. Peterson Institute for International Economics, Washington, DC.

Yeyati, Eduardo Levy. 2020. "COVID, Fed swaps and the IMF as lender of last resort." *VoxEu*, Center for Economic Policy Research, March.

Contributors

WOO JIN CHOI   is an assistant professor at the University of Seoul, Business
Administration. His research interests center on international finance
and economics. He was previously a research fellow in the Department
of Macroeconomic and Financial Policies at the Korea Development
Institute (KDI). His research has appeared in several economic
journals, including the *Journal of International Economics*. He is an
Economics Advisory Board Member of the Seoul Institute. He earned
his Ph.D. in economics from the University of Virginia.

DIANE COYLE   is the Bennett Professor of Public Policy at the University
of Cambridge and codirects the Bennett Institute for Public Policy.
Her latest book is *Cogs and Monsters: What Economics Is and What It
Should Be*. Her current research focuses on productivity, the digital
economy, and economic measurement. She is also a director of the
Productivity Institute, a fellow of the Office for National Statistics,
and adviser to the Competition and Markets Authority and the
National Infrastructure Commission in the United Kingdom.
She was awarded a damehood (DBE) for her contributions to
economic policy. She received a Ph.D. in economics from Harvard
University.

JOON-HO HAHM is a professor at Yonsei University and previously held positions at the University of California, Santa Barbara, and KDI. With experience spanning both the public and private sectors, including roles at the World Bank, Korean government ministries, and financial institutions, his work has focused on shaping economic policy. He served as a member of the Monetary Policy Board at the Bank of Korea and also as president of the Korea Money and Finance Association. He earned his Ph.D. in business from Columbia University.

BERNARD HOEKMAN is professor and director of Global Economics at the Robert Schuman Centre for Advanced Studies, European University Institute. He is a research fellow at the Centre for Economic Policy Research and an associate of the U.K. Centre for Inclusive Trade Policy. He served as director of the international trade department at the World Bank and held positions in the GATT Secretariat and at the Scienes Po, Paris. He has published widely on international trade policy and globalization. He holds a Ph.D. in economics from the University of Michigan.

DAEHEE JEONG is a senior fellow and director of the Department of Macroeconomic and Financial Policies at KDI. He previously led the Office of Global Economy at KDI and also served as a senior economist at the World Bank. With expertise in international finance, macroeconomic forecasting, and financial regulation, his research has appeared in KDI papers, studies, and academic journals, with a particular focus on Korea's macroeconomic management and policy planning. He holds a Ph.D. in economics from the Texas A&M University.

BRIAN JUDGE is a policy fellow at the Center for Human-Compatible Artificial Intelligence and the Berkeley Roundtable on the International Economy at the University of California, Berkeley. His research and teaching interests span politics, technology, and finance. His first book, *Democracy in Default: Finance and the Rise of Neoliberalism in America*, was published in 2024 by the Columbia University Press. He received a Ph.D. in political science from the University of California, Berkeley.

SIWOOK LEE is a professor at the KDI School of Public Policy and Management and is currently president of the Korean Institute of

International Economic Policy. He previously served as president of the Korean Association of Trade and Industry Studies, associate dean at the KDI School, executive director at the KDI Center for International Development, and editor-in-chief of the KDI *Journal of Public Policy*. He has also been a policy consultant to the Korean government and international organizations on international economic issues. He holds a Ph.D. in economics from the University of Michigan.

WONHYUK LIM is a professor at the KDI School of Public Policy and Management. He previously served as a senior fellow and vice president/director of Competition Policy at KDI. He is a former Center for Northeast Asian Policy Studies fellow at Brookings. He served on the Presidential Transition Committee and the Presidential Northeast Asia Committee in Korea. He has written extensively on development, corporate governance, and multilateral and regional cooperation, and his research also supports Korea's Knowledge Sharing Program. He holds a Ph.D. in economics from Stanford University.

JUSTIN YIFU LIN is dean of the Institute of New Structural Economics and the Institute of South-South Cooperation and Development and professor and honorary dean of the National School of Development at Peking University. He served as senior vice president and chief economist of the World Bank. His books include *Beating the Odds* (with Célestin Monga), *The Quest for Prosperity, New Structural Economics*, and *Demystifying the Chinese Economy*, among several others. He is a fellow of the British Academy and the Academy of Sciences for the Developing World. He holds a Ph.D. in economics from the University of Chicago.

CÉLESTIN MONGA teaches public policy and economics at Harvard's Kennedy School of Government and the University of Paris 1 Panthéon-Sorbonne. He has held senior positions in academia, international development institutions, and financial services, including serving as managing director at the United Nations Industrial Development Organization, vice president and chief economist at the African Development Bank, and senior economic adviser at the World Bank. He won the 2022 International Economic Association Fellow Award. He has published extensively, including several books, on various dimensions of economic and political development. He holds a Ph.D. in economics from the University of Pau, France.

ESWAR PRASAD is the Tolani Senior Professor of Trade Policy and Professor of Economics at Cornell University. He is also a senior fellow at Brookings, where he holds the New Century Chair in International Economics, and a research associate at the National Bureau of Economic Research. He is a former head of the IMF's China Division. His latest book, *The Future of Money*, was listed among the best economics books of 2021 by *The Economist*, the *Financial Times*, and *Foreign Affairs*. His articles have appeared in prominent media outlets. He holds a Ph.D. in economics from the University of Chicago.

ZIA QURESHI is a senior fellow in the Global Economy and Development program at Brookings. His research covers a broad range of global economic issues. He has recently led research projects at Brookings on technology, globalization, and the shifting growth and distribution dynamics in the world today. He previously worked in leadership positions at the World Bank and the IMF, including serving as director, Development Economics, at the World Bank. He led several World Bank and IMF flagship publications. He holds a D.Phil. in economics from Oxford University, where he was a Rhodes Scholar.

LAURA TYSON is Distinguished Professor of the Graduate School at the Haas School of Business, University of California, Berkeley, and chairs the Berkeley Blum Center for Developing Economies Board of Trustees. She was previously dean of the London Business School and the Haas School of Business. She was a member of the US Department of State Foreign Affairs Policy Board and served on President Obama's Council on Jobs and Competitiveness and Economic Recovery Advisory Board. She served in the Clinton Administration as Chair of the Council of Economic Advisers and as Director of the National Economic Council. She holds a Ph.D. in economics from the Massachusetts Institute of Technology.

JOHN ZYSMAN is Professor Emeritus at the University of California, Berkeley, and co-founder and co-director of the Berkeley Roundtable on the International Economy. He has authored several books on a range of topics in political economy, and his recent work covers the implications of digital platforms and intelligent tools, including AI, for economies and societies, as well as the challenges and opportunities of climate change and the green economy. He has also worked at leadership levels with governments and firms in Asia, Europe, and the United States on government policy and corporate strategy. He received a Ph.D. in political science from the Massachusetts Institute of Technology.

Index

economies and, 251–252, 257–261,
264–267; developing economies
and, 258–261, 279; EMEs and,
249, 251–252, 257–271, 279; GFC
and, 251, 253, 257–261, 265,
271–273, 279; imbalances of,
255–264; IMF and, 251, 255–256,
265–272, 279; overview, 250–255;
reforms, 250–251, 264–280; in the
United States, 228–229, 257–259,
261
global financial crisis (GFC) of
2008–2009, 5, 30–31, 61, 95, 127,
192–194; GFA and, 251, 253,
257–261, 265, 271–273, 279
global financial cycles, 261, 270,
274–275
global financial safety net (GFSN),
265–267
globalization, 54n38, 192–193; in
Asia, 61–88; barriers to, 64–67, 73;
cross-border data flows and, 5–6,
208; digital, 5, 13–14, 25–26,
30–31, 36–39; EMEs and, 35, 62,
73–75; financial, 17–19, 249–251;
future of, 3–8, 21, 26, 36–39,
51–53; GVCs and, 207–211;
neoliberal, 3, 13, 25–31, 35–37,
40, 43–44, 49; old and new logic
of, 28–32; overview of, 63–75;
positive-sum, 3, 26–27, 29, 40, 43,
51; supply chains and, 35–38, 100,
103–104; theories about, 66,
68–70; United States and, 25–26,
216; waves of, 70–75; zero-sum,
25–29, 42–43, 51–53
global supply chains. *see* supply
chains
Global Trade Alert, 160, 162
global value chains (GVCs), 8, 13, 30;
China and, 73–74, 196–203, 219;
climate change and, 17, 191–192,

206–207, 215–217; COVID-19
pandemic and, 200, 204–207, 211,
218; digital trade and, 15–17,
213–215; future of, 218–220;
globalization and, 207–211; ICT
and, 193, 207; recent trends in,
193–196; of semiconductors, 16,
35, 193; trade and, 191–195,
203–205, 221n4, 221n10;
transformation of, 205–211;
United States and, 197–198,
200–201; United States–China
rivalry and, 16, 202, 205, 211–213,
218; WTO and, 17, 219–220
Goldman Sachs (company), 47
Google (company), 33–34, 46,
102–103, 106
Great Depression, 7, 69, 72, 74–75,
250
Greater East Asia Co-Prosperity
Sphere, 78
green technologies, 2, 30, 52;
climate change and, 6, 22, 27;
in the United States, 37, 41–43.
see also climate change; renewable
energy
Group of Seven (G7), 252;
Hiroshima Process, 53
Group of Ten (G10), 251
Group of Three (G3), 268
Group of Twenty (G20), 11, 117, 252,
265, 277

Hamilton, Alexander, 131
Handbook on Measuring Digital
Trade, 159
Hayya (app), 55n51
Heckscher-Ohlin model, 66
Hiroshima Process, 53
Hong Kong, 78, 196, 241
Hsinchu Science Park, 41
hyperscaling, 33–34